W9-BIV-279

Katherine Anne Porter: Conversations

Literary Conversations Series
Peggy Whitman Prenshaw
General Editor

Katherine Anne Porter: Conversations

Edited by
Joan Givner

University Press of Mississippi
Jackson and London

© 1987 by the University Press of Mississippi
All rights reserved
Manufactured in the United States of America

The paper in this book meets the guidelines for permanence and durability of the Committee on Production Guidelines for Book Longevity of the Council on Library Resources.
89 88 87   4 3 2 1

Library of Congress Cataloging-in-Publication Data

Porter, Katherine Anne, 1890–1980.
  Katherine Anne Porter : conversations.

  (Literary conversations series)
  Includes index.
  1. Porter, Katherine Anne, 1890–1980—Interviews.
2. Authors, American—20th century—Interviews.
I. Givner, Joan, 1936–   . II. Title. III. Series.
PS3531.0752Z465 1987   813'.52 [B]   86-22387
ISBN 0-87805-266-6 (alk. paper)
ISBN 0-87805-267-4 (pbk. : alk. paper)

British Library Catalouging in Publication data is available.

Books by Katherine Anne Porter

Flowering Judas. Harcourt Brace: New York, 1930.
Katherine Anne Porter's French Song Book. Harrison of Paris: Paris, 1933.
Hacienda. Harrison of Paris: New York, 1934.
Flowering Judas and Other Stories. Harcourt Brace: New York, 1935.
Pale Horse, Pale Rider: Three Short Novels. Harcourt Brace: New York, 1939.
The Leaning Tower and Other Stories. Harcourt Brace: New York, 1944.
The Days Before. Harcourt Brace: New York, 1952.
Ship of Fools. Atlantic-Little, Brown: Boston, 1962.
The Collected Stories of Katherine Anne Porter. Harcourt, Brace: New York, 1965.
A Christmas Story: Seymour Lawrence: New York, 1967.
The Collected Essays and Occasional Writings of Katherine Anne Porter: Delacorte Press: New York, 1970.
The Never-Ending Wrong: Little, Brown: Boston, 1977.

For George Hendrick

Contents

Introduction   *Joan Givner*   ix

Chronology   xxi

What One Woman Is Doing to Help Children
    Gordon K. Shearer   3

Miss Porter Heads Clinic Campaign   *Kitty Barry Crawford*   6

Presenting the Portrait of an Artist   *Archer Winsten*   8

Katherine Anne Porter at Work   *Robert Van Gelder*   14

The New Invitation to Learning: "The Turn of the Screw"
    Katherine Anne Porter, Allen Tate, and Mark Van Doren   17

Reading and Writing   *Mary McGrory*   28

Miss Porter on Writers and Writing   *Winston Bode*   30

Desegregation Ruling Criticized by Author
    Richmond News Leader   39

Recent Southern Fiction: A Panel Discussion
    Bulletin of Wesleyan College   42

Katherine Anne Porter Comes to Kansas   *James Ruoff*   61

For Katherine Anne Porter, *Ship of Fools* Was a Lively Twenty-Two
    Year Voyage   *Elizabeth Janeway*   69

I've Had a Good Run for My Money   *Maurice Dolbier*   74

Katherine Anne Porter: An Interview   *Barbara Thompson*   78

An Interview with Katherine Anne Porter   *Roy Newquist*   99

A Country and Some People I Love   *Hank Lopez*   120

Katherine Anne Porter Makes a Feast of Life
    Josephine Novak   135

Katherine Anne Porter on. . . .   *John Dorsey*   139

Don't Scare the Horses, Miss Porter Tells Liberation
   Women   *Josephine Novak* and *Elise Chisholm*   155
Glimpses of San Antonio at Turn of the Century
   Mildred Whiteaker   158
Katherine Anne Porter: The Vanity of Excellence   *Henry Allen*   162
Katherine Anne Porter Reigns for Students   *Carl Schoettler*   173
Almost Since Chaucer With Miss Porter   *Mary Anne Dolan*   177
The Katherine Anne Porter Watch: After Sacco and Vanzetti, What?
   'The Devil and Cotton Mather'?   *Doris Grumbach*   184
A Fine Day of Homage to Porter   *Joan Givner*   189
Index   192

Introduction

Katherine Anne Porter often spoke of writing her autobiography and claimed to have amassed piles of notes to that end. The commemorative aspect of the project appealed to her. She loved to plan memorials—libraries to house her memorabilia, portraits, grave-markers, and burial rites. All the same, an autobiography was, in practical terms, an impossibility. In speaking of her past, her revisions were so extensive that they went far beyond the shaping that generally occurs in autobiographies. She was incapable of even approaching what Philippe Lejeune has called "the autobiographical pact"—the promise of sincere truth-telling.

The interviews which Porter gave over her lifetime contain her most extensive autobiographical statements. The interviewers—often journalists of unquestionable integrity—assume that she is telling the truth. Yet, she adds to the record a distinguished set of ancestors and an ancestral home complete with a well-stocked library, and staffed by devoted retainers. She speaks of her Catholic upbringing and convent education, and she invents an elopement at the age of sixteen from a New Orleans convent to marry a man much older than herself (her first husband was 21 when they were married) who shut her up. She suppresses her age, baptismal name, lowly origin as the daughter of a poor dirt-farmer, childhood religion, and at least one of her husbands.

Such extravagant departures from the truth disqualify the interviews as reliable sources of biography. At the same time they provide, in the manner of all autobiographies, an important record of a different kind. Of Laura, her character in "Flowering Judas," Porter wrote:

> She cannot help feeling that she has been betrayed irreparably by the disunion between her way of living and her feeling of what life should be.[1]

Katherine Anne Porter shared Laura's feeling. Her biography tells what her life was.[2] The interviews tell what she thought her life should have been. Because they span sixty of her ninety years (the first two predate her literary career), it is possible to trace the formation and development over the years of the public image she created. Some durable stories are elaborated and some details are dropped. For instance, the myth that she was descended from Daniel Boone was exploded. And as she grew older she cared less about changing her age and denying that she once had T.B.

Appropriately, this collection begins and ends near to her birthplace and burial site in the central part of Texas, the state which nurtured her and with which she had such an uneasy relationship. The interviews cluster in the early sixties. Then she had triumphantly finished *Ship of Fools,* achieved bestsellerdom, and gained at last the fame and fortune that had eluded her for so long. She was living in the Washington, D.C., area and, therefore, she was accessible to many skilled journalists. Accordingly, some of these interviews are in themselves masterpieces. The most artful is the one by Barbara Thompson which appeared first in the *Paris Review.* It comes closest of any in presenting Porter as she wished to appear before the world.

Unlike many writers, Porter was a cooperative subject. She was garrulous and uninhibited and basked in the attention. The exercise confirmed her sense of having amounted to something, and she was proud to show off her jewels and gowns and the treasures that filled the elegant homes she created with the earnings from *Ship of Fools.* Often, too, she was lonely and enjoyed her captive audience of a few hours, even while she protested the encroachment on her time. A library employee silently cataloguing books in the next room during one interview recalled hearing her repeatedly foil the attempts of the journalist to get away once he had his material. Porter, wound up to fever pitch, talked on and on as if unable to stop. When the young man finally escaped, Porter came in to the library worker and complained loudly about having her time and privacy eroded by anyone who could jimmy his way into her presence.

While Porter herself is highly repetitive—the same anecdotes and the same phrases recur at quite wide intervals—the interviews are remarkably diverse. Their territory is staked out by the different topical and geographical interests of the interviewers. Hence, although there are gaps in the early years when she was in Mexico and Europe, later interviewers with special interests in those periods recapture that time. Hank Lopez covers the Mexican experience and Mary Anne Dolan the German experience. Two interviewers from Texas, Winston Bode and Muriel Whiteaker, take her back to her childhood there.

She appears here in many guises. Teaching was the first job she undertook when she left school at fifteen, and she returned to it over the years. Before and after her first marriage she taught elocution, dancing, and dramatic arts in rooms she rented in small towns in Texas and Louisiana. When she was recuperating from tuberculosis in Dallas she organized a small school for the children in the sanatorium. She taught again when she was in Mexico in the early twenties. When she became an established writer, she embarked on a new career as a university teacher and lecturer, fond of boasting that the first time she entered a university was as a teacher. She was comfortable always with a student audience, which seemed to bring out her considerable didactic tendencies. Perhaps it was the effect of her early religious training that made her talks to young people often take the form of preaching rather than teaching. She preferred to inculcate broad moral values rather than dispense information or test the students' ideas.

Frequently asked to speak on the literary movements and figures of her time, she readily assumed the mantle of literary critic. Two panel discussions are included here. They show her as a critic, but they have been included also in order to show her slightly subdued as she often was when she was in the company of her distinguished peers rather than alone, under a single spot-light. Often asked to list contemporary writers she admires, she singles out for special praise such long-time friends as Glenway Wescott, Robert Penn Warren, Eudora Welty, Caroline Gordon, and Allen Tate. Her doing so is more than loyalty to durable friendships. It shows her conviction that the single important tradition in American literature is the mainstream Anglo-Saxon one. She firmly rejects the work of Saul Bellow and Norman Mailer on the one hand and of Richard Wright, Ralph Ellison, and James Baldwin on the other. Her explanation to Hank Lopez shows the racial bias that underpins her judgment:

Truly, the South and West and other faraway places have made and are making American literature. We are in the direct, legitimate line; we are people based in English as our mother tongue, and we do not abuse or misuse it, and when we speak a word, we know what it means. These others have fallen into a curious kind of argot, more or less originating in New York, a deadly mixture of academic, guttersnipe, gangster, fake-Yiddish, and dull old worn-out dirty words—an appalling bankruptcy in language, as if they hate English and are trying to destroy it along with other living things they touch.

A similar bias appears in her complaint to Roy Newquist about the American works shown in Europe in 1952:

> They would have these international festivals, where every country in the world would send something, presumably the best it had; whether the art was theater, dance, music, painting, the beautiful things would come. I'm thinking most about Paris in 1952, because I was there and took a great interest; I was one of our delegates.
>
> What did we send? *Four Saints in Three Acts*—or are the numbers the other way around?—with a Negro company. Can you imagine this as representing the American arts? I think Virgil Thompson is a very good composer, but this strange little trifle appalled me. And Gertrude Stein was American-born but got back to Europe as fast as she could and stayed there. She was an interesting phenomenon in her own right, but representative of anything American? I think not. The Negroes were extremely good singers and dancers, and it was an amusing little show; but was that the best we could send?

In fact, the American delegation to the *Congress de l'oeuvre du xxe siècle* was all she could have wished. Besides herself it consisted of James Farrell, William Faulkner, Allen Tate and Robert Penn Warren. Robert Lowell was also in attendance.

She speaks out without hesitation on political issues, considering herself an expert on the subject by virtue of her first-hand experience of many of the major events of the century. She experienced the anti-German hysteria in the United States during the first world war; she nearly died in the influenza plague of that time; she was in Mexico when Obregon was inaugurated as president; she was part of the protest against the execution of Sacco and Vanzetti; she claimed to have been in jail seventeen times for causes in Mexico, in France, and all over the United States; she was in Berlin during Hitler's rise to power and she was in Paris just before the Second World War. She prided herself on the range of her experiences and her astuteness in assessing the various situations and she often complains that she was never listened to or taken seriously.

All the same, the interviews show her to be confused on political matters. She is torn between her wish to identify with "the guilt-ridden white pillar crowd" on the one hand and with the rebels of the radical left on the other. Sometimes she tries to get the best of both worlds by depicting herself as someone of aristocratic origins who has turned her back on those origins. Hence Robert Van Gelder reports:

> But she has broken with the class from which she came completely. She has come over and taken out her card in the Guild of Artists. She considers that her class and no other.

In the same interview, she lists as her chief three interests friends, revolution, and cooking. In her 1942 entry for *Twentieth Century Authors,* she asserts "politically my bent is to the left." It becomes clear, however, in the later years that, if indeed her bent had ever truly been to the left, it had swung pretty far to the right. The conservative in her finally won out. In 1958 in Richmond, Virginia, she speaks out against the desegregation of schools:

> The down-trodden minorities are organized into tight little cabals to run the country so that we will become the down-trodden vast majority if we don't watch out.

She opposes the taking in of Asian refugees:

> We are bringing in their children and we have all those little Indian and Appalachian children. It is useless. What are they going to do? We should let each other alone.[3]

And in another peroration not included in this volume she comes out with a very old chestnut indeed:

> My grandmother, when she heard that Mr. Lincoln had abolished slavery and the Negroes were free, was heard to say "I hope it works both ways" and lived to realize that it did not.[4]

As might be expected, Porter is at her most interesting when she speaks out about her own work. She describes the origins of many of her stories and the origins of some stories—"Pale Horse, Pale Rider," "Flowering Judas," and "Noon Wine"—are described in more than one place. The accounts of the geneses of her fictions are invaluable to students of her work. Yet, important as they and the descriptions of her work habits are, the interviews provide something of even greater literary significance. They provide her self-portrait, her version of the

portrait of the artist as a woman. It is a picture riddled with
ambivalence and conflict. Her own remark indicates one fundamental
tension: "When they came to interview me, they wanted to know
something trivial or frivolous, wanted to make a Southern belle of
me."

Here, of course, she is externalizing her own deep-rooted conflict.
And it is perhaps not surprising that she should have experienced
those conflicts both as a woman and an artist. After all, a much
younger and better-educated woman, Sylvia Plath, in her portrait of
the artist expressed similar frustrations in the last half of the twentieth
century. She has her heroine in *The Bell Jar* tantalized by the
mutually exclusive destinies for which she longs—mother, wife,
homemaker, poet, academic, editor, world-traveller, and free spirit
with a pack of lovers.

How much more difficult it was for Porter to reconcile the roles
which she desired! Not only was she born at the beginning of the last
decade of the nineteenth century, but she was raised by a grandmother who was born in 1827. Porter was torn between wishing to
be an accomplished, independent woman, speaking out au-
thoritatively on literature and world events and wishing to be a
charmingly capricious belle, sought after for her beauty and arousing
chivalrous thoughts in every male breast.

There were few women in her own time to whom she could look
for patterns of resolving that conflict. She wrote glowing tributes to
the literary talents of Virginia Woolf, Willa Cather, and Gertrude
Stein, but her admiration stopped short of their personal lives. Her
distaste for Gertrude Stein's personal life was so strong that it ended
by warping her judgment of Stein's literary achievements. It was not
the literary women, so many of them blue stockings, who provided
models for the kind of life to which Porter aspired. Rather it was the
artists of the stage, such as Sarah Bernhardt, Lillie Langtry, and
Isadora Duncan, whose combination of talent and beauty earned
them a large following of fans and lovers.

Often Porter seems to fall back on the artist in an attempt to
reconcile the conflicts of the woman. She is able to do this as long as
she strips from the artist any suggestion of hard work, discipline, or
aggressiveness. The word must rather suggest a passive receptacle

into which a quasi-divine inspiration descends to work its will during brief intense visitations. In this way, the creator of great literature and the belle can be united. Thus Porter loved to quote a remark which she attributed to her fourth husband when she asked him if she was a failure as a wife. He told her: You just have a permanent engagement with a higher power.

A crucial part of her self-portrait as an artist is the rejection of any notion of a "career." The very word "career" to her smacks of opportunism and worldly ambition. She says of her family:

> We were never very ambitious people. . . . I suppose we did have a desire to excel, but not to push our way to higher places. We thought we'd already arrived.

Although her family never discouraged her from seeking gainful employment (her father depended on her for his support when she was fifteen) she attributes to them the nineteenth-century notion that a lady should never be contaminated by anything commercial:

> My family felt that if one had talents they should be cultivated for the decoration of life but never professionally. My father once said, "If you want to write, you can write just as well here at home. Besides, what business has a lady writing? Why not write letters to your friends? Look at Madame de Sévigné!"

Since her many jobs are a matter of record, she is at pains to reconcile these occupations with the idea of her family's disapproval. Typically she suggests that rather than acquiring the jobs aggressively, they were thrust upon her by accidents, such as could happen only to a winsome and improvident dreamer. Thus her explanation of her serious (but unsuccessful) attempt to become a movie star:

> There was a long line of people when I got there, and a man at the head of it telling some people to go one way and some to go the other. And I went up to him, and he said, "Here, little boy blue, you go over and get in that line." And I said, "But I'm from the newspaper." And he said, "Oh, go on, get in that line and go to the dressing room."
> And then one day the director came up to me and said, "Little boy blue, pack up your suitcase." And I asked why and he said we were going to Los Angeles to open a new studio there. And I said, "But I'm not going." He had started to walk away, and he turned round and just stared at me for a moment and said. "Do you mean you don't want to be an actress?" And I said "No." And he said, "Well, then, you must be a fool."

The selling of her first story (although she had been writing for money for several years) is also presented as an accident, the result of a friend's urging. The financial reward astounds her:

> I said to George, "I didn't realize there was money in this," and he said, "You might have hurried up a little if you had."

Porter, by her own strenuous efforts, raised herself from the poverty of a log cabin to great wealth. Her version of the American Dream, however, did not include Benjamin Franklin's precept that it is not enough to be industrious but necessary also to *appear* industrious.

In at least two places Porter tells how, in order to complete her first acknowledged story, she went into self-imposed confinement with her muse. She loves to speak of these periods of retreat, lovingly adumbrating the items on her spare but nutritious diet. She wrote "Noon Wine" and "Old Mortality" in an inn in Doylestown, Pennsylvania; she wrote the opening section of *Ship of Fools* at Yaddo and finished it in The Yankee Clipper Inn on Cape Ann. On the other hand, many retreats such as the five months on Bermuda in 1929, intended to see the completion of *The Devil and Cotton Mather*, produced no tangible results.

Another of her cherished myths is of dashing off works in one sitting or, for longer stories, in slightly longer gestation periods. Although the drafts of "Flowering Judas" date back over a period of ten years, she tells Barbara Thompson:

> I always write a story in one sitting. I started "Flowering Judas" at seven p.m. and at one-thirty I was standing on a snowy windy corner putting it in the mailbox.

Another interviewer reports:

> There was that autumn in 1927 when she sat down at 11 p.m. in her subleased apartment in West Fifty-Second street to write a story called "Rope." She wrote it, dressed, went out to mail it to the first American Caravan, where it was published; returned home, and it was 2:10 a.m.

Porter, of course, could not come to terms with her tendency to embroider her experiences sufficiently to explore the reasons that made her fantasies necessary to her. Yet she did think a great deal about the questions and problems inherent in sexual identity. She tells Mary Ann Dolan that she supposed everything in her life had to do with being female. Scholars in recent years have raised questions about the nature of her feminism. Her attitudes on the subject changed over the years, and while the interviews chart those changes they do not reveal a coherent stance. She lived through various feminist movements in her time. In fact, one of the earliest letters in the University of Maryland's Katherine Anne Porter archive is a 1909 letter from her brother upbraiding her for her vehemence on the subject of women's rights. But during the feminist movement of the sixties, when most of her own struggles were behind her, she dissociates herself from the individual crusaders and from the movement in general. She speaks scathingly of Simone de Beauvoir and derisively of Betty Friedan. As on so many matters, Porter is fundamentally ambivalent. Her own inner conflicts cause her contradictions.

Thus in 1962 she begins a luncheon interview with Maurice Dolbier with her favorite Mexican toast:

> Health and money!
> And more power to your elbow—
> Many hidden love affairs
> And time to enjoy them!

In the course of the interview she makes the following statement:

> I've never felt that the fact of being a woman put me at a disadvantage, or that it's difficult being a woman in a "man's world." The only time men get a little tiresome is in love—oh, they're OK at first, but they do tend, don't they, to get a little bossy and theological about the whole business?

In an interview published a year later, she makes to a woman journalist the following more thoughtful statement:

> You're brought up with the notion of feminine chastity and inaccessibility, yet with the curious idea of feminine availability in all spiritual ways, and in giving service to anyone who demands it. And I suppose that's why it has taken me twenty years to write this novel; it's been interrupted by just anyone who could jimmy his way into my life.

The difference in the two statements indicates one factor which always has to be taken into consideration in assessing her opinions on feminism and other subjects. She has an overriding desire to entertain and woo her audience, whether that audience consists of one person or a crowd of hundreds in an auditorium. She is always the actress and she is always ready to sacrifice consistency and truth for a laugh or a burst of applause. This is the characteristic of the "belle," whose reflex is to make a conquest.

The excesses of Porter criticism have been often noted. Her critics often jumped to her side like knights errant vying for their lady's favor. When *Pale Horse, Pale Rider* was published she was compared with Dante, Milton, and Henry James. Later she was elevated to the position of "First Lady of American Letters." Her supporters strove not merely to praise her considerable qualities as a stylist and short story writer, but they competed in making exaggerated claims for her stature as brilliant political commentator and moral prophet. Often, the most impassioned admirers of her work were those who had been exposed not only to the works but to her physical presence as well. Thus one reviewer who ends by declaring her to be "the greatest moralist and satirist of her times" includes in his list of credentials the fact "he spent several days as a guest of Miss Porter's in College Park."[5]

To read these interviews is to understand the cause of that adulation. They show the interviewers, both men and women, falling under her spell. And these are not naive observers but case-hardened journalists, used to casting cold eyes over celebrities. Yet, they tax all their lyrical resources in order to rhapsodize her charms, singling out for special praise her eyes, hair, voice, and laugh. Thus Mary McGrory:

> Miss Porter somehow still commands the aura of a Southern belle. Her snow-white hair frames her delicate features and an elegant gray dress brought out her beautiful deep-set gray eyes. Her throaty drawling conversation is sprinkled still with the "La me's" of her Texas and Louisiana girlhood.

Winston Bode finds her eyes a "deep-lustered ageless grey green," while for Henry Allen they "swim behind thick glasses, and they are fierce and violet." James Ruoff elaborates further:

> . . . . this initial impression of frailty and serenity was off set by the shock of wild gray hair, the alert blue eyes that flared like blown coals, and the firm eloquence of the voice falling on our ears like strange music.

Elizabeth Janeway sees her as the guardian of a great talent, like a priestess, like a tiger, like a dragon "but a most charming and exquisite dragon, Chinese porcelain of the best period, with the purr of an affectionate tiger."

To Janeway, Porter's chuckle sounds like "a soda-water syphon which has just learned to talk and is delighted with the sound." Carl Schoettler, on the other hand, finds it "oddly metallic as if created by a toy-maker to a Byzantine emperor." To Barbara Thompson "its tone is that of someone talking to a bird, or coquetting with an old beau—light and feathery, with a slight flutter."

Sometimes Porter's frailty and small stature are used to suggest heroism, as when the last interviewer sees her as "a small gallant Texan, whose only wish is to be read and remembered" or when Doris Grumbach signs off with this elegaic note:

> Then it is time to go and Miss Porter is left standing at the end of a long hall, dressed all in white, quiet and alone, with one arm folded behind her, the other resting at her side. Seeing that small, indomitable figure standing at the door, her head held in the same erect, jaunty, graceful way it is in her youthful pictures, it seems that she will be here to do it all. Even the Cotton Mather biography.

The reader does not, however, depend on the commentators for an appreciation of Katherine Anne Porter's charms. The supreme virtue of these interviews is that her presence and her vibrant voice irradiate them. She lives in these conversations as the brilliant raconteur and wit that she was. Quite apart from their value in documenting the conflicts and triumphs inherent in being a woman writer in her time and her country, they are fun to read. She is a delight to listen to as she speaks out with grace, originality, and humor. After all, who else could sweep away her evasions and indiscretions with a line like this one?

"I have no hidden marriages. They just escape my mind."

JG
July 1986

---

[1] Katherine Anne Porter, *The Collected Stories of Katherine Anne Porter* (New York: Harcourt, Brace & World, Inc., 1965, p. 91.

[2] Joan Givner, *Katherine Anne Porter: A Life* (New York: Simon & Schuster, 1982).

[3] Mary Corddray, "Miss Porter Is An 'Optimist' Who Believes No System Works," *The Baltimore Sun,* 5 May 1975.

[4] Katherine Anne Porter, "Notes On The Texas I Remember," *Atlantic Monthly,* March 1975, pp. 102–106.

[5] Carl Griffin, "How Facts of Life Became Porter's Fiction," *The Atlanta Journal, The Atlanta Constitution,* 9 January 1983.

[6] Any quotation not documented is to be found in this text.

All interviews have been reproduced as they originally appeared.

Chronology

1890   Callie Russell Porter born 15 May in Indian Creek, Texas, fourth of the five children of Harrison and Mary Alice Porter. Baptized in the Methodist Church.

1892   Death of the mother. Harrison Porter's mother, Catherine Anne, takes the family to her home in Kyle, Hays County.

1901   Death of the grandmother

1906   Porter marries John Henry Koontz of Inez, Texas

1910   Porter converts to Catholicism, the faith of her husband's family

1914   Departure for Chicago to work in the movies

1915   Divorce from Koontz; ill with T.B.

1917   Employed by the *Forth Worth Critic*

1918–19   Employed by the *Rocky Mountain News* in Denver; ill with influenza

1919–20   Works in New York as publicist for a movie company; ghost-writes a novel; publishes stories in children's magazine *Everyland* and elsewhere

1920   First visit to Mexico

1921   Forced to leave Mexico, spends a few months in Fort Worth

1922   Returns to New York; publishes "María Concepción" in *Century* Magazine; trip to Mexico to write catalogue for exhibition of folk-art

1926   Brief marriage to Ernest Stock

1929   Spends five months in Bermuda in vain effort to com-
            plete *The Devil and Cotton Mather*

1930   Publication of *Flowering Judas*

1930   Begins her longest period of residence in Mexico; meets
            Eugene Pressly with whom she spends the next six years

1931   Sails from Vera Cruz to Bremerhaven; lives in Berlin

1932   Visits Paris, Madrid, Basel

1933   Settles in Paris, marries Eugene Pressly

1936   Returns to U.S.A.; spends productive writing period in
            Doylestown, Pennsylvania

1937   Separates from Pressly; goes to New Orleans and begins
            relationship with Albert Erskine

1938   Spends the winter writing in Houston; marries Albert
            Erskine and lives in Baton Rouge

1939   Publishes *Pale Horse, Pale Rider,* collection of three short
            novels

1940   Separates from Albert Erskine and goes to Yaddo

1942   Divorced from Erskine

1944   Publishes *The Leaning Tower & Other Stories*

1945   Brief stints as scriptwriter in Hollywood; stays on in
            California

1948–9   Teaches at Stanford; returns east to live in New York

1953–4   Teaches at University of Michigan

1954   Fulbright lectureship at University of Liége terminated by
            illness; returns to U.S.A. and lives in Connecticut

1959   Settles in Washington D.C.

1962   Publication of *Ship of Fools*

1965   Publication of *The Collected Stories of Katherine Anne
            Porter*

1967   Establishment of Katherine Anne Porter Room at the
            University of Maryland

1970   Publication of *The Collected Essays and Occasional Writ-
            ings of Katherine Anne Porter*

1976   Last year of travelling and lecturing before a series of
            strokes leaves her bedridden

1977   Publication of *The Never-Ending Wrong,* the account of
            her experiences during the last days of Sacco and Vanzetti
            in 1927

1980   Death; burial beside her mother in the Indian Creek
            cemetery

Katherine Anne Porter: Conversations

What One Woman is Doing to Help Children

Gordon K. Shearer/1916

From *The Dallas Morning News*, 16 December 1916. Reprinted by permission of *The Dallas Morning News*.

"Academy Oaks" is a fitting title for Dallas County's first outdoor school. It has twelve pupils, and instruction is being given in all branches, from the primary department to fourth-grade lessons.

Back of the outdoor school is the heart of a free-air-loving girl. She is teaching this school under the trees she loves so well. Last summer, this girl, Miss Katherine Anne Porter, was ill for several months. She chafed at the idleness of illness, at her inability to continue the outdoor life to which she had been accustomed since her childhood.

Then fate played her part. Miss Porter paid a visit to the Woodlawn Sanatorium, three miles north of Dallas. There she became interested in the tubercular children who were leading outdoor lives in a battle for health. They, too, were idle as she had been forced to be during her illness.

She saw the inviting meadow ground about the sanatorium, with its large shade trees and soft turf. She saw the children playing there, their screened galleries between the storm buildings where they sleep, and all the modern equipment which has been supplied to assist them to grow strong. Seeing all this, the question suggested itself:

"What is being done for the growth of their minds?"

From that question sprang the Woodlawn Woodland School. The need of teaching for the children had been considered before, but teachers hesitated to risk health in such close association with the children. Miss Porter volunteered to become their teacher. She trusted to fresh air and a sunny disposition as her germicides. The teaching she knew she could master, for at one time she had been an instructor in elocution and folk-lore dancing in Corpus Christi.

It's a school without desks. The children gather under this tree or that, following the shade. The ground is the bench. A swing in one of the trees is an honor seat. Good pupils have it as a reward. Punishment? Of course. Discipline is required in this as in other schools. But it is not ordinary punishment. Whipping or a task to learn is not punishment therapeutically suited to a child whose temperature must not be raised. Miss Porter solved the punishment problem. If the pupil does not behave, the rest cure is applied. The pupil stays in bed instead of coming to school. Truancy is unknown.

Sunday was appointed by Miss Porter for a visit to her outdoor school. She could not have it interrupted weekdays by newspaper interviewers and cameramen. But the children gladly staged their outdoor school on Sunday, just as during the week, though some difficulties presented themselves.

"Jimmy" (that is not his real name, but all of the pupils are waiting to see their pictures and read this story, and he might be embarrassed if he were correctly named) hesitated to sit down as the pupils took their places on the soft turf under the afternoon oak.

"That's all right; sit right there on the ground!" said teacher.

Still he stood and said, "I can't."

"Yes, you can," replied Miss Porter. "Sit right down!"

"Naw, I can't," said Jimmy, grown desperate. "These are my other pants!"

He was assured that for once he might sit down in the dirt in his Sunday clothes, and school was called to order.

Remarkable aptitude is shown by these little outdoor scholars. Part of their progress is due to the personal attention the small class makes it possible for Miss Porter to give to each one, but she modestly attributes it to the fresh air and their natural brightness.

There's a touch of sadness, too. A tablet leaf is caught up by the breeze and goes sailing away with its unfinished "sum." A little girl starts after it, and you feel a tug at your heart, for she limps painfully.

Strangely precocious are some of these nature pupils. With the example of some of the grown-ups about them, they have strange, old-fashioned, hospitable ways.

"How have you been?" was the diagnostic greeting of a tiny curly-headed girl, not "Glad to see you!" or "Hello!"

If there's illness all about, Miss Porter counteracts it with cheerfulness and life. The children never are permitted to tire. At the slightest sign of fatigue or worry there is a turn to a new topic—

maybe lessons are cast aside altogether and there is a folk-dance with easy steps requiring not too much exertion. Bright colors, too, are favored for their cheering effect.

To the casual visitor the apparent hardihood of these children who are under medical care comes as a surprise. On bright December days many of the boys go barefoot. On cold days, of course, there are wraps; but it's a severe day indeed that prevents the outdoor school.

Gary methods are used to a considerable extent. The books prescribed in other public schools are in use, and the course in other schools is followed. In this way it is hoped to keep the children apace with the boys and girls who go to ordinary school, so that when their cures are effected they may go on with pupils of their age.

Miss Porter Heads Clinic Campaign

Kitty Barry Crawford/1921

From *The Fort Worth Record,* September 1921. Reprinted by permission of *The Fort Worth Star-Telegram.*

"I can do everything a publicist does except write about myself."

That is what Miss Katherine Anne Porter, just the instant before I began to write this bit of copy, declared to me. And incidentally, that is why I am writing it at all.

Miss Porter is to have charge of a modest kind of campaign to create a fund for a clinic for the tuberculars in Fort Worth. She is to plan and direct efforts to obtain this fund along natural lines that will not interfere with the activities of other organizations already depending on public support. It is not to be a general drive, or solicitation from the public at large. More than one novel means of obtaining the money necessary to the equipment is being considered by Miss Porter and when the finance committee for the clinic has its full list of members, she will begin to put her plans into action.

Aside from a friendship of longstanding with me, Miss Porter has a special interest in the work she will undertake in Fort Worth. She was once a rest cure devotee herself, and spent several years in sanatoriums and resorts for the tuberculous. She believes that a well-conducted clinic for those whom it is not advisable to send away from home is a basic, necessary thing in every sizable city.

"There are hundreds here and in this vicinity, I am sure," said Miss Porter, "who cannot afford to pay the prices demanded by our best institutions, and who yet might bear the full expense of expert advice at home."

"A tuberculous patient is sent away from home always upon a chance. The doctor who advises a removal from familiar surroundings can never fully determine what effect this radical change will have upon the individuals moved. Altitude often affects people harmfully, causing insomnia and heart irregularity. Absence from home has a bad mental effect."

"In more than the majority of cases it would be better for the tubercular persons to stay at home if they might have proper care and direction. Getting well is a long, tedious business, full of minute detail, and mistakes are always dangerous. Only the most expert attention will bring about the best results, and a clinic, with authoritative medical and nursing facilities, and modern equipment, will provide such attention."

"While I think that often it is best to send patients to other climates and environments, long experience has convinced me that hardly more than 10 per cent of those actually expatriated should have been removed from their familiar atmosphere."

Miss Porter will organize a finance committee immediately, and begin work on the creation of the fund.

Presenting the Portrait
of an Artist
Archer Winsten/1937

From *The New York Post,* 6 May 1937, p. 17. Reprinted by permission of *The New York Post.*

When the Book of the Month Club recently found itself with extra cash and a kindly impulse to give $2,500 to an author of outstanding merit whose work had not been appreciated by the great public, it chose Katherine Anne Porter for the award.

Her reputation, wide spread among connoisseurs, was based on eleven short stories written and published during the past thirteen years and brought together in a volume called *Flowering Judas.*

In strong and simple prose they brought to the reader Mexico and Mexicans, the failure of a marriage, a quarrel, a few days in the making of a motion picture, the death of an old woman.

There were no tailor-made plots to gratify one's detective instinct with a tricky end. Something happened, something was said, some people live and, after the story was read, lived on. There was always the inescapable quality of the single observation, of the character portrayed, a capture of the truth.

She has been thought of as one who took a year to write three thousand words, a whole day to fit ten words into a sentence and half of another to weigh, polish, rearrange, and think about it. Editors, having read some of her stories, wrote in the editorial manner ". . . surely you have something on hand that we would like to see." But there was nothing, except maybe once a year. And editors considered her a most extraordinary writer. How strange not to have something on hand. And how much stranger not to sit right down and bat it out if the desk drawer happened to be depleted.

In such a case editors and others are apt to decide they are up against a stylist—that is, one to whom the manner of writing is so important that it is only by a major miracle that anything ever gets written. Ordinarily stylists can be identified by their thin volumes, rare publication, a small but appreciative public and an independent income.

Miss Porter had no independent income. Moreover, she has found it annoying to be called a stylist and what that implies.

In rebuttal she cites a recent twenty-one-day period in which she wrote 62,000 words, part of five short novels, which will soon appear under the Harcourt Brace imprint as *Pale Horse, Pale Rider.* There was also that autumn in 1927 when she sat down at 11 P.M. in her subleased apartment in West Fifty-second Street to write a story called "Rope."

She wrote it, dressed, went out to mail it to the first American Caravan, where it was published; returned home, and it was 2:10 A.M.

There are also the four complete novels and forty short stories she burned because she did not like them.

Do you understand? She is an artist.

She is now living in a first-floor apartment in a brownstone building on Perry Street in the Village. Her living room has a wall full of books, pale, unpainted furniture low to the floor, and a spinet.

The spinet, with its pearwood body, ebony and boxwood keys, a sounding board of 150-year-old fir, and its beech table and cover, is an exact copy of a French museum piece dated 1550. When she brought it from France last October, the steam heat and sea air warped the delicate instrument so that it has had to rest ever since.

She is a small woman with hair grayed almost to white and a young face. She has traveled far and done many things and remembers much because she has "an ungodly memory that won't let me forget anything except telephone numbers and the time of day."

When she was six years old she wrote, bound and hand-printed what she spelled "A Nobbel—The Hermit of Halifax Cave." There were no writers in the family—though she may have been very distantly related to O. Henry (Sidney Porter). No one encouraged her to become a writer. It was not done in those days in Texas, her native State.

She says, "My family felt that if one had talents they should be cultivated for the decoration of life, but never professionally."

From the beginning there was a determination to write. In school she learned proper things—dancing, elocution, penmanship. At home a grandmother born in 1827—sixty-six years old when Katherine was born—took the place of her dead mother and insisted, "Children should be seen and not heard" or "Handsome is as handsome does."

So at the age of sixteen the convent girl ran away and was married, was divorced at the age of nineteen. A year later she left Texas.

She says "I had to leave the South because I didn't want to be regarded as a freak. That was how they regarded a woman who tried to write. I had to make a revolt, a rebellion, and I don't mean 'living your own life' either. When I left they were all certain I was going to live an immoral life. It was a confining society in those days."

In due time that society will find itself in the first part, "Legend and Memory," already completed, of a novel to be called *Many Redeemers*.

She went to Chicago and worked as an extra in the Essanay studios the very week that Gloria Swanson broke in as an extra. She was asked to go to the Coast with the company as a "guaranteed" extra when it moved. She refused, and she had a reason. Just as she had a reason for refusing to go to the Coast six years later when she was doing publicity work under Hunt Stromberg at the Selznick studios in New Jersey.

She says, "I knew. I just knew what it would do to me. I'm very luxury-loving. I have all the expensive tastes. I could fall into it like a cat into an empty pillow. I knew I was corruptible."

So she stayed in Chicago that time, was desperately poor, for she has always made her own way, and didn't get enough to eat all the time. Pretty soon she went back home with tuberculosis.

A few years later she was making good her recovery in Denver and working on the Rocky Mountain News as movie reviewer, drama critic and sob sister.

In 1920 she went to Mexico to study Mayan art, and found herself instead in the center of the Revolution. Being something of a rebel in her own quiet way, it was easy to plunge in on the side of Liberty, Equality and Fraternity. She taught dancing and physical culture in four of the new schools.

The experience provided her with a couple of stories and she stayed there off and on for eight years. In 1922 she brought the work of a couple of unknown Mexican artists to New York. They were Diego Rivera and Miguel Covarrubias.

One of the later stories she wrote with a Mexican setting was the one called "Hacienda," which told the events of a few days during Eisenstein's filming of "Thunder Over Mexico."

From the lips of one of the Russian characters she quoted the following: "Ah yes, I remember," he said on meeting some Southern women, "you are the ladies who are always being raped by those dreadful Negroes."

It is the kind of quotation that is unexpected in the writings of a woman trained in the Southern tradition, rebel though she was. But she has broken with the class from which she came, completely. She has come over and taken her stand, taken out her card in the Guild of Artists. She considers that her class, and she wants no other.

She feels that her life has had one pattern, the determination not to make writing a career—that is, not ever to allow her serious writing to be in any way influenced by demands of editors or public, as it would have to be if it were her livelihood.

"If I began to look upon it as a means to make money—I mean, for me it wouldn't do," she says.

Ghost writing, rewriting, editing, revising, all the different ways in which a writer works on other people's material—these she has done in order to keep going and to keep herself free.

She wrote steadily for years without ever an attempt at publication. Unlike the familiar tale of writers who collect basketfuls of rejection slips, she never had one. At the age of thirty she thought she had written a story worth printing and she sent it out and it was accepted. Since then she has had only one rejection. An editor asked her to send something to him. She sent the story she had just finished. It didn't please her and it didn't please him either.

There is a powerful element of self-confidence in her makeup. A story is written at fever heat, fast and without a break in the mood if she can help it. She goes over that copy with a pencil, marking out a few words and changing some. A clean copy is made, and that's the way it goes out. No one sees it but the editor to whom it is sent. She is the only one who knows what she is trying to accomplish, and therefore, logically, she is the best judge of whether or not she succeeds.

One of her greatest obstacles to increased production is libraries. Set her down in the midst of the dusty stacks of a big library and she is utterly content. In Basel, Switzerland, where she was able to go on a Guggenheim Fellowship in 1931, she found herself in the midst of the original documents of the Reformation. She wanted never to leave, never to stop her orgy of researching.

This side of her talent will be expressed in a book to be published after her next. It is "The Devil and Cotton Mather," the writing of which is almost finished. The next story of hers to appear, if you are interested, will be "Noon Wine," in *Story* magazine for June.

Besides writing, three things interest her: friends, revolution and cooking.

Friends—She likes them, can't resist; sees more of them than is good for work.

Revolution—She has been a so-called Fellow Traveler for many years, but whenever on the verge of joining up, some small thing prevented her, an incident, a statement, a person. It was always something that made her afraid for her mental freedom. A larger-scale example would be the Trotsky trials, which were profoundly disturbing to her. "Why," she asks, "should I have rebelled against my early training in Jesuit Catholicism only to take another yoke now?"

Cooking—"I'm a fanatical cook. I'm proud of the fact that I could hire out and be a good cook. I'm an imaginative cook. Some day, when I've finished all my books, I'm going to write a cookbook. I'm a perfectionist in cooking."

She thinks it would be wise for artists to be good cooks, since they seldom have enough money to eat in good restaurants and since their health and energy may depend on the food they eat.

An additional but purely personal interest is her husband, Eugene Pressly, whom she married in Paris in 1933 when he was in the United States Diplomatic Service.

This, quite by the way, is said by Miss Porter to be, with one exception, the only time she's ever been interviewed. Seeing the pencil and copy paper, she exclaimed, "It's going to be a real interview. You're going to take notes." And then, with marvelous restraint, she failed to add, "You'll have to let me see what you write before it's published."

The other interview occurred in Mexico City. Then, as now, she protested there was no reason to interview her. No one ever did. But the Mexican reporters and photographers insisted, taking a flock of

pictures and jotting down terse statements about the beauties of
Mexico and Mexico City. Finally they asked her to write her name on
a piece of paper so it would be spelled correctly.

That done, they put their heads together. "Then you are not," they
accused gravely, "Gene Stratton Porter?"

No, she was not.

This time, though, there has been no mistaken identity. A portrait
of a sincere artist has been intended. It is a portrait of a woman who
says about writing, "I don't think people really know what they do,
and when they finish they don't know what they've done. We start
out to do a particular thing of course. But what you write is a sum of
your experience and yourself."

Katherine Anne Porter at Work

Robert Van Gelder/1940

From *The New York Times Book Review,* 14 April 1940, p. 20.
Reprinted by permission of *The New York Times.*

Katherine Anne Porter stated with evident surprise that her papers are now in order, and in her own house. Formerly she traveled a great deal with a suitcase for personal effects and a steamer trunk filled with manuscripts and notes. "Always I was up to my chin in paper." Now she has burned numerous short stories and four novels that she decided not to publish. But the material that she kept to work over is enough to occupy her well into her eighties. There are notes for novels, for a biography of Cotton Mather, and for some forty short stories.

Miss Porter's books are long anticipated. Each season Harcourt, Brace hopefully announce the coming publication of her study of Cotton Mather. Each season publication is postponed. Now she has completed eleven of the twenty chapters. And more, she expects to have a novel finished in June.

One difficulty is, she explained last week—when she came here from her home in Baton Rouge, La., to receive a gold medal in recognition of her work—that she requires absolute privacy when she does her writing, and as she likes people very much and thoroughly enjoys everyday living, she finds the gift of privacy not much to her taste.

Her neighbor in Baton Rouge, Robert Penn Warren—poet and author of the powerful novel, *Night Riders*—amazes Miss Porter with his ability to make full use of even thirty minutes of free time. "He simply goes to his typewriter, picks up where he left off, and pounds ahead. *Night Riders* was a tremendously complicated book to write. He went through it as though he was simply making notes in a journal."

Miss Porter is generally thought of as a stylist—her writing as a "connoisseur's product." Actually she is not much interested in writing for connoisseurs, and certainly she does not strive as a maker of phrases or wielder of rhythms. To write a story she goes through a long "brooding period." then stocks a room—preferably a rented room in a place where she is a stranger—with oranges and coffee, and goes to work, writing as rapidly as possible. Each of her three novelettes, "Old Mortality," "Noon Wine," and "Pale Horse, Pale Rider," was written in a week.

"I was just back from Europe and had no ties, no immediate responsibilities. Carl Van Doren told me of an inn at Doylestown, Pa., and I went there and took a room and started writing on a Saturday. I worked all week and on the next Saturday that first story was finished. I immediately commenced the second story and finished it on the Saturday after. Then it was necessary for me to return to Baton Rouge. I took a room in New Orleans on a Monday and finished the third story on the next Monday."

In the interest of speed she works on a typewriter, has evolved a kind of typewritten shorthand. When the first version is down she revises by interlining the script, makes more changes in a clear copy, and that is all. The crystal clearness of her style, the perfect imagery, are achieved at white heat.

Miss Porter never shows her manuscripts to anyone until they are ready for publication. "If you go about showing what you do and asking advice and perhaps taking it, then the work isn't yours any more, isn't entirely your own." Through her long apprenticeship she said nothing about her work. She earned her living by writing—but that was writing done on order. Once on order she wrote an entire Mexican issue for a magazine. That issue continued to sell for eleven years, according to Paul Crume, who wrote on Miss Porter recently in *The Southwest Review.* Miss Porter hadn't heard of this record sale.

During her apprenticeship Miss Porter made a living for a time here in New York as a book reviewer. She also "ghosted" books and articles. While she was ghosting books, she said, she was bewildered and even a little frightened. "It seems perfectly incomprehensible to me that any one should want to sign a book that some one else had written. I think it a kind of insanity. I hated to be alone with people like that."

Miss Porter is a Texan, the descendant of soldiers and scholars. One of her ancestors was a colonel on Washington's staff and she is "quite proud of him; it seems that he went where he was needed and did the best he could. There is nothing in the record to suggest that he was a careerist or politician." Other ancestors established Porter Academies in various parts of the country.

Miss Porter started work as a newspaper reporter in Dallas—"but they let me go after a brief time." She had more success on a newspaper in Denver, but the influenza epidemic of the armistice year brought her so close to death that she believes she learned that it is true that the moment of death holds something like revelation. "Pale Horse, Pale Rider," is an attempt to record that experience; Miranda looks over the precipice that she recognizes as death:

> There it is, there it is at last, it is very simple; and soft, carefully shaped words like oblivion and eternity are curtains hung before nothing at all. I shall not know when it happens, I shall not feel or remember, why can't I consent now. I am lost, there is no hope for me. Look, she told herself, there it is, that is death and there is nothing to fear. But she would not consent, still shrinking stiffly against the granite wall that was her childhood dream of safety, breathing slowly for fear of squandering breath, saying desperately, Look, don't be afraid, it is nothing, it is only eternity.

Miss Porter believes that this is the best story she has yet written. But she never has written anything that was not "the best I could do at the time."

The New Invitation to Learning:
"The Turn of the Screw"
Katherine Anne Porter, Allen Tate, and Mark Van Doren/1942

From *The New Invitation to Learning,* ed. Mark Van Doren,
New York, The New Home Library, 1942, pp. 223–225.

Van Doren: This great and famous story is told by a governess, who
lets us know how she saw two children under her charge, a little boy
and a little girl, in an English house of indeterminate antiquity and
solitude, corrupted by the ghosts of two evil servants, recently dead.
Now the first question we shall be expected to settle, if we can, is the
question whether all that happens, all that is seen, is in the mind of
the governess, or whether—or to what extent—there are objective
existences here over which she has no control.

Tate: Mr. Van Doren, if you mean by "objective existences" only
those existences which can be seen visually, I would say no, except in
so far as the governess sees them; but I think there are objective
existences which don't manifest themselves visually. Again, I think
that these apparitions, in so far as they become agents in the action
affecting human lives, are just as real as if they were people in the
sense that we are people around a table. I don't want to quibble
about it, but I think that a discussion along that line is the way to get
at it.

Van Doren: Is that true for you, Miss Porter? Does it seem to you
a false problem if I state it by asking whether everything happens in
the mind of the governess or nothing does?

Porter: When I first read this story, I accepted the governess's
visions as real, that is, the ghosts were real in themselves, and not
only the governess, perhaps, but others might have seen them; they
had a life of their own. But as I went on reading the story and
studying it through the years, and I read Henry James's notes on it, I
decided that the ghosts were a projection of the governess's imagination and were part of her plot.

17

Tate: It is evident, Miss Porter, isn't it, that nobody actually sees these people but the governess?

Porter: Nobody.

Tate: James is very adroit in convincing the readers that perhaps they can be seen by other people, or have been, but if you look closely it is perfectly evident that nobody sees them as physical existences but the governess. I don't say that that destroys their reality.

Porter: Not at all.

Van Doren: And, of course, there's no possible doubt that she does see them. The statement "the governess sees the ghosts" is a true statement.

Tate: Oh, there's no question of that.

Van Doren: Not only does she have no doubt herself, but it never occurs to her that anyone else could question their presence.

Tate: She has a momentary doubt of a certain kind, Mr. Van Doren. Doesn't she say toward the end that if Flora goes out into the world and people come in from outside—for example, her employer, the uncle of the children—and look at the situation and find that the apparitions don't visually exist, then she will have to say: "Where am I?" Those are her exact words.

Van Doren: Yes, and there is one moment when Mrs. Grose, the housekeeper, the plain and simple woman of the story, fails to see Miss Jessel, the evil governess who has died.

Tate: That is one of the most interesting moments in the whole story.

Van Doren: The present governess even then, as you say, seems to understand that she may be lost if she can't make Mrs. Grose see this woman who is "as big as a blazing fire," for then she has no case. She does seem, at that moment, to think of herself as one having a case.

Tate: She has been so hard-pressed that she feels she must build the case herself even at the expense of the children. That is the sinister note which enters the second half of the story.

Porter: In her attempt to vindicate herself she's doing the whole thing really at the expense of the children—I have always believed for the sake of destroying them, of putting them out of the way in some manner or other in order to clear a road to the master.

Tate: I agree with Miss Porter. But does the governess realize that consciously?

Porter: No, never.

Van Doren: Well, this is the question then that frames itself in my mind: are we to take the story as a piece of psychology, as an exploration of a peculiar temperament, namely, the governess', suffering under illusions and hallucinations? I prefer not to take it that way. It seems to me that the story would shrink a great deal in power and significance if it were merely a story which psychoanalyzed an old maid.

Tate: I think we've got to take it that way and the other way, too—both at once—and perhaps if we take it both ways, we've got to take it in a third way which will explain the fact that the story is a unified thing, a single thing which is neither psychological wholly nor a mere attempt on the part of this governess to protect her children.

Van Doren: You see, I am interested in Miss Porter's statement that the first time she read the story she believed the governess. This is certainly true for me.

Tate: And for me, too.

Van Doren: And it still is. The first time Miss Porter read the story, it never occurred to her that the evil personified in these two persons—at least these two, because Miss Porter would add a third, or . . .

Porter: Even a fourth, perhaps—

Van Doren: . . . all right, that the evil somehow was there. Now, I think we must take that as a fact. If the story were merely—I'm agreeing with you, Mr. Tate—if the story were merely a clever piece of psychology, no reader, even a child, would feel in it the powerful presence of evil.

Tate: That's absolutely right. It seems to me that given the time in which James lived and the growing interest then in the processes of the mind, we have to see James as taking that peculiar interest as a medium through which to set forth the reality of evil; because the reality of evil in this story is not destroyed, or made a false issue, by explaining it psychologically. In James's time the psychological basis was necessary. In the past, treatment of ghosts, the material projection of evil in earlier literature, didn't follow a psychological bent; it wasn't done psychologically; the evil creatures were presented in their

full physical body and the public accepted them at their face value.
We have become more sophisticated, and perhaps a little more
decadent in our literature—certainly more critical. Don't we demand
that all of these allegorical effects, all of these realities of evil, be set
forth on some level that will also satisfy the critical point of view?

Porter: Yes, that is important. James himself confessed that he
wished to catch those not easily caught.

Van Doren: Exactly.

Porter: And he made in effect booby-traps of a very high order,
with a great deal of wit and a great deal of good humor. But I was
thinking that one of the really interesting levels of analysis in this story
is theological, admitting the existence of original sin, of the fact that
we really are conceived in sin, brought forth in iniquity. I think that is
a very interesting point in the study of this story.

Tate: Wasn't James always preoccupied with evil?

Porter: Yes.

Van Doren: That is one reason we call him a great writer.

Tate: But wasn't his problem then to make that evil as dramatically
convincing as possible?

Van Doren: Yes, but I think of him as suffering under the
limitations which modern literature and the critical mind imposed
upon him. He wasn't able to ask us to believe that anything like
Furies or devils existed. Aeschylus could put the Furies on his stage,
and even Shakespeare could put on a ghost. All James was able to
do was to ask us to believe in the return—somehow—of two very evil
individuals. They are not devils; they don't represent evil; they simply
are evil. A very bad man, Peter Quint.

Porter: Known to have been bad, yes. And the woman, known to
have been bad.

Van Doren: A very tragic and dishonored woman, Miss Jessel.

Tate: Now, are they described as necessarily evil during their lives?
My feeling is that they were merely "bad." Couldn't we make this
distinction: that this story is not about good and bad, but about good
and evil? The question of the way in which James makes evil
dramatic and convincing has always fascinated me in this book. If
you will remember, Quint first appears dressed in the master's
clothes; it is the first thing the governess notices about him. Then she
notices that he has red hair, and strange pointed eyebrows, and . . .

Porter: All the physical attributes of the legendary devil.

Tate: Exactly.

Porter: The evil eye.

Tate: Precisely. And I think James is playing with us a little there—bringing in an additional dimension of the imagination. But when she tells Mrs. Grose about Quint, it seems to me that James's dramatic powers, his powers as a writer of fiction, are at their very highest, because his job is to insert Quint into the scene and make him an actor in it, and that is very difficult. In order to do that, he must have the governess get some objective verification for her vision, and the way in which the governess makes the simple Mrs. Grose identify Quint established him in the scene. Well, that is—if you wish—a trick of fiction. It is the novelist's technique. Actually, at the same time, it doesn't invalidate Quint as an evil person. That's the ambivalent thing in the story.

Van Doren: And of course there are some wonderful strokes as Quint is painted. Remember, his first two appearances do not reveal anything except the upper half of him. Once he is standing behind a sort of balustrade on top of the tower; another time he is merely looking in a window, but the lower half of him is not there—it is as if he were in some ghastly way truncated. I am also interested in the fact that he is pale—that he has a pale face with light hair. If he is the devil, at least he is a very special sort of devil; he's not swarthy or grimacing; his face is rigid. He has a thin face and light curly red hair.

Tate: He never changes his expression. I recall something that James says in his preface to this book about the presentation of supernatural creatures in fiction. We must remember that neither Quint nor Miss Jessel ever does much of anything; they just appear; they just stand there and look—and their mere appearance is enough to set all this machinery of horror into motion.

Van Doren: That's enough, incidentally.

Tate: Yes. He says supernatural creatures should do as little as possible, as little as is "consistent with their consenting to appear at all."

Van Doren: Exactly. The awful thing is that they should appear.

Porter: The one thing we haven't talked about yet is the role of the children in this story. This, I think, is terribly important, because the governess persistently tries to fix upon the children evil motives and base actions, and takes seriously an accusation made against the little boy by the head-master of the school when he is sent home with a note saying that he had been an immoral influence. She was using this accusation as a weapon against the little boy—a kind of moral blackmail. The girl, who was in some ways a simpler nature, I think, and of a more positive mind than the little boy, was uncomplicated by the fact that she had had no sad experiences. Well, their simplest and most natural acts are interpreted by the governess as being of a suspicious nature, even when they got up in the night and went out to look at the moonlight, and that sort of thing. The governess constantly attempts to draw the children into her orbit of evil and force them to share it and prove them guilty. She transfers her guilty motives to them, making them accomplices to justify herself. But it seems to me that their conduct is perfectly simple and intuitive. They surmise the purpose and the enormous threat to them . . .

Tate: But the threat was real, wasn't it, Miss Porter?

Porter: Very real. The children were frightened for good reasons, though they did not understand anything; they acted with the curious reserved defensiveness of children who don't know what is happening to them. They surmised evil, surmised the threat and were trying to escape. They even tried to get together to confide in each other, but the governess made constant efforts to keep them separate so that they would never be able to work up a common defense against her.

Van Doren: She assumes that when they are together they talk unspeakably evil things.

Porter: Yes.

Van Doren: But I wonder if we're not a bit misleading about the governess. I quite agree that the children are in some sense innocent, beautiful and clear. But so is the governess. We are suggesting that she is more sinister than she ever, at any rate, knows herself as being.

Tate: She never knows herself as being sinister.

Van Doren: We almost have imputed to her a plot to corrupt the children herself. Now I'm willing to believe that it is she who corrupts the children and brings about the death of the little boy. Nevertheless, that is precisely my way of understanding how potent the evil in this story is. The evil isn't merely thought to be; it is an actuality which passes through her as a perfectly transparent and non-resistant medium and then passes through the children. The evil is somehow there.

Porter: And finally it is projected to an immense distance.

Van Doren: Yes, for she has great power. If it were merely a story of what she thought, of what she could fool herself into seeing, she wouldn't have the power she has over us as readers; she wouldn't be able, as you say, to project Quint and Miss Jessel to great distances, across lakes, to the tops of towers, and so on.

Tate: Mr. Van Doren, couldn't we put it this way? The governess doesn't invent these apparitions; they merely use her as a medium. Because, obviously, the monstrous proportions of the evil are so great that they are beyond the power of any individual imagination to invent. There is something much stronger than the governess operating through her. She has her own innocent later existence, as is proved, I think, by the prologue of the story, where we learn that after this terrible incident had passed, she went on to other posts and nothing like it occurred again. It was some peculiar conjunction of forces which permitted this evil to emerge through her here.

Van Doren: That is extremely interesting, Mr. Tate. You suggest to me another reason why James is a great writer. Living as he did in our time, which usually does not take stock in either good or evil, he was able to construct in the governess a creature almost like Cassandra, through whom evil tears its way without any instigation on her part at all—without, so to speak, her permission.

Tate: Don't you feel then that the governess, at the end of the story, in spite of the fact that you see what she's done, has a certain dignity of her own, that she is a person of great proportions? She is not in the least an insignificant creature.

Van Doren: She is no such creature as a story-teller makes his victim when he wants to deal in mere delusion. She is not ridiculous or trivial. As a matter of fact, she becomes tragic.

Tate: Exactly. It's her tragedy.

Van Doren: Of course, individual creatures can be the vehicles or channels of great good also. Just as Cassandra is a person through whom evil tears, so a saint may be a person through whom good pours in floods.

Porter: An illuminant is not always an illuminant for good. The most dangerous people in the world are the illuminated ones through whom forces act when they themselves are unconscious of their own motives. And yet, no force has ever acted through either a saint or an evil person that wasn't somehow directed to further the ends and the ambitions and the hopes of that person, which makes me feel that the instrument is not altogether so innocent and so helpless as we have been saying. Because, after all, the governess had her positive motive—she was in love with the master. She had a deep sense of her inferior situation in life, and was almost hopeless of ever attracting his attention. And I do think that this love, which was quite hopeless, which was an ingrown thing, took this form; she herself, in her imagination—yes, unconscious of her motives—designed all this drama to make the desired situation possible—that she would arrive somewhere at a level with the man she loved and create some sort of communication with him.

Tate: I agree with you, Miss Porter, but it has always seemed to me that that level of the governess's experience—that is, her personal motivation, what she expected to get out of it and all that—has a perfectly naturalistic basis. Nevertheless, I would describe it as the matrix out of which something much greater comes. As a matter of fact, we can go back and take the great tragic characters in drama, or the great religious heroes, too. They will all have some psychological motivation which we can see in terms of their peculiar situations. At the same time, are we agreed that in the case of the true saints, of the great tragic heroes, possibly in the case of the governess here, the psychological basis doesn't explain it all?

Porter: The popular psychological explanation is too superficial.

Van Doren: Otherwise we should be aware that an explanation is ready and easy as we read along, whereas the truth is—we all grant this—that as we read along we're not explaining anything to ourselves at all. We're not saying: Well, a dreadful, dreadful thing is happening, yet we know the reason. In a very important sense we don't know the reason. Somthing is loose here in the world, if only in the mind of a woman. Something is loose in the world which is very powerful and beyond the control of any human being.

Porter: I would say quite beyond the Freudian explanation.

Van Doren: Oh, decidedly.

Porter: Here is one place where I find Freud completely defeated.

Tate: James knew substantially all that Freud knew before Freud came on the scene.

Porter: All major artists do.

Van Doren: Any great story-teller has to, because a great story-teller has for his subject good and evil.

Tate: There is an aspect of this story which has always interested me very much. It is what we might call the technical aspects. I should think readers of the story would be very much interested in how James established the realities of these things which would otherwise be incredible. Consider the fact that the story is told by a governess and the fact that, as Mr. Van Doren said some time ago, in reading it we tend to forget that the governess is telling it; we think we are actually participating. That is due, I think, to the great art of James. Isn't it true that one trouble with the first-person narrative, the story told by somebody in the story, is that the authority of that person is usually not quite established? We say usually of such a person: she is participating in it, you can't expect her to give us an unbiased version of it; she's not sufficiently detached; she's not disinterested. But, while that's a liability in most first-person narratives, it seems to me that James's triumph consists in the fact that he has been able to take the defect of the method and use it for a positive purpose. The very fact that the governess is biased becomes a dramatic factor. The bias becomes a part of the story.

Porter: Yes, and because she has no understanding at all of her real motive, she gives herself away completely and constantly.

Tate: Constantly. There are two levels: the level at which she sees the action and the level at which the reader can see it, and this creates an irony of which the governess is not aware.

Van Doren: She is not aware, for instance, of how much it is against her own nature and her own desire to plague the little boy at the end, to make him tell more and more and more about the bad things he has done. They turn out to be rather slight things, don't you think? No reader assumes that the little boy has done anything very bad.

Tate: Nothing bad at all.

Porter: Some vague little offense against Victorian morality, no doubt.

Van Doren: Yet the governess all along has wanted to spare the children. Indeed, her declared intention was to protect, to shield them. Here she is forced by the irony of her character and fate to torture this little boy into confessions which he doesn't want to make, which he doesn't even know how to make because he has nothing to confess.

Tate: Isn't that a wonderful scene in Miles's room at night? The governess comes—it bears out just what you were saying, Mr. Van Doren—she comes to have a talk with him, as you will remember, and to try to get out of him what he did at school. It's a general stock-taking of Miles's situation. It is one of the most powerful pieces of irony I've ever read, because the governess is actually making love to the little boy and she doesn't know it. But he knows it in a curious instinctive way; he blows the candle out to get rid of her.

Porter: And the scene is wonderfully written—his terror at this visit in the night, with what for him was ghost or devil, all evil in fact, everything that he had reason to be terrified of, coming into his room with that unpardonable invasion of his privacy—this is all projected with such admirable simplicity and directness that the reader forgets the words and shares the impression.

Van Doren: His very childish understanding of the fact that she is in love with him comes out, it seems to me, in the conversation in which he suggests that he should be going back to school now, because, after all, he's just a "fellow," and has no right to spend all of his time with a lady.

Tate: He shows something perfectly wonderful there. It is so simple that the implications are sometimes lost on the reader. He is sitting with her and there's silence. The governess says, "Well, here we are." And Miles says, "Yes, we're here." Just like that.

Van Doren: That's right. But again it seems to me that the fame of this story among all of James's stories is justified by the fact that the evil in it somehow remains pure and general, remains undefined. All of the attempts on the part of the governess to find out what it is, after all, are frustrated. There is never any danger that evil will shrink here into vice, into misdemeanor.

Tate: James says that evil is never credible in fiction if it is presented in "weak specifications."

Van Doren: We have all had the experience of reading a story about some villain whom we can believe to be unspeakable—we like to believe in unspeakable villains—and then of being shocked by the discovery that all he did was murder his grandmother. That never is enough.

Porter: Yes, nearly always the specific act, the crime, does seem inadequate compared to the great force of evil which produces it.

Van Doren: I am reminded of Iago, whose evil is never explained by the specific motives he is said to have, and even himself thinks he has. Iago thinks that he is jealous of Othello, but it isn't jealousy, it isn't ambition, it isn't anything you can name at all. That is why Iago is a force. He is one of these figures who are being used.

Tate: But he's an evil figure, not merely a bad one. There's a fundamental difference between the evil and the bad.

Van Doren: Good and evil is the distinction. I wonder if everyone agrees with us that the great theme is good and evil. We keep saying so.

Porter: Yes, or rather the conflict between them in the minds of men.

Van Doren: Do you suppose anyone doubts us?

Tate: Otherwise we get merely social literature, the literature of social problems, political and economic literature.

Porter: I think that during the nineteenth century, when the perféctibility of man was an accepted doctrine, James was one of the few who had this genuine knowledge of good and evil, and the courage to take it as his theme.

Tate: I would like to read the very last paragraph of this story. It is the moment after Miles has died. He is lying there dead and the governess is looking at him.

"But he had already jerked straight round, stared, glared again and seen but the quiet day. With the stroke of the loss I was so proud of, he uttered a cry of a creature hurled over an abyss, and the grasp with which I recovered him might have been that of catching him in his fall. I caught him; yes, I held him, it may be imagined with what a passion. But at the end of a minute I began to feel what it truly was that I held. We were alone with the quiet day and his little heart, dispossessed, had stopped."

Reading and Writing

Mary McGrory/1953

From *The Washington Star,* 12 April 1953. Reprinted by permission of *The Washington Post.* All rights reserved.

Katherine Anne Porter, the distinguished short-story writer and essayist, who used to be here as a fellow in American Letters at the Library of Congress, returned to town briefly last week. Winding up a reading tour, she was obviously flurried and in her words "broken-bones tired."

Although of an age to be a grandmother, Miss Porter somehow still commands the aura of the Southern belle. Her snow-white hair frames her delicate features and an elegant grey dress brought out her beautiful deep-set gray eyes. Her throaty drawling conversation is sprinkled still with the "La me's" of her Texas and Louisiana girlhood. Miss Porter charmed the audience right out of their seats at her reading at the Institute of Contemporary Arts.

Though frail and small, Miss Porter takes pride in the toughness she exhibits on these barnstorming tours. She regards herself as a pioneer in the new craze of authors reading from their own works. She hit the road all sole alone some 12 years ago and has been trouping the universities and colleges all over the country ever since. She says it's more profitable than writing, and, of course, more fun.

Has she noticed, she was asked, any reaction toward the congressional inquiries into university life. After first submitting it might not be discreet to say, Miss Porter suddenly recollected she had never been discreet in these matters and spoke her mind.

I think those Senators' ears would fall off if they could hear the contempt and anger with which the students speak of them. They are more angry than frightened and more disgusted than either, and they aren't dupes or cowards. They are very sincere and intelligent about the danger of communism.

"When I think," said Miss Porter warming to her subject, "that the life of the mind and the spirit—the fine arts are the only things that

28

outlive everything else—are being mauled and pawed over by people who are not only perfectly ignorant but perfectly malignant . . ."

"We will pay a big price for this kind of foolishness," she finished.

Miss Porter, whose last book, *The Days Before,* was published last fall, has at the moment nothing ready for press. She was hurrying back to New York to make a tape recording for a radio broadcast, which will be devoted to a reading of American poetry of the last 125 years. With that out of the way she hopes to get to her typewriter for an extended session with four long short stories she has in mind and a couple of essays.

Miss Porter on Writers
and Writing
Winston Bode/1958

From *The Texas Observer*, 31st October, 1958. Reprinted by
permission of Winston Bode and *The Texas Observer.*

"Yes, I remember you," said the voice of Katherine Anne Porter. I
had asked for an interview. "I've been answering the phone all
morning with my mouth full of toothpaste. But I've finally got it out."
She laughed a belly laugh. "It's the most amazing thing. Apparently"—the t's sharp—"the whole place is populated by old friends of
mine. But they're all widows. Isn't that funny? All the uncles and
brothers and fathers gone now."

We met in the dim tall-ceilinged lobby, she in her fur and rich hat,
64 and sporting lorgnette-type glasses ("I have others, but these are
so much easier, don't you know"), looking at a letter we had opened
on the way down, from the *Southwest Review.*

Her eyes are wide and a deep-lustered ageless grey green: "This is
good. Write for the little magazines first . . . Some of the battles we
won and you don't have to fight them again. When I was young
there was a slick formula that was being used by the magazines and
being practiced with great skill by a handful of craftsmen. But I wrote
honest, and it was hard to get an honest story published. I think one
man was responsible for the change. James Joyce with *Dubliners*
broke the formula . . . Katherine Mansfield didn't write formula. Of
course, I'd been writing my own kind of stories for years. But I was
just a little girl from Texas in New York. My first story was published
in *Old Century,* a respected magazine, like the *Atlantic Monthly.* That
was "María Concepción," the first story I had finished. First finished,
first published—in 1923. I had started many other stories, but I
hadn't finished them. I was 29, and I had been writing since I was six
or seven, and had been an apprentice for 15 years. But nobody ever
saw a manuscript of mine except the editor I sent it to. There was an

exception of a friend or two, whom I would show a manuscript to after it was all done and ready to be sent off.

"And then came the era of the little magazines. For 25 years I saved the stories for the poor dears because I wanted to keep them going. But now *Mademoiselle* will take the same stories and pay me $1,000, and you know, I'm going to take it. That's the battle we won for you. You don't have to starve in garrets and cellars as many of us did . . . The big magazines got the idea that people would read these stories and they started publishing them without changing a line. But they will not buy you if you are not known. You must send to the good small ones and then the big rich ones will buy your stories. They'll try to sidetrack you once they have you and make you write their way, but if you're strong and hold out they'll buy the same stories the small magazines do . . . But it's a long haul. It takes about 40 years!" She laughed.

"In the early days people would say, 'I will go to Hollywood and save money and then write the way I want to.' But they never did. In the first place they didn't save money, and they ruined themselves. You can't hold yourself in contempt and do anything worthwhile.

"I would say to the young writers, You shouldn't side-step suffering if you have to go through it to get where you're going."

What did she mean by suffering?

"I mean whatever your human problem is. I mean facing it in life—not turning it into literature. Facing it, and not turning into a hobo like the beat generation, or a stuffed shirt . . . You'll have to write what you are. I wish I could remember who it was who said, 'If you don't want to give yourself away, don't write.' "

We discussed writers. I mentioned James Agee. She responded: "A first-rate artist, a wonderful example of the regional, the particular, used in such a way that the meaning is universal.

"He worked hard, and he played hard, and he used himself up all too soon. But he lived to the full, and perhaps that was the only way he could be. He just went over the dam chin first. I'm just awfully glad we had him while we did. But if someone could have stopped him and said, 'Look, save yourself. . . .' I regret him bitterly, as I do John Peale Bishop, who I think had so much promise and who had not reached his height.

"And I like Allen Tate." She smiled. "He has that sense of, of 'local

habitation' . . . I don't like to quote Shakespeare, but sometimes we
have to, don't we? . . ."

Her tone changed. "And then there are those like Jesse Stuart,
who stay in one place—But I don't want to talk about other writers!
After all, dog does not eat dog!

"I've come nearer getting exactly what I wanted than anyone I
know. What is it? Not fame or notoriety, just having the people you
want to read and like you. I have so little complaint. I haven't done as
good work as I had hoped or expected to do. But that's why we don't
quit. We're expecting the next one to be a masterpiece. You can't
expect us to quit a way of life, to quit writing, any more than you can
expect us to quit reading. I'll probably go on writing more and more.
I've been so busy making a living, teaching and trouping the country,
and I've had so many human calls on me."

Our interview was cut short. "I'm afraid I've made a terrible
mistake," she said. "The people from the University are coming for
me at 11:30 and I thought they said 12. You know on these lecture
assignments, they put you on a treadmill. . . . But would it be
convenient for you to call me here at the hotel at 2:30? Would you
do that please? I could tell you all my life in ten minutes. I talk very
fast. But I know you have those questions there you haven't asked
me, and I talk just as fast on the telephone." She laughed.

"I'm relaxed," Miss Porter said on the telephone, "but my voice is
hoarse. I've been talking since early this morning, and I simply must
save myself for tonight. You know I got up much earlier than I
thought and people have been calling me constantly. But go ahead,
let's answer your questions."

A few "feature story" type questions, we said. Age?

"Of course I don't mind. You can find it in the backs of any
number of books in the library. I was born May 15, 1894. That's a
beautiful time of the year. I have a friend who says, You must feel
awfully lucky being born right smack dab in the middle of May in
Texas."

"You know," she said, "I have a lot of friends who were born in
April and May. . . . Of course, as someone has pointed out, that's the
lambing season!"

How did she feel about prolixity in writers?

"I don't have anything against prolixity. I hate that word! I don't have anything against abundance. But if you have a selectiveness, you don't publish so much. I've written bushels but I publish only what I choose to publish. Your output can be small, but you can be world famous on one little book of poems. After all, say you write 50 or 60 books. Out of that there are going to be only five or six that are really good."

Miss Porter said she started lecturing in 1936 when she came back from abroad. "Before that I did articles and that sort of thing. I was married part of the time. I did book reviews for the New York newspapers, and one way or another I made out. I wrote every day of my life and still do even on these little old trips. I write not to be taking notes, you understand, but because I like to get a thing down. Of course, it's a great change, to get out of the whirl and sit down and face that blank wall to write." Her musical voice rang. "But nobody promised us the great things would all be wonderful."

"I've been a total widow for 16 years," she said, "and I intend to stay that way. My maiden name is Katherine Anne Porter, Porter is my family name. I never used my husbands' names except for social purposes. I'm not going to talk about my private life. It's not that I mind, but you understand there is nothing to tell. The only thing that counts is my work."

We asked where she was born.

"Why do you ask that? I thought everybody around here knew all that."

We discussed the fact that she was not written about too much in Texas. There was some joke about a revival.

"Yes I realize that! Well they know me elsewhere! I was born in Indian Creek, I think that is the name of a Community, in Brown County, and I was raised around Kyle . . . No, I didn't attend college, I went to girls' schools, convents, that type of thing."

"I feel about revival like whoever it was who heard that Henry James was being revived. He said, 'I hadn't heard he was dead.' I hadn't heard I was dead."

"Texas has no serious writers. I am the first serious writer Texas has produced. That is, up to now. There are two young writers who are very promising. William Humphrey has written a good book. 'Home is the sailor' . . . How does it go? 'Home from the sea And the hunter home from the hill.'[1]

"Robert Louis Stevenson was not a good writer but that was a good poem. Now William Humphrey is really young—in his mid-thirties. If you start when you're 18 and work your head off, you're doing good to amount to something at that age."

"I thought William Goyen had a really brilliant and strange talent. When his first works came out I thought he had a first rate talent. But he seems to have—gone off. But maybe he will come back and produce more good work . . . I am the first and only serious writer that Texas has produced. These young people may turn out to be first rate. The woods are swarming with writers. In all this ferment, we're bound to get more good ones. But so far I am the only one. If you can show me others, I'll be glad to see them!"

In the hotel she had said, "What is more 'regional' than 'Noon Wine'? Than 'Old Mortality'?" I asked, "Are you a regional writer?" "Of course I'm not a regional writer. I think you ought to write about what you know. But I don't know any first rate person who is a regional writer.

"I don't think we ought to have American lyric writers or French provincial writers or English country writers . . . I think we ought to drop two words: Americanism and regionalism. They are coins with the design rubbed off. They are cramping people with perfectly good instincts. Let the artist write what he can. I think we should be good writers."

The lecture hall was filled up, some sat in folding chairs in the aisles, and they piped the sound to two rooms upstairs. Miss Porter came out in a blue gown, stiffly and formally engaged the crowd, and bowed low. Her hair was dressed brilliantly. Her heart-shaped face looked sculptured, delicate and beautiful, and her lovely eyes were steady as they met the audience.

Dr. William Eckman of the English staff had introduced her as the first in the current series of lectures in the University's Program in Criticism and as a woman who has "one of the solidest literary reputations in America." He said she would talk on "Noon Wine: The Sources."

"Noon Wine" had been bandied about in the papers all week as a story laid near Austin, around Buda.

Miss Porter fumbled in her purse and coughed a little and seemed apologetic and said, "You know, I've been meeting people all day and signing things and before I go a step further I want to say that . . . more fumbling . . . "I got away with a perfectly good grey Parker pen!" She went into a deep laugh. More fumbling. "No, that's mine" . . . She lifted her chin. "I look upon this as a kind of beautiful family gathering. I shouldn't be surprised if there are some of you who know the place where I was born. It isn't on the map at all . . . I was taken away when I was 18 months old, and I haven't been back there for 45 years. I lived until I was ten years old with my grandmother, who died in the little farm town of Kyle . . . I think my first sight of the great world was when my grandmother brought me up here to be vaccinated . . . My first look at a work of beauty was when she took me into the Capitol rotunda. We went all the way up to the top of the Capitol then. I understand they won't let you do that now."

"The people I knew accepted art . . . Van Cliburn doesn't seem a surprise to me. He's the sort of person I recognize. I can remember the school teacher who would catch the train once a week and come into Austin for piano lessons . . . They studied from the Germans, who came down on the piano from above . . . not like they do today all with the fingers . . . And the girls who taught school would go to Europe for the summer. Nobody thought much about it."

"People ask me what I write from, and I say, I write from experience, but I say experience is anything that happens to me. . . . a flash of memory, a nightmare, a daydream . . . You can't start a work of art anywhere except where life starts. . . ."

". . . But many an experience that I use in a story happened to me so early I can hardly put it together . . . People ask me, 'Who was the person in real life who inspired you to write about the Swedish hired hand named Helton in "Noon Wine"?' I say, 'Why, his name was Helton and he was a Swedish hired hand.' He was someone I saw once propped up against the side of a shack playing tunes on a mouth organ. A lonely figure with thatched bleak hair between his eyebrows. And that's all I knew about him."

She prepared to read from her text and said perhaps the best way

she could tell about the sources of "Noon Wine" would be to read
what she had written Allen Tate about them.[2]

She reached for her glasses and said: "You know I have wonderful
eyes and can count the hairs of your eyebrows at 60 paces. I think it
is perfect irony that I can see everything except print at 17 inches."

She looked up from the text. "I think everyone lives a story three
times over . . . The first time is when the events occur . . . then when
you remember them . . . and the third time is when you begin to put
them into art . . . And there is a fourth time when people ask how it
happened when they ask artists to explain themselves . . . Tracing the
art through the labyrinth of experience . . . childhood memory . . . is
really an impossible undertaking, a little like tapping one's own spinal
fluid."

She read: "By the time I wrote "Noon Wine" it had become real to
me almost in the sense that I felt not as if I had made that story out of
my own memory of real events and imagined consequences, but as if
I were quite simply reporting events I had heard or witnessed. This is
not in the least true: the story is fiction; but it is made up of thousands
of things that did happen to living human beings in a certain part of
the country at a certain time of my life; things that are still remembered by others as single incidents; not as I remembered them,
floating and moving with their separate life and reality, meeting and
parting and mingling in my thoughts until they established their
relationship and meaning to me. So I feel that this story is "true" in
the way that a work of fiction should be true, created out of all the
scattered particles of life I was able to absorb and combine and shape
into new being . . ."

". . . The story wove itself in my mind for years before I intended
to write it at all . . . When the moment came to write this story, I
knew it; and I had to make quite a number of practical arrangements
to get the free time for it, without fear of interruption. I wrote it as it
stands except for a few pen corrections in just seven days of trance-
like absorption in a small inn in rural Pennsylvania, from the early
evening of November 7 to November 14, 1936. Yet I had written the
central part, the scene between Mr. Hatch and Mr. Thompson, which
leads up to the murder, in Basel, Switzerland, in the summer of
1932."

". . . I had been in Mexico, Bermuda, Spain, Germany,

Switzerland and, best of all, in Paris for five years . . . And while I was there I was making notes of my own place . . . the south. (Looking at other countries) gave me back my past and my own home." She remembered "all the life of that soft black farming land . . . the rivers . . . the honey suckle . . . the heavy tomatoes, eaten ripe from the vine . . . the savory corn."

She told how she remembered her people, poor but not poverty-stricken, with origins in Kentucky and Tennessee, with a violence potential that broke through without warning . . . the feuds. She recalled their faces, with the prominent handsome noses with the diamond-shaped figure at the bridge, "I saw Pope Pius's picture in death the other day and I said, 'I know that nose. It looks like a Kentucky nose to me'."

The incidents in "Noon Wine"? She didn't in the least remember the tobacco-chewing incident. But the men were always gathering in small knots, day after day, whittling and chewing and talking. She never had the courage to go close enough to hear what they were saying. She always wondered what could they find to talk about, day after day. But all her childhood around Kyle there were sharp blades slicing tobacco. She remembered her father's knife was so sharp he could peel a pecan with four cuts through the hull, taking the meat out whole. There were blades everywhere—hoes, axes, knives, plow shares. But the children, for some reason, scarcely ever got hurt. She remembered her tall darkhaired booted relatives from West Texas, with guns in their shirts . . . You would go into a closet and there would be the long cold barrel of a shot gun or rifle, put there because the gun closet was full . . . She remembered shooting at targets and clay pigeons with her father . . . she could identify the sound of any kind of gun. And she remembered being on the patch of grass at the side of the house in a yard that was ever shrinking in size as her world became wider, and the town became smaller. She supposed she must have been small because of the way she remembered the way a table and people's legs looked to her . . . and she knew that there must have been others around her because there were always relatives around her. But all she remembered clearly was a shot gun shot breaking the stillness, followed by a wail of death.

She told of the bleary-eyed, slack, wild-talking man who came to her grandmother's one day after the shooting and the funeral. She could remember hearing him; "I swear it was in self-defense!"

"Lady, if you don't believe me, ask my wife. She won't lie."

The pitiable, shamed, bent figure sat and hoarsely said, "Yes, that's right. I saw it."

Was this the man who killed Pink Hodges? She didn't know. She remembered asking about the murder. But all she was sure of later was that it was in her ninth year.

"Suppose now," said Katherine Anne Porter, "I really saw all these persons in the flesh at one time or another? I saw what I have told you, a few mere flashes of a glimpse here and there, one time or another; but I do know why I remembered them, and why in my memory they slowly took on their separate lives in a story. It is because there radiated from each one of these glimpses of strangers some element, some quality that arrested my attention at a vital moment of my own growth, and caused me, a child, to stop short and look outward, away from myself; to look at another human being with that attention and wonder and speculation which ordinarily, and very naturally, I think, a child lavishes only on himself . . . This was a spiritual enlightenment, some tenderness, some first wakening of a charity in my self-centered heart. I am using here some very old-fashioned noble words in their prime sense. . . . I know well what they mean, and I need them here to describe as well as I am able what happens to a child when the bodily senses and the moral sense and that sense of charity are unfolding, and are touched once for all in that time when the soul is prepared for them; and I know that the all-important things in that way have all taken place long before we know the words for them."

Notes

1 Under the wide and starry sky
Dig the grave and let me lie
Glad did I live and gladly die
And I lay me down with a will.
This be the verse you grave for me
Here he lies where he longed to be
Home is the sailor home from the sea
And the hunter home from the hill.

—Robert Louis Stevenson's poem for his tombstone.

2 Robert Penn Warren and not Allen Tate requested the essay which appeared in the *Yale Review* (XLVI [1956], 22–39) as *"Noon Wine: The Sources,"* and was subsequently included in *The Collected Essays and Occasional Writings of Katherine Anne Porter.*

Desegregation Ruling Criticized by Author

Richmond News Leader/1958

From the *Richmond News Leader,* 20 November 1958. Reprinted by permission of the *Richmond News Leader.*

Katherine Anne Porter said here today the Supreme Court acted "recklessly and irresponsibly" in the school desegregation decision.

Her opinion on that issue popped up unexpectedly when deploring pressures to conform in the modern world, she said:

"I belong to the school of thought that believes the Supreme Court acted recklessly and irresponsibly in precipitating this crisis at the worst possible time when we already had enough crises on hand."

In the midst of saying it, the famous novelist paused to add, "I wonder what kind of trouble this may get me in, but I don't care."

("That's one of the pleasant things about growing old," she said. "As you perhaps have accomplished a little something, you feel more at home with yourself and the world and lose whatever fears you may have had.")

Miss Porter said she believed the justices "acted with moral irresponsibility because apparently they are ignorant of the true situation."

"That thing was taking care of itself very well," she added.

There is little conformity in Miss Porter.

She delivers fire-cracker opinions in soft, tentative tones, sometimes almost childlike, sometimes as if telling an engrossing fairy tale to a child.

She was dressed stylishly in black, a big silver filigree rose from Mexico on her lapel, a pizza-size gray felt hat from Paris over her soft white hair. She speaks with a wide-eyed verve and gaiety of a literary Tallulah Bankhead.

Asked what disappointed her most in contemporary America, she replied she didn't like "the way we have of taking on all the evils we were supposed to be fighting in Nazism, Fascism and Communism the oppression of the human spirit through the multiple making of petty, niggling laws."

("Although," she added, in an aside, "it's always been true that, in the strangest way, you tend to become like the thing you fight.")

What disturbs her, she said, is the tendency "to put the human spirit in a mould . . . to compress the individual into the lowest common denominator in human life."

Everything, she went on, is being organized into kinds of cartels, being done on a chain from education and government to motels and restaurants. In the attempt to make everything alike as possible, there is no room left for exploring and experimenting.

"The down-trodden minorities," she said, "are organized into tight little cabals to run the country so that we will become the down-trodden vast majority, if we don't look out."

The only things that make the world interesting, she said, "are the differences in nations and people. Why destroy that?"

Miss Porter, who likes to write of broad and subtle differences, says her favorite work always is her latest and the latest at the moment is "a great big smacking book. 200,000 words long" that will appear in late spring: *Ship of Fools.*

She got the idea when she won a Guggenheim Fellowship in 1931 and left Mexico, where she had been "attending and assisting a revolution," and traveled by ship to Europe "with the most unpleasant gang of people I ever knew."

Everything was "getting ready for the long fall," she recalls and all those aboard ship disliked each other for a variety of reasons.

"That's going to be my story," she said, "the time aboard ship from Vera Cruz to Bremerhaven, August 22 through Sept 17, 1931, an allegory of the ship of this world on a voyage to eternity."

It's going to depict the "inertia good people have toward the evils of this world, the things they allow to happen through indifference, laziness and confusion, too."

"Without knowing it," she said in another aside, "we are sometimes half in love with evil and don't stop it because it adds color and excitement to life."

She's "dead certain," she said, that the book is "the best thing I ever did," adding, laughing, "If I didn't think it was good, I wouldn't be doing it."

Her friends sometimes tease her, she said, because she is quite frank to agree when others praise something she owns and likes.

"If I didn't love it, I wouldn't have it around," she said. "And so it is with writing, I wouldn't waste my life on it if I didn't think it worthwhile. It's hard work and there are too many other wonderful things. I like too much just plain human living."

Sometimes plain living interferes. Her "lasting regret" is that she didn't have a better sense of management of life, time, and energy to finish her many projects.

"I'm leaving just bales," she said.

At times, she feels she has been wasteful, extravagant, and strewn herself around. But, she says, that has been her temperament from the restless activity of her childhood when, earlier than she can remember, she began writing, coloring, and sewing together little books.

"I was not a worldly person." she said, "but I was of this world in the sense that I wanted to touch, smell, see and be. I didn't figure it out. I just did it."

Recent Southern Fiction: A Panel Discussion

Wesleyan College/28 October 1960
Panelists: Katherine Anne Porter, Flannery O'Connor, Caroline
Gordon, Madison Jones, Louis D. Rubin, Jr., Moderator

From *Bulletin of Wesleyan College* [Macon, GA], 41 (January 1961). © 1960 by Wesleyan College. Reprinted by permission.

Despite the widespread scholarly attention given to the "Southern literary renaissance" in the twentieth century, a number of misconceptions and unanswered questions remain. In the first place, who qualifies as a Southern writer and on what grounds? If Thomas Wolfe, Ellen Glasgow, Erskine Caldwell, and William Faulkner, to name just a few, are all Southern writers, what does their work have in common? If we say that they are all products of a "Southern way of life," what elements in this complex heritage have shaped them and have caused so great a variety, on the surface at least, in their writing? How is the work of the present generation of Southern writers related to that being done in the 1920's and 1930's?

The following discussion, held at Wesleyan College on October 28, 1960, touches on these questions but does not, of course, settle any of them once and for all. (It is doubtful whether a single significant question has ever been settled to anyone's complete satisfaction during a panel discussion.) This discussion is valuable, however, because it contains the views of four Southern writers themselves. And they are writers of such stature that even their random remarks command close attention. While it is probably true that the serious writer's aims, methods, and basic concerns are best revealed in his published literary works, no one could deny the genuine interest which even his informal comments hold for the dedicated reader.

The discussion gains additional dimension from having several points of view represented. Two of the panelists, Miss Porter and Miss Gordon, long established as important writers, have done much of their writing while living outside the South. Miss O'Connor and Mr. Jones, on the other hand, represent a new generation of South-

ern writers, and they speak from the point of view of
those still living and writing in the South. Professor Rubin,
a Southerner with a sensitive awareness of the literature
of his native region, provides the broad perspective of the
literary critic and historian.

Rubin: I suppose you know what a panel discussion is—for the first
thirty minutes the moderator tries his best to get the panel members
to say something and for the last thirty minutes he does his best to
shut them up. I hope we can do that tonight. My own position here
with these four distinguished Southern writers on my left is something like the junior member of that famous and often narrated legal
firm—Levy, Ginsberg, Cohen, and Kelly. Kelly presses the suits. I
thought the first thing we might talk about, if we may, would be
writing habits. That is something everyone has one way or another.
Mr. Jones, suppose I ask you, how do you write?

    Jones: Well, you mean just physically speaking?

    Rubin: Yes. What time of the day?

    Jones: Well, I usually write from about 8:30 to 12 or 12:30 in the
morning.

    Gordon: Every day?

    Jones: Well, every day except Sunday.

    Gordon: You're a genius.

    Rubin: How about you, Miss Porter?

    Porter: Well, I have no hours at all, just such as I can snatch from
all the other things I do. Once upon a time I tagged a husband
around Europe in the Foreign Service for so many years and never
lived for more than two years in one place and never knew where I
was going to be and I just wrote when I could and I still do. Once in a
while I take the time and run away to an inn and tell them to leave
me alone. When I get hungry, I'll come out. And in those times I
really get some work done, I wrote two short novels in fourteen days
once ["Noon Wine" and "Old Mortality"] but that was twenty-five
years ago.

    Rubin: How about you, Miss Gordon?

    Gordon: I made a horrible discovery this summer. I had a great
deal of company and they all wanted to help me with the housework

and I discovered I would have to stop writing if I let them do it because my writing and my housework all go together and if they washed the dishes then I didn't get any writing done. That's just my system that I have developed over the years—it works for me except it maddens my friends, because they like to help me wash the dishes.

Rubin: You mean your whole day is part of a very closely worked in regimen?

Gordon: I didn't discover it until this friend came and insisted she wanted to help me.

Rubin: How about you, Miss O'Connor. Do you do your writing along with the dishwashing?

O'Connor: Oh, no. I sit there before the typewriter for three hours every day and if anything comes I am there waiting to receive it. I think there should be a complete separation between literature and dishwashing.

Porter: I was once washing dishes in an old fashioned dishpan at 11 o'clock at night after a party and all of a sudden I just took my hands up like that and went to the typewriter and wrote the short story "Rope" between that time and two o'clock in the morning. I don't know what started me. I know I had it in mind for several years but the moment came suddenly.

Rubin: If that's what dishwashing does, then I'm going to buy a box of Duz in the morning. What I think you all seem to show is that there is no right way or wrong way, I suppose.

Porter: I think Grandma Moses is the most charming old soul. When they asked her how she painted—and they meant, I am sure, how she used the brush—she said, "Well, first I saw a masonite board to the size I want the picture to be." And I think that is what we do.

Rubin: It all sounds like alchemy to me.

Gordon: That is one question that people always ask a writer. How many hours he or she puts in a day. I've often wondered why that is and I just discovered fairly recently. I think they expect you to say you are writing all of the time. If you are mowing the grass you are still thinking about what you are going to write. It is all the time.

Rubin: I always remember reading something the late Bernard DeVoto remarked—that one of his hardest jobs was keeping his wife from thinking that if he looked up out of the window, then that meant he wasn't doing any work at the moment, so that she could ask him about some spending money or something of the sort.

Gordon: I used to have a dentist—an awfully good one—but I quit him because when he was going to hurt me he would say, "Now just relax and think about your novel." I couldn't take that.

Jones: I have always found that when something is going well, I can't think about it at all unless I am right over the paper. Unless I am at work, I can't even get my mind on it away from my environment.

Rubin: Let me change the subject. I'll let Miss Porter answer this one. Miss Porter, do you consider yourself a Southern writer?

Porter: I am a Southerner. I have been told that I wasn't a Southerner, that anyone born in Texas is a South-westerner. But I can't help it. Some of my people came from Virginia, some from Pennsylvania, but we are all from Tennessee, Georgia, the Carolinas, Kentucky, Louisiana. What does it take to be a Southerner? And being a Southerner, I happen to write so I suppose you combine the two and you have a Southern writer, haven't you? What do you think? I do feel an intense sense of location and of background and my tradition and my country exist to me, but I have never really stuck to it in my writing because I have lived too nomadic a life. You know my people started from Virginia and Pennsylvania toward the West in 1776 or 1777 and none of us really ever stopped since and that includes me. So why should I stick to one place or write about one place since I have never lived just in one place?

Rubin: Miss O'Connor, how about you?

O'Connor: Well I admit to being one. My own sense of place is quite unadjustable. I have a friend from Michigan who went to Germany and Japan and who wrote stories about Germans who sounded like Germans and about Japanese who sounded like Japanese. I know if I tried to write stories about credible Japanese they would all sound like Herman Talmadge.

Rubin: Does the State Department know about *this*? How about you, Mr. Jones?

Jones: I feel more or less like Miss O'Connor. No matter where I was or how long I might live there—although my attitude might change—I still have the feeling that everything I would write would be laid in the country that I feel the most communion with, that is the central Tennessee area, or at least a part of it. My imagination just

feels at home there. Other places I have been have never tempted
me to write about them so I think I am a Southern writer.

Rubin: Miss Gordon, how about you?

Gordon: I agree with him. I wouldn't think about writing anything
about anybody from Princeton. They just don't seem to be important. That's dreadful but that's the way I feel. Your own country—
that's the first thing you knew—that's important. I did write one story
once that was laid in France but it was fifteen years after I lived there.
But I think the thing about the Southern writer—I believe there is
such a thing—and I think he is very interesting because he knows
something that not all other writers in America today know. I feel that
very strongly.

Porter: He usually knows who he is and where he is and what he
is doing. Some people never know that in a long lifetime. But you
see, I write out of my own background about what I know but I can't
stay in one place. I write about a country maybe ten years after I
have been in it. But that is a part of my experience too, and in a way
it is an egotistic thing to do because it is what happened to me. I am
writing about my own experience, really, out of my own background
and tradition.

Rubin: What do you mean by a sense of place? Do you mean
simply your geographical knowledge?

O'Connor: Not so much the geography. I think it is the idiom.
Like Mrs. Tate said, people in Princeton don't talk like we do. And
these sounds build up a life of their own in your senses.

Gordon: And place is very important too, I think.

Jones: And I think it is a check in a way, too, of the honesty in
your writing. Somehow in writing you have a way to check yourself
by the kind of intimacy you have with your community and home.

Rubin: I don't think myself there is any doubt that there is such a
thing as a Southern Writer—capital S, capital W—and that when you
pick up a book, a novel, a short story, it doesn't take you very long
before you have the feeling that this is by a Southerner. I suppose
there are Southern writers that fool you. I mean that you don't think
are Southerners. I think that you could pick up some Erskine
Caldwell for instance, particularly his later work, and you would
never think that this man is from 50 miles from where Flannery
O'Connor lives but at the same time—

Gordon: But he says things which are not so. For instance, I forget in what story he has the best hound dogs in the neighborhood down in the well and all of the men are just sitting around talking. None of the men are getting the dogs out of the well. That just couldn't happen. Simply couldn't happen. You can't trust him on detail.

Rubin: I like some of the things in the early Caldwell work.

Gordon: Oh, at times he's very amusing.

Rubin: I was thinking about this the other day. Let's take writers such as Caldwell and Faulkner or Eudora Welty. You think of them as being poles apart. But when you compare either of these writers, with, let's say, Dos Passos, you notice that the Caldwell people and the Welty people are more or less responsible for their own actions. In the stuff Caldwell wrote about 1930 or so he was trying to show, for example, that what was wrong with Jeeter Lester was society and the share cropping system and things like that, but when he wrote about Jeeter Lester you couldn't help feeling that the main reason Jeeter Lester was what he was was because he was Jeeter Lester. Whereas in a book like *USA* I don't think you had this feeling—I think you do accept the author's version of experience that society is what causes it. I think that the individual character somehow being responsible for his own actions is very typical of the Southern writers, and I think this is why we have produced very few naturalists as such. Do you think there is something to that?

Gordon: Why I think we have produced wonderful naturalists.

Rubin: Well, I was using the word in the literary sense.

Gordon: I just don't think you can use it that way. Every good story has naturalistic elements. Look at the sheep, cows and pigs in Miss Porter's story, "Holiday."*

Rubin: Well, I was using the word in the philosophical sense of the environment-trapped hero and such as that.

Porter: Don't you think that came out a great deal in the communist doctrine of the locomotive of history—you know, rounding the sharp bend and everybody who doesn't go with it falls off it— that history makes men instead of men making history, and it takes away the moral responsibility. The same thing can be said of that cry

---

* *"Holiday,"* read by Miss Porter on the preceding evening, appears in the December, 1960 issue of *The Atlantic.*

during the war that nobody could be blamed because we are all guilty until we stopped realizing that one has been guiltier perhaps than the other. This whole effort for the past one hundred years has been to remove the moral responsibility from the individual and make him blame his own human wickedness on his society, but he helps to make his society, you see, and he will not take his responsibility for his part in it.

Rubin: Well, that's very interesting. I think right there is the difference between Caldwell and Dos Passos. Caldwell was consciously writing out of just that propagandistic position. He wanted to show that these people were victims. Yet because he was a Southerner, because he was writing about these people, they wouldn't behave. They became people instead of symbols.

Gordon: I would like to say one other thing about the Southern writer. I think we have some awfully good Southern writers and I believe one reason they are so good is that we are a conquered people and we know some things that a person who is not a Southern writer cannot envisage as happening. For him they never have happened. We know something he does not know.

Rubin: You know that this isn't necessarily the greatest nation that ever was or ever will be.

Gordon: Well, we know that a nation can go down in defeat. A great many men committed suicide after the Civil War and anyone I have ever heard of left the same note. He said, "This is a great deal worse than I thought it was going to be." Some of them eighty years old. Edmund Ruffin, for example.

Rubin: Tell me this now. Do you think that this is as true of the young Southerner growing up today as it was for the generations of Southerners who wrote the books in the 1920's and 30's?

Gordon: I think the most terrible thing I have ever read about the South was written by my young friend here [Miss O'Connor]—worse than anything Faulkner ever wrote. That scene where that lady, I forget her name, but her husband is dead and now she gets in a tight place and she goes into the back hall behind some portieres. I can just see them, too. Some of my aunts had portieres. And she sits down at a roll-top desk which is very dusty and has yellow pieces of paper and things, and communes with his spirit. And his spirit says to her. "One man's meat is another man's poison" or something like

"The devil you know is better than the devil you don't know." I think that's the most terrible thing that's ever been written about the South. It haunts me.

Rubin: Do you really think that this is changing?

Gordon: Well, I would say here is a young writer who has this terrible vision and such a vision could only come out of great concern.

Rubin: I wonder though. Nowadays I go to my own home town of Charleston, South Carolina, and it still looks the same downtown but you go outside of the city and everything about it looks just like, well I won't say Newark, New Jersey—it's not that bad—but let's say Philadelphia, and I just wondered if the same environment that operated even on Miss O'Connor will still have the emotional impact that it has had on Southern writing, whether the sense of defeat that we were just mentioning is still going to prevail. I think the notion that the South alone of the American sections knew that it is possible to lose a war, that it is possible to do your very best and still lose, is something that has been very true of Southern life, but I wonder whether in the post-Depression prosperity this is still going to be so? I have a feeling that it isn't.

Gordon: I do too.

Porter: It is happening already. There are some extremely interesting young writers. Walter Clemons—I don't want to speak of Texas writers altogether—there is one named George Garrett and there are several others—William Humphrey, Peter Taylor, among them, and I think they are probably the last ones who are going to feel the way they do. And I think these young people are probably the last because I don't see anyone coming after them at all and even they have changed a great deal because they don't have the tragic feeling about the South that we had, you know.

Gordon: One of Peter's best stories, and he says it is his best story, is "Bad Time." Do you know that story? It's a beaut.

Porter: Yes. But I don't see anybody else coming after and these are greatly changed. You think of young Clemons and then think of ones just before and they are changed. More of them are city people; they are writing about town life. And a kind of life that didn't really interest us, even though we were brought up partly in town. It was the country life that formed us.

Gordon: Peter is kind of a missing link. But he writes about country people going to town.

Jones: I noticed that in the collection of new Southern writings more than half were set in urban areas.

Rubin: You mention William Humphrey and to me he is symptomatic of this change. That book [*Home From The Hill*] to me started off extremely well and then suddenly nose-dived, and it nose-dived precisely at the point where the protagonist could no longer do the Faulknerian sort of thing, the hunt and things like that, and was just an adolescent in the city, and it seems to me we just couldn't take the person seriously enough. Humphrey was still trying to write like Faulkner in a sense—the wrong kind of milieu in the wrong kind of place—and to me the book failed, and this is symptomatic.

Porter: He is an extremely good short story writer. He preceded that book with a number of very good short stories, I think, but he did want to write a successful book if he possibly could, you know, and he got the idea of what is success mixed up with what would be good sales and so he spoiled his book by trying to make it popular.

Rubin: He succeeded in that.

Porter: He did and good luck to him. He was my student for years and I thought he was going to turn out better than that, I must say.

Rubin: I have a feeling about the Southern writing in the last ten years, and that includes Miss O'Connor by the way—and I certainly don't mean it as an insult, Miss O'Connor. There is a kind of distance to the life you describe, a kind of esthetic distance, as if the people are far away from the writer, and this sometimes produces an extremely fine emotional effect. Take for example the difference in Styron's *Lie Down in Darkness* and Faulkner's *The Sound and The Fury,* where in both cases you have someone walking around in a northern city holding a time piece getting ready to take his or her life. Somehow or other the protagonist in the Faulkner novel is still a Yoknapatawpha County citizen. Somehow the protagonist in the Styron novel is away from that, she has left it, she couldn't go back to it if she wanted to or anywhere like that, and to me this feeling runs through so much of the most recent Southern writing. The Southern community is moving farther and farther away. You write about it and do it beautifully, but the distance is farther. You can't take it as seriously.

Jones: But don't you think in *Lie Down in Darkness* that as long as he is at home, Styron makes you feel closer to the character? I mean, that last business about the girl seems to be pretty bad.

Rubin: What I think about that book is that the book takes place in a Southern city, Port Warwick—something like Newport News, but I don't feel that the family in the book are essentially what they are because of the community at all. I think that is what Mr. Styron wanted them to be. He wanted Payton Loftis to suffer because of several generations, etc., but I don't think she does. I think it is purely because of these particular people involved. Their little private things are apart from the community, and I don't get the same sense of community even when they are writing about things in Port Warwick that you would have in a Faulkner novel.

Porter: I have a feeling about Styron, you know the way he develops piles of agonies and horrors and that sort of thing, and I think it masks a lack of feeling. I think he has all the vocabulary of feeling and rhythm of feeling and knows he ought to feel but he does not. I can't read him with any patience at all. I want to say, "Take off those whiskers, come out of the bushes and fight fair."

Rubin: I find him a very provocative writer myself.

Porter: Well, you remember the story about the man and the two people who come to play cards, I think this was in Rome. They are terrible card cheats and everybody gets frightfully drunk and he winds up perfectly senselessly without any clothes on, robbed and beaten, in a horribly filthy hotel and his wife has to come and get him and you say—now let me see, what was it about? What did it mean? It means absolutely nothing. One feels, well, the police just should have put this one in jail until he sobered up. And such a thing is not interesting for the simple reason that the man to whom it happened is of no interest. That is my quarrel with him, and it is a quarrel, too.

Rubin: If there is anything to this feeling of distance, I have the feeling that the Southern writer now isn't taking the things that go on in the community with the same kind of importance. He takes it with equal importance, but with a different kind of importance than, let's say, Faulkner did. Take someone like Sutpen in Faulkner, or Colonel Sartoris. What they did seemed to Faulkner to be very logical and important, even though it may be mad, but at the same time he wasn't writing about it in the sense that he thought he was handling a sort of primitive, or something like that.

Jones: Well, in that kind of community I guess that when someone jumps in the water you feel the ripple, but now it is hard to feel it.

Porter: I think Styron's trouble may be he really is alienated, you know, from that place and he can't get back home himself. Thomas Wolfe said, "You can't go home again," and I said "Nonsense, that it is the only place you can go. You go there all the time."

Rubin: He certainly can't write about Southerners in the sense that they are importantly in the South acting on Southern concerns. His last one takes place in Italy.

Porter: It's curious. He may be able to do it. He has been living there for years. But I don't know what is happening to him.

Rubin: Miss O'Connor, I know this is a question that writers don't think of and only literary critics like myself think of and ask, but do you think that the Southern community you see, that your relationship to it, is different from the way that Eudora Welty or Faulkner looks at the Southern community?

O'Connor: Well, I don't know how either Eudora Welty or Faulkner looks at it. I only know how I look at it and I don't feel that I am writing about the community at all. I feel that I am taking things in the community that I can show the whole western world, the whole edition of the present generation of people, of what I can use of the Southern situation.

Rubin: I surely agree with that.

Porter: You made that pretty clear yesterday. You know that was one of the things you talked about. It was most interesting.*

O'Connor: You know, people say that Southern life is not the way you picture it. Well, Lord help us, let's hope not.

Rubin: Well, I think that this is one of the tremendous appeals that Southern writing has had—the universality of its creative materials— but to me there has been some relation between this universality and the particularity with which it is done. You couldn't have one without the other. But I think the fact that you are all writing about the South in the sense that this is the way the people talk, etc., somehow does make possible a meaningful, broader reading that people give it.

Jones: It does give you something to check yourself against.

---

*Miss O'Connor's talk was entitled "Some Thoughts on the Grotesque in Southern Fiction."

Rubin: I think that is a very good notion. It is the thorough grounding in actuality.

O'Connor: Well, the South is not the Bible Belt for nothing.

Porter: Someone said that the resemblance of the real Southerner to the Frenchman was that we have no organized, impersonal, abstract murder. That is, a good Southerner doesn't kill anybody he doesn't know.

Rubin: I wonder if even that isn't changing. Speaking of the Bible Belt, I think that it has more than one relevance to what we are dealing with. I think it also involves this question of language. I think that Southerners do and did read the Bible a great deal and somehow, more in the King James Bible, this rolling feeling for language comes through.

Gordon: They read a lot of Cicero, too.

O'Connor: More than the language it seems to me it is simply the concrete, the business of being a story teller. I have Boston cousins and when they come South they discuss problems, they don't tell stories. We tell stories.

Rubin: Well look now, how about our audience? I am sure that our panel will be glad to parry any questions you would like to throw at them. Doesn't someone have a question or two to ask?

Question: Would someone care to comment on the great number of old people and children in Southern writing?

Porter: Well, they are very much there.

Gordon: How many children in that family you were reading about last night?

Porter: Well, there were eight under the age of ten—counting one not yet born—belonging to two women. That isn't bad, is it? And I have known them to do better than that. And with the old people who always seem to live forever and everybody always lived in the same house, all the generations. It was one way of getting acquainted with the generations. We simply would have old people and we would have children in the house together, and they were important, both ends of the line. It was really the ones in mid-life who took the gaff, didn't they? Because they had the young on one side and the old on the other.

Rubin: They were too young to be tolerated and not old enough to be characters.

Porter: A friend of mine said the other day, "Now there are only three degrees of age—young, mature and remarkable."

Question: Miss O'Connor, you said yesterday that the South was Christ-haunted instead of Christ-centered. I don't quite understand this and how it affects our Southern literature. Would you please explain this?

O'Connor: I shouldn't have said that, should I? Well, as I said, the South didn't seem to me as a writer to be Christ-centered. I don't think anyone would object to that at all. I think all you would have to do is to read the newspapers to agree with me, but I said that we seemed to me to be Christ-haunted and that ghosts cast strange shadows, very fierce shadows, particularly in our literature. It is hard to explain a flat statement like that. I would hate to talk off the top of my head on a subject like that. I think it is a subject that a book could be written about but it would take me ten or twelve years to do it.

Gordon: When I was young, old gentlemen sat under the trees reading. That was all they did all of the time, and shall we call it the movement which is sometimes called The Death of God, that controversy that Hegel the Philosopher had with Heine the Poet. There was quite a lot of talk about the death of God, but God crossed the border, and I think that is what you are talking about. It's cast its shadow.

O'Connor: It's gone underneath and come out in distorted forms.

Question: I would like particularly Miss Porter to comment on religious symbolism in her work—if you think there is any and how you go about it in your work.

Porter: Symbolism happens of its own self and it comes out of something so deep in your own consciousness and your own experience that I don't think that most writers are at all conscious of their use of symbols. I never am until I see them. They come of themselves because they belong to me and have meaning to me, but they come of themselves. I have no way of explaining them but I have a great deal of religious symbolism in my stories because I have a very deep sense of religion and also I have a religious training. And I suppose you don't invent symbolism. You don't say, "I am going to have the flowering Judas tree stand for betrayal," but, of course, it does.

O'Connor: I would second everything Miss Porter says. I really didn't know what a symbol was until I started reading about them. It seemed I was going to have to know about them if I was going to be a respectable literary person. Now I have the notion that a symbol is sort of like the engine in a story and I usually discover as I write something in the story that is taking on more and more meaning so that as I go along, before long, that something is turning or working the story.

Rubin: Do you ever have to try to stop yourselves from thinking about your work in terms of symbols as you are working?

O'Connor: I wouldn't say so.

Porter: No. May I tell this very famous little story about Mary McCarthy and symbols? Well, she was in a college and she had a writers' class and there was a young person who wrote her a story and she said, "You have done a very nice piece of work. You are on the right road, now go on to something else." And the young person said, "But my teacher read this and said, 'Well, all right, but now we have to go back and put in the symbols."

Rubin: How about you, Mr. Jones?

Jones: Am I a symbol man? Well, I don't think so. The story is the thing after all and I don't see how a writer can think about anything but the story. The story has got to carry him. I think it is bound to occur to you finally that something you have come across—maybe in the middle of coming across it it might occur to you—that this has certain symbolic value and maybe you would to a certain extent elaborate it in terms of this realization, but I don't think it is a plan of any kind where you say I am heading for a symbol and when I get there I am going to do so and so to it. It just comes out of the context. Of course, writing is full of symbols. Nearly everything is a symbol of some kind but some of them expand for you accidentally.

O'Connor: So many students approach a story as if it were a problem in algebra: find X and when they find X they can dismiss the rest of it.

Porter: Well, and then another thing, everything can be used as a symbol. Take two of the most innocent and charming sounding, for example, just in western Christianity, let us say the dove and the rose. Well, the dove begins by being a symbol of sensuality, it is the bird of Venus, you know, and then it goes on through the whole range of every kind of thing until it becomes the Holy Ghost. It's the same way with the rose which begins as a female sexual symbol and ends as the rose of fire in Highest Heaven. So you see the symbol would have the meaning of its context. I hope that makes sense.

Question: Is tradition an important part of contemporary Southern writing?

Rubin: What about you, Miss Gordon, do you have a tradition you go back to when you are writing? You told me today that you are writing an historical novel.

Gordon: All novels are historical. I don't think I told you I was writing an historical novel. I said it went back to 1532.

Rubin: Well, that sounds pretty historical.

Gordon: The word has become so debased. I wrote two novels, one in Civil War times and one in pioneer times, but people didn't know how to read them. I wouldn't like to be accused of writing what is known as an historical novel.

Rubin: Well, instead of saying tradition, do you think Southerners do things in certain ways because that is the way they have always been done rather than thinking about it at all, and if so, is this the way you see the Southerner in what you write?

Gordon: Well, I don't see it that way. I sit there or I walk around or I wash dishes until I see these people doing something and hear them and then I record it as best I can.

Rubin: It is very hard to get people to talk in terms of these abstractions because I don't think anyone uses tradition with a capital T. And yet there is a lot of tradition in what they do.

Question: I meant white columns, magnolias, worship of family—tradition in his sense.

Gordon: Well, after the Civil War there was a school of literature foisted on us by Northern publishers. They demanded moonlight and magnolias and a lot of people furnished it to them and that idea stuck in peoples' heads ever since. If a Southerner writes a novel now, whoever is reviewing for the *New York Times* will make a point of saying it isn't moonlight and magnolias. It's all nonsense. We are a conquered nation and abominably treated and we paid the greatest tribute perhaps ever paid by any conquered nation. Our history was miswritten and our children were taught lies and therefore the Northerners could not bear the image of us as we were and therefore the Northern publishers would publish only novels full of white columns and magnolias.

Porter: But this very place right this minute is absolutely filled to the chin with moonlight and magnolias. All you have to do is look outside.

Rubin: I think the position of that particular role of moonlight and magnolias tradition in Southern literature is very true. In the case of someone like George Washington Cable, for example. He tried to write one book without it and it was a flop. Nobody paid any attention to it so he went back and wrote the flowery sort of war romances. This was the only thing he could write. I must say that this ain't so no more, and I think it has been people like Miss Porter who ended all that. Many people read their books for what the books *say,* instead of what the people *thought* they should say. I think that the tremendous importance of Southern literature in our own time represents a breaking away from the stereotype. Writers who have done this, having published their first books in the 20's and 30's, have performed a great service for future generations of Southern writers. Not that that was what you were trying to do at the time, but I think the young ones are going to be eternally grateful for it.

O'Connor: Walker Percy wrote somewhere that his generation of Southerners had no more interest in the Civil War than in the Boer War. I think that is probably quite true.

Rubin: I think there is something to that and yet I heard many an argument in the Army during the last war. You get one or two Southerners in a barracks with a bunch of Northerners and maybe the Southerners were just kidding but let anyone say anything too outrageous and the fight was on.

Jones: That's true. They'll still fight but they don't know what they are talking about. They have no real information and so it is more a matter of just being a personal insult.

Question: Do you think that the South is being exploited now for its immediate fictional gains, let's say commercial gain, etc., is it too popular? Is it too much *Southern* writing?

O'Connor: I don't know any Southern writers who are making a big killing except Faulkner, you know. We are all just limping along.

Rubin: I think when you have a group of very fine writers who approach a group of people and subjects in a certain way, it is then easier to imitate that than to do something on your own. And therefore a lot of second rate writers will come along and imitate it, and I know—I see the publisher announcement sheets every fall. On one page of almost all announcement sheets from every publishing house there is announced a new Southern writer and most of them are never announced more than once. But I do feel very definitely there is a great deal of writing about the South, because these people here have shown how it can be done, and therefore someone is not going to do something on his or her own when this is the best lead to follow.

Question: I would like to know if your writing is strictly for a Southern reading audience or if you have in mind any reading audience.

O'Connor: The *London Times Literary Supplement* had an issue on Southern writing once and they said that Southerners only wrote books, they didn't read them.

Porter: Well, that's just the opposite from the old South because they only read them, they never wrote them. At least before The War Between the States writing was not really a gentleman's occupation except as privately. He wrote letters, memoirs, and maybe essays. But they all had libraries and collections of books.

Rubin: The South has long had the reputation for being the worst market for books in the U.S., per capita, among the publishers. I think any Southern writer who wrote primarily for Southerners would have to write a syndicated column for a newspaper or he would starve to death. I don't really think that these people think in terms of who is going to read what they are going to write, unless I am mistaken.

Jones: I was just going to say that I don't know who I write for but it seems to me that I have a person or two who is my audience rather than an group. But I think about one person and perhaps the standards that I absorbed from that person and maybe that person tends to be my audience rather than any group. I hope that a group will buy a book but I don't think I direct a book at any large group of people.

Rubin: John Bishop wrote that he wrote his books to be read by Edmund Wilson and Allen Tate.

Gordon: But you see he never wrote but one novel. Well, I know I have one reader, a Frenchman. He is the only person I know of who understands my work and I think that is why I think about him but I don't think I would under other circumstances. He knows a great deal about techniques of fiction and, perhaps this is a little off the subject, but people very much dislike any revolution in technique. If an author uses a technique that has never been used before, everybody will dislike it. And there is no record of any literary critic ever recognizing an innovation in technique. It has never happened. It is always recognized by another artist. So I have gotten to the point that I write for the person who will know what I am doing.

Question: Mr. Jones, you mentioned this afternoon that Southern writers have a stronger than usual sense of guilt and natural depravity. If this is so, what means of redemption do you see as possible?

Jones: You asked me a very complex question. I don't know whether I can answer the whole thing or not. You said that Southern writers have a sense of natural depravity. Do I think they do? Well, I do have the feeling that if it is not still, it certainly was the case with the first important Southern writers in that there was very little question about the sense of man's guilt. There was a consciousness of that and a perfect willingness to accept it and I think that is very notable in all the best Southern writers of the last generation. I don't know why that should particularly be the case with Southern writers except partly because, as I said, of Southern Fundamentalism, which has kept that fact before them. And perhaps the Civil War had something to do with it. Not that I feel that the Southerners felt guilty about the Civil War but perhaps even though we felt we were right before the war, nevertheless we were defeated and didn't achieve all we thought we could, even though we thought we were right and something must be wrong. I am sure there would be a great many other reasons that someone else could elaborate on. Man is of a less than perfect nature.

Porter: I am sure that we are all naturally depraved but we are all naturally redeemable, too. The idea, Calvin really put it into action, that God somehow rewarded spiritual virtue with material things, which is to say that if you were living right God would reward you with health and money, a good reputation, or the goods of this world is to me an appalling doctrine. I happen to have a faith that says the opposite, you see, that goods of this world have nothing to do with your spiritual good and your standing with God, and I think that this attitude of the South, when you say they felt that if they had been right, God would not have permitted them to lose that war is dreadful, you know. I think it is a terrible fallacy and a terrible mistaken way to feel because some very good people have had the worst times in this world and have lost all their wars, don't you know, have lost everything altogether. Defeat in this world is no disgrace and that is what they cannot understand. If you really fought well and fought for the right thing.

Rubin: That is a very good point. You know, I think it is about time we finished. I would like to question you a bit on that Calvin business if it weren't. I think we had better say one thing. We have been talking about a number of characteristics and we say, now *this* is Southern, and *this* Southern, and then somebody comes along and says, well don't you think that New England writers, or Western writers, have a notion about the natural depravity of man? Is this something that was invented in the South? I think the answer would be is that there are a number of qualities that people assign to Southern writing and say, "This is true of Southern writing." It isn't the uniqueness of the qualities, but I would say the combination of a certain number of qualities at one time, which has made this achievement possible and I think that whatever the achievement is, it has been a considerable thing; and I, myself, am not particularly pessimistic about it continuing, what with the people seated at the table with me tonight. We have hashed over the problems of writers and writing in the South for about an hour now and tried to answer some questions, and I think we'll quit. I would like to say on behalf of the panel what a wonderful time we have had and how grateful we are to Wesleyan College and to everybody for coming.

Katherine Anne Porter
Comes to Kansas

James Ruoff/1961

From *The Midwest Quarterly*, IV (1963) 205–234. Reprinted by permission of *The Midwest Quarterly*, Pittsburgh State University.

In September 1961, Katherine Anne Porter spent several days at the University of Wichita talking informally with students and faculty about everything from segregation to symbolism, but what especially interested her audience were her comments regarding the forthcoming novel *Ship of Fools*. In the following conversation she discusses with characteristic candor and eloquence the origins of the novel, the difficulty she experienced as a short story writer working in a new form, and the paradoxical relationship of the ideas in the novel to her actual experiences and moral values.

Pale, thin, diminutive, archly erect and poised, her small freckled hands folded sedately in her lap, she seemed at first glance to resemble a chic version of Whistler's mother. But this initial impression of frailty and serenity was offset by the shock of wild gray hair, the alert blue eyes that flared like blown coals, and the firm eloquence of the voice that was falling on our ears like strange music. "As a little girl in Texas I was brought up a Catholic," she was saying. "But my father, Harrison Boone, now, he was a free-thinking man. One morning he stopped me as I was on my way to church to celebrate the Immaculate Conception. 'Immaculate Conception!' he said, "Girl, d'you know what in thunder that means?' When I told him I did, he pointed to the *Complete Works of Voltaire* on the shelf. 'See those?' he said. 'Now you go ahead and read 'em so you and I will have something to talk about!' "

It was late afternoon, September 28, 1961. We were gathered in the Provincial Room of the Campus Activities Center at the Univer-

sity of Wichita. The speaker was Katherine Anne Porter, author of
Flowering Judas, Ship of Fools, and a half dozen or so of the greatest
short stories written by an American. Erect as a Buckingham guards-
man, she sat in a straight-back chair and smiled calmly at the college
students and faculty packed three-deep along the walls and jammed
together at her feet. The small room was acrid with cigarette smoke
and the odor of black coffee left unattended in a hundred cups.
Somewhere in the room a student stirred to ask a question: "Miss
Porter, where do you find your material?"

"It's wherever *I* am—in fact, dearie, I'm finding it right now," she
responded quickly. And then, as if in pursuit of an elusive idea behind
the laughing faces, her energetic eyes searched out the student who
had asked the question, and she began to talk directly to him, as if
they were completely alone. "You don't get material by peeping or
prying or looking over transoms," she said quietly. "You live and it
comes. Life's kicking you in the britches all the time, if you only know
it. If you go looking for your material you may put into your writing
what really doesn't belong to *you.* I didn't look for Laura in
"Flowering Judas"—she was then and is now a very dear friend who
never *did* anything in life—like the man in Henry James' story 'Beast
in the Jungle'."

She was a superb teacher. There was candid affection in her eyes
and voice, and every word seemed to arrange itself behind the other
with compelling force and accuracy. The subject turned to her
contemporaries. Robert Penn Warren, she declared emphatically, was
a great poet but not a true novelist. He was sacrificing poetic genius
to satisfy his readers' demands for novels. "I've told Red a hundred
times to leave fiction alone and go on with his poetry, but he won't
listen to me." The real masters of fiction were Ernest Hemingway,
Joseph Conrad, Eudora Welty, and James Joyce. She owed so much
to Joyce, she said, that she could never be critical of him. "Like Eliot
and Pound, Joyce was one of my important experiences. *Dubliners*
was a revelation to me—it showed what could be done with the short
story. To my generation, Joyce was a tremendous influence. He gave
us courage and confidence. I can't tell you what a breath of fresh air
he was. It was time for a break, and he made it. I don't know what
we would have done without *Dubliners* and *Ulysses*."

She still read Hemingway, she said, for his short stories. "Go back to the 'Big Two-Hearted River.' All of his good things are right there!" As for Mary McCarthy, her explorations into childhood were best, the rest of her work too caustic. "About her early times, as in *Memoirs of a Catholic Childhood,* she has a sense of wonder. But Eudora Welty is more sunny, more radiant." The University bell rang through the halls outside and she added wryly: "Ah, Mary's bell tolls for us!"

What about William Saroyan and F. Scott Fitzgerald? She considered the question for a moment. "I don't care for Saroyan at all," she said at last. "He will not discipline himself. He runs off the edges, and he can't *think!* I know he's one of the sweetest, gentlest people, but he doesn't know how to stop to ask himself what he's doing. . . . As for Scott Fitzgerald, well, for a long time I couldn't read him because I knew the people he was writing about too well. In fact, I stayed in Mexico to avoid that crowd in New York. *Tender is the Night* has some good passages, and so has *The Great Gatsby.* But poor Firtzgerald!" She bristled indignantly. "An artist has no *right* to have such feelings about those cheap, nasty, rich people he was so afraid of!"

What writers had influenced her most? "Laurence Sterne was the first one who made me think I could write," she recalled affectionately. "That wonderful style with all the dashes! It looks easy, but it's terribly difficult. Through the years, though, I've had greater sympathy for Henry James than for almost any other writer. . . . You know, I first started writing when I was five. I started a novel called 'The Hermit of Halifax Cave.' I had my hero going fishing and doing other such things until I couldn't think of anything more for him to do and had to quit the novel." As she talked about her own writing habits, her hands suddenly came to life and stroked the air as if they were molding clay. "For many years I had to work up a story slowly, and with many revisions—one story I revised seventeen times—but now I've learned to be a first-draft writer. I write at top speed and then go over the story again with a pen and there it is." She laughed with a kind of triumphant gaiety, then suddenly became serious. "The speed is not important, because I never intended to be a fifty-book writer—why should I print my studio litter? I haven't published a fraction of what I've written. I have four bushels of manuscripts I've never tried to publish—forty short stories, and five novels I started when I was young and didn't know I was a short story writer. Once in a while a story can be brought out of storage and revived, though. Recently I printed one that had been lost for thirty-five years. It was based on something that happened to me when I was twenty, something that presented a powerful problem to me, something I couldn't avoid. A long time ago I made three revisions but somehow couldn't bring it off. Then, thirty-five years later, I rewrote it in twenty days from the first version, which, after all, was the right one. It was a long story called 'Holiday,' published in *The Atlantic Monthly*."

A student asked how she came to write the collection *Flowering Judas*. "I was so sure of the title story I wrote it in one day and part of a night," she said. " 'María Concepción' took seventeen days. 'Flowering Judas' began one night in Mexico as I was walking down a street and passed a window where I saw a young girl I knew sitting in a chair, a book in her lap, and in another chair there was a great fat man plucking a guitar. I went inside and sat with the girl until the man left. I didn't write 'Flowering Judas' until ten years later, but the whole story began with that glimpse through the window. The publisher printed the manuscript just the way I wrote it, with all kinds of mistakes in punctuation and capitals." She laughed. "I understand that edition is now quite a collector's item!"

Of her story "Rope," she stated: "I'd heard lots of quarrels among couples I knew and found in them all the same pattern—a structure like a five-act drama. 'Rope' is the distilled essence of all those fights I'd heard." Of "Noon Wine" she said it had taken but seven days to write, but "thirty-five years before that to *prepare* for it. And the genesis of that final version," she added, "took me one whole summer." She referred to one of her most popular stories, "Theft." "It's about a woman who leads a sacrificial life," she observed: "She had a strange sense of alienation. No one could get near her. Someone gave her a purse with gold pieces and it was lost. She accused the waitress. The woman *really* wanted to commit suicide but didn't know it, so she killed herself bit by bit. But this isn't the story," she concluded: "There's a transmutation, a chemical change that makes it fiction."

A student posed the question every English instructor hears in his sophomore literature courses: do authors employ symbols con-sciously? "Well, you don't *put in* the symbols," she replied kindly. "You see, symbols take care of themselves. Anything can be a symbol, but it must never be forced. I'm often asked about the symbolism of the silver dove and the engraved ring in 'The Grave.' I used these symbols only because they were really there in the experience on which the story was based. My brother and I found those objects in my grandfather's grave. Of course the dove is a symbol. It's symbolic of peace, security, love, and lechery. But it's also the Holy Ghost and the innocent love of children. The ring is the serpent biting its tail, a symbol of immortality." She paused, adding reflectively: "At the time I wrote 'The Grave' I didn't know the ring was also symbolic of exploring the past. . . ."

But what about obscurity? "Well, you don't have to know every-thing about a work the first time you read it," she countered easily. "I wonder now what there could have been about T. S. Eliot that *ever* puzzled me! As for my own stories, I wrote strange and rather weird things, so that at first they wouldn't even publish me because I was such a recondite writer." She laughed. "Recondite! Look at me now—I'm no more mysterious than a goldfish floating in a bowl!"

Obscurity was one thing, isolation from society quite another. A writer, she insisted vehemently, must never be alienated from the community, and the deliberate isolation of writers like J. D. Salinger she considered as enervating as alcohol or drugs. "Any such aliena-tion from society is death," she asserted. "You may live in an attic, and you'll probably have fine company if you do, but first you have to become a human being. . . ." It was equally dangerous for a writer to become so involved in one corner of society as to lose his perspective. As examples she cited Richard Wright, Ralph Ellison, and James Baldwin. "I can't read them," she declared. "I'm so tired of all that hatred and poison that I think I'll just sit this one out, if you don't mind. They've all had such horrible lives—such horrible experi-ences—that it's left them with dreadful minds. Baldwin, I think, is nearly crazed—not at all sane." She suddenly grinned, and one could tell from the expression in her eyes that she was laughing at herself. "You see? I just won't talk about them at all!"

Everyone was curious about her new novel, *Ship of Fools,* which was to be released by the publisher later that month. Now that the long work was finished, she could talk about it, and she approached the subject with all the enthusiasm of a fisherman describing the big catch that did *not* get away. "Nobody ever fought a novel as I did that one. It took me twenty-one years to get that novel written, and I quit every chance I found. But it won," she said and then, wonderingly: "460,000 words! Is it possible? The title *Ship of Fools* I borrowed from Sebastian Brant's *Narrenshiff*, published in Basel in 1494. I found the title when I was in Basel reading about Erasmus of Rotterdam, and I thought 'That's *my* title—I'll just borrow it. Brant doesn't need it anymore.' "A question from an English instructor: "Did *Ship of Fools* end the way you had originally planned it?"

"It's exactly the same," she replied. "In fact, I wrote the last three pages first and kept working toward that conclusion. The idea of the novel is basic and simple—the ship of this world on its voyage to eternity. But this was a real ship that started from Vera Cruz and went to Bremerhaven. It was my first voyage to Europe, just after *Flowering Judas* came out and I'd received a Guggenheim. . . . I'd been on voyages before, but there was something about this one that was totally different. For one thing, 1931 was a crucial year, with revolutions in Mexico and South America, and Mussolini in power in Italy. In Cuba the bottom had fallen out of the sugar market and there were shipping strikes. Sugar fields were burning, idle ships choked the harbours, and all the workers brought to Cuba from Spain and the Canary Islands were being deported by the government. In Havana we saw them driven aboard ship like cattle. . . . We had a twenty-eight day voyage. Aboard ship were a half dozen nationalities and as many religions and castes. That ship was like a basket of snakes on a hot stove. People were drawn together by religion, separated by language or nationality; drawn together by nationality, separated by caste or politics. You see, all my life I'd been a completely free agent experiencing one thing and then moving on to experience something else, but aboard that ship I was stuck—stuck with people I never dreamed existed—and I started keeping a diary of everything I saw and heard. Strangely enough, I don't think I spoke a half dozen words to as many passengers, yet I couldn't take my eyes and ears off them. . . .

"When we arrived at Bremerhaven I sent my ship's log to Caroline Gordon—Allen Tate's wife—in the form of a long letter, and afterwards, in Berlin, I wrote a poem abut the voyage, but it was interrupted after forty-two lines. Three or four years ago I added some lines to the first version and published it as 'After A Long

Journey.' A few years after I left Germany, Caroline Gordon returned my letter because she thought I might find use for it in my writing. Although the voyage was still working in my mind, I put the letter away and never looked at it again except to get the time right, the phases of the moon, the tides, and so forth. All the rest was novel. At first, though, I tried to make it a short story. With 'Pale Horse, Pale Rider'; 'Noon Wine,' and 'Old Mortality,' *Ship of Fools* was to be the fourth in a group, but it simply ran away from me. . . ."

"Why did you experience such difficulty with it?" someone asked. "Were there too many characters in it to fit the short story form?"

"No, I just didn't *want* to write a novel," she said emphatically. "I was baffled and frustrated because I wasn't able to work my material into the shape it wanted to become. And *I* was wrong, of course. It grew and developed, and with its growth my own view of the world changed. I came to see that something had happened aboard that ship which was quite stupid—that it wouldn't have happened if the people opposed to it had taken hold and not let it happen. The point is, I had seen these criminals—these *clowns*—like Hitler, and was stricken by an idea: if people like this could take over the world! Of course there were all the good people who didn't believe in the clowns, but they still let the clowns commit the crimes good worthy people would commit if only they had the nerve. How else to account for the collusion in evil that enables a creature like Mussolini, or Hitler, or Huey Long, or McCarthy (make your own list, petty or great) to get hold of things? Who permits it? We *know* we're not criminals—we're not evil. We don't *believe* in that sort of thing, do we?" Her penetrating eyes made a swift arc among the young faces gathered on the floor around her. For a brief moment the room was so quiet the clock on the wall could be heard throbbing like a drum.

A student cleared his throat to phrase a mindless but heart-felt question: "Miss Porter, what can we do about the world situation today? What do you think we ought to be doing to avert disaster?"

"Oh, dearie, it's too late now. It's too late!" She smiled grimly. "The tragedy of our times is not an accident but a total consent. Any way, my novel is a tiny drop of water to illustrate this vast ocean of accord. For me as a writer, being on that ship was a godsent experience, although I wouldn't have been able to see any of these things if I hadn't seen them first in Mexico. Still, in Mexico there was always something good about it—in Mexico there was always a *chance* of salvation. As for all the evil that threatens us here and now, I must say we haven't an alibi in the world. We let all the evil come upon us." She paused for a moment, then added: "Well, that's the theme of my novel. And it's not mentioned once in the story. Find it for yourself."

Having almost reached her four score and ten years, she would never, in all probability, witness the ultimate consequences of our human folly on this planet. We who would live after her were already eager to begin picking her frail bones. "What about all those manuscripts you mentioned?" someone asked.

"I'm leaving my papers to the University of Texas," she replied. "They seem to think I'm the only writer Texas has produced. Actually, there are plenty of young ones coming up—George Garrett, Walter Clemons, William Goyen—who have perfectly wonderful talents. The University of Texas is naming a big new library center after me, with a special room for my papers—and, well, I have to do *something* in return, don't I?" She sighed and folded her gnarled but delicate hands in her lap. She seemed then to become as tiny, shy, and incredibly fragile as the little girl who had stood before her towering father and tried to explain to him the meaning of the Immaculate Conception. "So I guess I'll wind up in a dark, tight place after all," she said. "Too bad—I have a terrible case of claustrophobia!"

But it was impossible to sustain even for a moment the incongruous idea of her death. Through her well-wrought works of art the firm voice would go on forever reassuring us that "Beauty is truth, truth beauty." And to the many Kansans who listened to her on that September day, she will be remembered not as an aged woman but as a youthful artist still head over heels in love with living.

For Katherine Anne Porter, *Ship of Fools* Was a Lively Twenty-Two Year Voyage
Elizabeth Janeway/1962

From *The New York Times Book Review,* 1 April 1962. Copyright © 1962 by The New York Times Company. Reprinted by permission.

Who is it who is being interviewed? We are sitting in the front parlor of a house in Georgetown, in the District of Columbia. The damp afternoon outside is hinting faintly at spring, and a black and white gentleman cat in the window is looking thoughtfully at the grounds of Dumbarton Oaks across the street. His name is Bela Bartok and he is not a lodger, merely a boarder who knows a good cook when he meets one. His hostess and mine has just received the first bound copies of her novel, a novel for which readers have been waiting twenty years, and which cynics declared would never see the light of day. But here it is, a strong, healthy, beautiful child. Miss Porter picks up the copy lying on the tea table and turns it over. "I still don't quite believe it," she says. "Oh dear, I don't like that picture! It makes me look like a little old lady."

This, of course, is nonsense. Both the picture (those eyes!) and the presence deny it. Miss Porter was born in 1890, but whoever is being interviewed, it is not a little old lady. Indeed, she knows better herself, for she chuckles—when she does, she sounds like a soda-water syphon which has just learned to talk and is utterly delighted by the knack—and remarks that she went coasting last week in Connecticut, and not on anything as conventional as a sled: "It was a Flying Saucer, my dear, a metal thing like the top of a garbage can, you know, and you sit in it and whizz down hill. It was wonderful. People who didn't know me were stunned, but not my friends."

Anyone who was stunned can't have read her books. They are marvelous books, at once feminine and fierce; not aggressive, just

completely uncompromising. From them, it is clear that the author is
not afraid of anything in the world. Once she has seen that something
is true, she cannot un-see it, any more than an accurate thermometer
can fail to register the temperature.

Perhaps this is one way to say what she is: imagine a most delicate
and sensitive apparatus constructed a world or two ago in West
Texas, when the Civil War and its aftermath were still remembered
and operative forces, an apparatus set to read the truth of events in
our time. Its outer housing is a beautiful, merry little person skilled in
traditional female arts; who is, none the less, first and foremost the
priestess of this seismographic machine. To it, she will sacrifice
anything without a moment of hesitation. She is its guardian and its
servant, a very tiger of a guardian, a dragon of a servant; but a most
charming and exquisite dragon, Chinese porcelain of the best period,
with the purr of an affectionate tiger; unless you encroach on her
hoard, her treasure, her talent. "If I have *that,*" she says, "I have
everything, and if I don't, I have nothing."

Clearly this gift is the core of her life, and its cross. In 1940 she
wrote, "I did not choose this vocation and if I had any say in the
matter, I would not have chosen it. I made no attempt to publish
anything until I was 30, but I have written and destroyed manuscripts
quite literally by the trunkload. I spent fifteen years wandering about,
weighted horribly with masses of paper and little else. Yet for this
vocation I was and am willing to live and die and I consider very few
other things of the slightest importance."

When she was young, she remembers now, she tried upon
occasion to stop writing, for perhaps she had no talent. She had gone
to small convent schools in Texas and Louisiana, where young ladies
were taught deportment and not much else: "We were told never to
look a gentleman right in the eyes for more than a second, but to
look over his shoulder, or at his necktie, and then flash the eyes
up"—they flash now. So how on earth was she to know whether she
had talent? There was no one to tell her. Even after she went to
Mexico to live, her friends were not writers but painters and compos-
ers; which was just as well, she thinks now, for she dislikes writers "in
huddles and heaps."

Just the same, she could not stop writing. She felt under a

compulsion. It was not fretful, or feverish or anxious—simply, she could not stop. It was a thing laid upon her to do.

So she wrote, but she wrote "in private." She would finish a story and put it away. One of the first to be published reached the magazine that welcomed it only because a friend commandeered it and sent it off before its author could tuck it away in a drawer. And still she writes privately, inside herself, never thinking of other writers, uninfluenced, and hating "competition" so much that she can't bear to hear children quarrel. "I never quarreled as a child," she says. "I just went somewhere else." Though it might be noted that her characters know how to quarrel, even if their maker disavows an ability to do so and writes of it as hateful. Why quarrel, when one can so easily be at home in a big world full of pleasant people and surprising events?

"I have never known an uninteresting person," she says now. She likes Washington, where she settled two years ago, but she could write anywhere, and almost has. She is an "obstinate" writer, she thinks, or "persistent," or even "willful," but she rejects the word "arrogance" because it has an overtone of that competition which she hates. The world has room for all kinds of good things, and they should not compete. Her good thing is to write as her talent bids her.

It is a very pure talent, limpid and unarguable, and it has its own laws. Her characters, she says, "are drawn from life." Take one from *Ship of Fools,* La Condesa. In a boatload of humans blown about by winds of banal and cruel convention, she is a center of courage and individuality, who makes her own rules and trusts her own thoughts. She is tragic, impossible, and valuable.

"I have ruined my life," says another character to her, a good man, the best in the book, who has made this discovery by falling in love with her. "My life was ruined so long ago I have forgotten what it was like before," says La Condesa, equably and indomitably. Miss Porter knows her so well that she must surely have dreamed her up out of the depths of her subconscious?

Not at all. She was a real woman, a passenger on the very ship that Katherine Anne Porter boarded in 1931 in Veracruz for her first trip to Europe. Thirty years later, she is aboard it still. But by what magic has the real, remembered, fellow-passenger, seen in glimpses and snatches for a couple of weeks, turned into this vivid, capricious creature on whom, as much as anyone, the book turns? How has the outward reality of fact turned into the inner truth of art? It is as mysterious as the ability of a Byzantine master to construct a brooding Madonna out of little bits of tile and pebble. Is it perhaps why the book took so long to write?

"I knew what was going to happen," says Miss Porter. "That is, I knew what the people in the book were going to do. But there were times when I didn't know why they were doing it, and so I would have to wait until I could find out."

"Was it alive all the time, the book?"

"Oh yes. I didn't have to revive it. Of course, I was interrupted. There were years when I didn't touch it. But it is the same book that it started out to be."

"And when was that?"

"I wrote the first and last pages in 1940 in Louisiana. It was to be another short novel, like the three in *Pale Horse, Pale Rider.* I wrote those very quickly after I came back from Europe. Of course, I'd been making notes for years. But I wrote them each in a week—no, a week for 'Old Mortality' and 'Noon Wine,' nine days for 'Pale Horse, Pale Rider.' Then I started 'Ship of Fools,' and wrote straight ahead, fifty pages very quickly, before I realized that it was going to be something else, something long. But none of that fifty pages is lost. It is all in here." She leans forward and opens the book at the beginning. "This is as I wrote it," she says, "the square in Vera Cruz and the men drinking limeades on the terrace, but I put the dead boy in later. The last page is the same too, where the German boy cries out 'Gruss Gott' to the town when the ship has docked. I expanded it and wrote bridges from scene to scene. Yes, I can write ahead, write scenes that I haven't really come to yet, if I see them clearly."

"What happened with *Ship of Fools* is that I knew, after the first fifty pages when I thought it would need only one draft, that I would have to change the original structure. So all the scenes are here, but I moved them around. The movement of the ship, forward, the movement of the waves," (her hands gesture a rocking back and forth), "the movement of the passengers as they walk about the decks, all these got into the structure of the book. It moves in all these ways. It takes planning, of course. But you can plan and plan, and then it's all useless unless the big thing happens, and that can't be planned for. Only—" she stops for a moment, questioningly. "Only would it happen without the planning, the solid foundation?" It is the same voice speaking which, years ago, replied to a questionnaire from a magazine with these words: "I choose Henry James, holding as I do with the conscious, disciplined artist, the serious expert, against the expansive, indiscriminating, 'cosmic' sort."

It is a humanist voice, the voice of a creature who knows about life and can't be fooled, and loves it. There were times, finishing this book, when she was in despair, when it seemed like an Old Man of the Sea. Would she never be rid of it! And at the same time, she was certain it would be done one day. "I never worried," she says, "it's so unnecessary to worry. There are always half a dozen people eager to do it for you." If that is hard on other people—well, she isn't easy on herself. Her only debt and obligation is to the talent that impels her, and there she will not fail. It is her treasure and her justification.

To keep it from the breath of corruption (and she has seen writers corrupted, she remembers), she has worn herself out lecturing and reading, taken on teaching jobs, accepted grants and gifts, and refused to write faster, to write for money, or to change a manuscript in a way that would cheapen it. She has waked in a hospital and found that three weeks of readings were delivered while "a bad cold" turned into pneumonia. She has been to Hollywood and found it amusing and absurd and a fine place to grow flowers, for by the time she went she knew how to guard her talent.

What of the future? Will there be another novel?

"Heavens, no," she says, not at all regretfully. "I don't have time for another. Thirty years of living went into this one. But upstairs in my workroom I must have forty stories that were interrupted one way or another. First I'm going to have a vacation, I'm going to Ireland and then to Rome and to Paris, but when I come back, I'll go over the stories. Why, you know," she adds suddenly, "I can hardly wait." Meanwhile, we may all be content that this wonderful tapestry of a book has finally been woven down to the last stitch, unmistakably her own, unmistakably a witness of our time.

I've Had a Good Run for My Money
Maurice Dolbier/1962

From the *New York Herald Tribune Books,* 1 April 1962,
pp.3,11. © I. H. T. Corporation. Reprinted by permission.

Katherine Anne Porter was born in 1894 at Indian Creek,
Tex., brought up in Texas and Louisiana, and educated in
small southern convent schools. She is the author of
Flowering Judas (1930), *Hacienda* (1934), "Noon Wine"
(1937), *Pale Horse, Pale Rider* (1939), *The Leaning
Tower, and Other Stories* (1944), and a collection of
essays, *The Days Before* (1952). A collection of stories
was published in paperback in the Armed Services editions during the war ("I had 600 letters from boys on
every battlefront; warm, friendly letters, and I answered
every blessed one"). In 1943 she was elected a member
of the National Institute of Arts and Letters.

This luncheon interview began with a Mexican toast
which Miss Porter translated as: "Health and money,
more power to your elbow, many secret love affairs and
time to enjoy them."

Interviewer: And now the notebook appears. I hope you won't
mind if it stays here on the table during lunch. Authors' attitudes vary.

Miss Porter: Not at all. Once I interviewed a beautiful opera
singer named Anna Case. She told me that she loved to eat steak
and young green onions, and I reported it. Next day her manager
came and complained bitterly; he said that I was destroying the aura
of romance about her.

Interviewer: Where are you living now?

Miss Porter: I've sometimes given my address as *The Atlantic
Monthly.* People say, "You're not stopping there, are you?" No. I'm
not stopping anywhere. I've been living in Washington. I had my eye
on a house near there that I wanted to buy, but everytime I make up
my mind to do something, friends seem to jump up from every
corner, in the world, saying, "Don't Don't!" and stamp the life out of

the project. I love my friends. I'm not mad at them. They just make it impossible for me to live where they are. Meantime, I'm travelling. I'm going to Ireland May 10, and will be back by July 6.

Interviewer: Could you tell me something of the history of this novel—your first? It's been announced for publication several times in the past. In fact, under the title "No Safe Harbor," it was to have been published in 1942?

Miss Porter: Yes. I think sometimes you've got to be a saint to be a publisher. I'm the last person in the world to be a troublemaker, or a tiresome prima donna, but when I'm asked if I can turn in 4,000 words before such-and-such a date four weeks away, for some insane reason I always think I can do it, and say "Yes." Then I'm absolutely paralyzed, and can't work at all until the deadline passes.

Interviewer: How long was *Ship of Fools* in the writing?

Miss Porter: In the act of writing, perhaps two years. But the history of the novel goes back to 1931. In that year I made the ocean voyage that's the basis of the story. I kept a log during the voyage, and continued to make further notes for the novel in the years that followed. In 1936, I had a contract for four short novels, and when I came back from Europe that fall I packed a suitcase, went to a little inn in Pennsylvania, wrote "Noon Wine" in seven days and "Old Mortality" in another seven. Then I went to New Orleans, and wrote "Pale Horse, Pale Rider" in nine days. But for some strange reason, I couldn't get at the fourth, which was to be "Ship of Fools." So the book came out with three stories only.

Interviewer: This was 1936? How long an interlude was there before *Ship of Fools* did get under way?

Miss Porter: I continued to add to my notes. I kept on thinking about it, and in June, 1940, when I went to Yaddo, I began writing it, and have been writing it, off and on, ever since. I've been stopped in the middle of a paragraph and gone back a year later to start again where I left off, with no break in the novel's continuity or style.

Interviewer: What has stopped you?

Miss Porter: All kinds of things. Telephone calls, those friends I mentioned, the necessity to earn money by going on speaking tours and public reading engagements, and housekeeping chores.

Interviewer: Did you use a synopsis for keeping the story's continuity?

Miss Porter: No. The novel has had an organic growth. It's been like making a tapestry, really. Weaving on a shuttle. You use threads of different colors, but the work itself is all of a piece. The first fifteen or twenty paragraphs I wrote at Yaddo in 1940 and the last three paragraphs, and they're exactly the same now, but they have been separated—there's later work added between them.

Interviewer: Your story "Holiday" has won first prize in the current O. Henry Awards selection [published by Doubleday]. Isn't there a coincidence here . . . some family connection?

Miss Porter: Yes, O. Henry [Sidney Porter] was my father's first cousin. But I gather he was a timid man, and in my family that's a terrible thing to be. By the way, while we're on the subject of family, perhaps we can set the record straight. Some biographical notices say that I'm a descendant of Daniel Boone. Not so. I'm descended from his younger brother, Jonathan.

Interviewer: The record is now straight. What is your favorite reading?

Miss Porter: Well, of course, the short story is my love. I'm excited when new stars keep appearing in the skies. I remember reading a short story called "The Conversion of the Jews" by a young man named Philip Roth. I'd never heard of him before, but when I read that, I said, "Well, here he is." And a publisher asked me for comment on a story he received from another young writer. He thought he wanted to publish it, but worried over whether it was too obscure. I advised him to ask the author to try to make it clearer, but said, "If he won't, publish it anyway. Don't lose him." That author's name was J. F. Powers. I'm all for new, young, fresh writers, with a will to do what they want to do.

Interviewer: Are there writers you're against?

Miss Porter: I despise Sartre. First, because of his attempt to Germanize French thought. And second, because he doesn't seem to know anything about human beings.

Interviewer: What about Simone de Beauvoir?

Miss Porter: It's a pity. She seems to be an intelligent woman, but I thought "The Second Sex" was a stupid performance. Whenever I find a book that begins "Women are . . ." or "Women do . . ." or "Women think . . .," I say "That's enough." Not that I think it's a bore being a woman. It's exciting, and I wouldn't know how to be anything else. But I just can't bear to read about it.

Interviewer: You're no crusading feminist, then?

Miss Porter: No, I've never felt that the fact of being a woman put me at a disadvantage, or that it's difficult being a woman in a "man's world." The only time men get a little tiresome is in love—oh, they're OK at first, but they do tend, don't they, to get a little bossy and theological about the whole business? I've had a very hard life, but it's not other people who have made it hard for me. I did that for myself. But I've had a good run for my money—a free field in the things that matter: the will to be an artist and to live as a human being. When my friends want to compromise with the universe, I say: "Go right to the mat and fight to the finish!"

Katherine Anne Porter: An Interview
Barbara Thompson/1963

Interview with Katherine Anne Porter by Barbara Thompson
from *Writers at Work: The Paris Review Interviews*, Second
Series, edited by Malcolm Cowley. Copyright © 1963 by The
Paris Review, Inc. Reprinted by permission of Viking Penguin
Inc.

The Victorian house in which Katherine Anne Porter lives
is narrow and white, reached by an iron-railed stairway
curving up from the shady brick-walked Georgetown
street. The parlor to which a maid admits the caller is an
elegant mélange of several aspects of the past, both
American and European. High-ceilinged, dim and cool
after the midsummer glare, the room is dominated by a
bottle-green settee from the period of Napoleon III. Outside the alcove of windows there is a rustle of wind
through ginkgo trees, then a hush.

Finally, a voice in the upper hallway: its tone that of
someone talking to a bird, or coquetting with an old
beau—light and feathery, with a slight flutter. A few moments later, moving as lightly as her voice, Miss Porter
hurries through the wide doorway, unexpectedly modern
in a soft green suit of woven Italian silk. Small and elegant, she explains her tardiness, relates an anecdote of
the morning's mail, offers a minted ice tea, and speculates
aloud on where we might best conduct our conversation.

She decides on the dining room, a quiet, austere
place overlooking the small enclosed garden. Here the
aspect is a different one. "I want to live in a world capital
or the howling wilderness," she said once, and did. The
drawing room was filled with pieces that had once been
part of the house on rue Notre-Dame des Champs; this
one is bright with Mexican folk art—whistles and toy
animals collected during a recent tour for the Department
of State—against simpler, heavier pieces of furniture. The
round table at which we sit is of Vermont marble, mottled
and colored like milk glass, on a wrought-iron base of her
own design. There is a sixteenth-century cupboard from
Avila, and a refectory table of the early Renaissance from

a convent in Fiesole. Here we settle the tape recorder, under an image of the great god Horus.

We try to make a beginning. She is an experienced lecturer, familiar with mircrophone and tape recorder, but now she is to talk about herself as well as her work, the link between, and the inexorable winding of the tape from one spool to the other acts almost as a hypnotic. Finally we turn it off and talk for a while of other things, more frivolous and more autobiographical, hoping to surprise an easier revelation.

Interviewer: You were saying that you had never intended to make a career of writing.

Porter: I've never made a career of anything, you know, not even of writing. I started out with nothing in the world but a kind of passion, a driving desire. I don't know where it came from, and I don't know why—or why I have been so stubborn about it that nothing could deflect me. But this thing between me and my writing is the strongest bond I have ever had—stronger than any bond or any engagement with any human being or with any other work I've ever done. I really started writing when I was six or seven years old. But I had such a multiplicity of half-talents, too: I wanted to dance, I wanted to play the piano, I sang, I drew. It wasn't really dabbling—I was investigating everything, experimenting in everything. And then, for one thing, there weren't very many amusements in those days. If you wanted music, you had to play the piano and sing yourself. Oh, we saw all the great things that came during the season, but after all, there would only be a dozen or so of those occasions a year. The rest of the time we depended upon our own resources: our own music and books. All the old houses that I knew when I was a child were full of books, bought generation after generation by members of the family. Everyone was literate as a matter of course. Nobody told you to read this or not to read that. It was there to read, and we read.

I: Which books influenced you most?

P: That's hard to say, because I grew up in a sort of mélange. I was reading Shakespeare's sonnets when I was thirteen years old, and I'm perfectly certain that they made the most profound impression upon

me of anything I ever read. For a time I knew the whole sequence by
heart; now I can only remember two or three of them. That was the
turning point of my life, when I read the Shakespeare sonnets, and
then all at one blow, all of Dante—in that great big book illustrated by
Gustave Doré. The plays I saw on the stage, but I don't remember
reading them with any interest at all. Oh, and I read all kinds of
poetry—Homer, Ronsard, all the old French poets in translation. We
also had a very good library of—well, you might say secular phil-
osophers. I was incredibly influenced by Montaigne when I was very
young. And one day when I was about fourteen, my father led me
up to a great big line of books and said, "Why don't you read this?
It'll knock some of the nonsense out of you!" It happened to be the
entire set of Voltaire's philosophical dictionary with notes by Smollett.
And I plowed through it; it took me about five years.

And of course we read all the eighteenth-century novelists, though
Jane Austen, like Turgenev, didn't really engage me until I was quite
mature. I read them both when I was very young, but I was grown up
before I really took them in. And I discovered for myself *Wuthering
Heights;* I think I read that book every year of my life for fifteen
years. I simply adored it. Henry James and Thomas Hardy were
really my introduction to modern literature; Grandmother didn't
much approve of it. She thought Dickens might do, but she was a
little against Mr. Thackeray; she thought he was too trivial. So that
was as far as I got into the modern world until I left home!

I: Don't you think this background—the comparative isolation of
Southern rural life, and the atmosphere of literary interest—helped to
shape you as a writer?

P: I think it's something in the blood. We've always had great letter
writers, readers, great storytellers in our family. I've listened all my life
to articulate people. They were all great storytellers, and every story
had shape and meaning and point.

I: Were any of them known as writers?

P: Well, there was my sixth or seventh cousin once removed, poor
William Sidney. O. Henry, you know. He was my father's second
cousin—I don't know what that makes him to me. And he was more
known in the family for being a bank robber. He worked in a bank,
you know, and he just didn't seem to find a talent for making money;
no Porter ever did. But he had a wife who was dying of TB and he

couldn't keep up with the doctor's bills. So he took a pitiful little sum—oh, about three hundred and fifty dollars—and ran away when he was accused. But he came back, because his wife was dying, and went to prison. And there was Horace Porter, who spent his whole eight years as ambassador to France looking for the bones of John Paul Jones. And when he found them, and brought them back, he wrote a book about them.

I: It seems to me that your work is pervaded by a sense of history. Is that part of the family legacy?

P: We were brought up with a sense of our own history, you know. My mother's family came to this country in 1648 and went to the John Randolph territory of Virginia. And one of my great great grandfathers was Jonathan Boone, the brother of Daniel. On my father's side I'm descended from Colonel Andrew Porter, whose father came to Montgomery County, Pennsylvania, in 1720. He was one of the circle of George Washington during the Revolution, a friend of Lafayette, and one of the founders of the Society of the Cincinnati—oh, he really took it seriously!—and when he died in 1809—well, just a few years before that he was offered the post of Secretary of War, but he declined. We were never very ambitious people. We never had a President, though we had two governors and some in the Army and the Navy. I suppose we did have a desire to excel but not to push our way to higher places. We thought we'd *already* arrived!

I: The "we" of family is very strong, isn't it? I remember that you once wrote of the ties of blood as the "absolute point of all departure and return." And the central character in many of your stories is defined, is defining herself often, in relation to a family organization. Even the measure of time is human—expressed in terms of the very old and the very young, and how much of human experience they have absorbed.

P: Yes, but it wasn't a conscious made-up affair, you know. In those days, you belonged together, you lived together, because you were a family. The head of our house was a grandmother, an old matriarch, you know, and a really lovely and beautiful woman, a good soul, and so she didn't do us any harm. But the point is that we did live like that, with Grandmother's friends, all reverend old gentlemen with frock coats, and old ladies with jet breastplates. Then there were the younger people, the beautiful girls and the handsome young boys, who were all ahead of me; when I was a little girl, eight or nine years old, they were eighteen to twenty-two, and they represented all glamour, all beauty, all joy and freedom to me. Then there was my own age, and then there were the babies. And the servants, the Negroes. We simply lived that way; to have four generations in one house, under one roof, there was nothing unusual about that. That was just my experience, and this is just the way I've reacted to it. Many other people didn't react, who were brought up in very much the same way.

I remember when I was very young, my older sister wanted to buy some old furniture. It was in Louisiana, and she had just been married. And I went with her to a wonderful old house in the country where we'd been told there was a very old gentleman who probably had some things to sell. His wife had died, and he was living there alone. So we went to this lovely old house, and, sure enough, there was this lonely beautiful old man, eighty-seven or -eight, surrounded by devoted Negro servants. But his wife was dead and his children were married and gone. He said, yes, he had a few things he wanted to sell. So he showed us through the house. And finally he opened a door, and showed us a bedroom with a beautiful four-poster bed, with a wonderful satin coverlet: the most wonderful, classical-looking bed you ever saw. And my sister said, "Oh, that's what I want." And he said, "Oh, madame, that is my marriage bed. That is the bed that my wife brought with her as a bride. We slept together in that bed for nearly sixty years. All our children were born there. Oh," he said, "I shall die in that bed, and then they can dispose of it as they like."

I remember that I felt a little suffocated and frightened. I felt a little trapped. But why? Only because I understood that. I was brought up in that. And I was at the age of rebellion then, and it really scared me. But I look back on it now and think how perfectly wonderful, what a tremendously beautiful life it was. Everything in it had meaning.

I: But it seems to me that your work suggests someone who was searching for new—perhaps broader—meanings . . . that while you've retained the South of your childhood as a point of reference, you've ranged far from that environment itself. You seem to have felt little of the peculiarly Southern preoccupation with racial guilt and the death of the old agrarian life.

P: I'm a Southerner by tradition and inheritance, and I have a very profound feeling for the South. And, of course, I belong to the guilt-ridden white-pillar crowd myself, but it just didn't rub off on me. Maybe I'm just not Jewish enough, or Puritan enough, to feel that the sins of the father are visited on the third and fourth generations. Or maybe it's because of my European influences—in Texas and Louisiana. The Europeans didn't have slaves themselves as late as my family did, but they *still* thought slavery was quite natural. . . . But, you know, I was always restless, always a roving spirit. When I was a little child I was always running away. I never got very far, but they were always having to come and fetch me. Once when I was about six, my father came to get me somewhere I'd gone, and he told me later he'd asked me, "Why are you so restless? Why can't you stay here with us?" and I said to him, "I want to go and see the world. I want to know the world like the palm of my hand."

I: And at sixteen you made it final.

P: At sixteen I ran away from New Orleans and got married. And at twenty-one I bolted again, went to Chicago, got a newspaper job, and went into the movies.

I: The movies?

P: The newspaper sent me over to the old S. and A. movie studio to do a story. But I got into the wrong line, and then was too timid to get out. "Right over this way, Little Boy Blue," the man said, and I found myself in a courtroom scene with Francis X. Bushman. I was horrified by what had happened to me, but they paid me five dollars for that first day's work, so I stayed on. It was about a week before I remembered what I had been sent to do; and when I went back to the newspaper they gave me eighteen dollars for my week's non-work and fired me!

I stayed on for six months—I finally got to nearly ten dollars a day—until one day they came in and said, "We're moving to the coast." "Well, I'm not," I said. "Don't you want to be a movie actress?" "Oh, no!" I said. "Well, be a fool!" they said, and they left. That was 1914 and world war had broken out, so in September I went home.

I: And then?

P: Oh, I sang old Scottish ballads in costume—I made it myself—all around Texas and Louisiana. And then I was supposed to have

TB, and spent about six weeks in a sanatarium. It was just bronchitis, but I was in Denver, so I got a newspaper job.

I: I remember that you once warned me to avoid that at all costs—to get a job "hashing" in a restaurant in preference.

P: Anything, anything at all. I did it for a year and that is what confirmed me that it wasn't doing me any good. After that I always took little dull jobs that didn't take my mind and wouldn't take all of my time, and that, on the other hand, paid me just enough to subsist. I think I've only spent about ten percent of my energies on writing. The other ninety per cent went to keeping my head above water.

And I think that's all wrong. Even Saint Teresa said, "I can pray better when I'm comfortable," and she refused to wear her haircloth shirt or starve herself. I don't think living in cellars and starving is any better for an artist than it is for anybody else; the only thing is that sometimes the artist has to take it, because it is the only possible way of salvation, if you'll forgive that old-fashioned word. So I took it rather instinctively. I was inexperienced in the world, and likewise I hadn't been trained to do anything, you know, so I took all kinds of laborious jobs. But, you know, I think I could probably have written better if I'd been a little more comfortable.

I: Then you were writing all this time?

P: All this time I was writing, writing no matter what else I was doing; no matter what I *thought* I was doing, in fact. I was living almost as instinctively as little animal, but I realize now that all that time a part of me was getting ready to be an artist. That my mind was working even when I didn't know it, and didn't care if it was working or not. It is my firm belief that all our lives we are preparing to be somebody or something, even if we don't do it consciously. And the time comes one morning when you wake up and find that you have become irrevocably what you were preparing all this time to be. Lord, that could be a sticky moment, if you had been doing the wrong things, something against your grain. And, mind you, I know that can happen. I have no patience with this dreadful idea that whatever you have in you has to come out, that you can't suppress true talent. People *can* be destroyed; they can be bent, distorted, and completely crippled. To say that you can't destroy yourself is just as foolish as to say of a young man killed in war at twenty-one or twenty-two that that was his fate, that he wasn't going to have anything anyhow.

I have a very firm belief that the life of no man can be explained in terms of his experiences, of what has happened to him, because in spite of all the poetry, all the philosophy to the contrary, we are not really masters of our fate. We don't really direct our lives unaided and unobstructed. Our being is subject to all the chances of life. There are so many things we are capable of, that we could be or do. The potentialities are so great that we never, any of us, are more than one-fourth fulfilled. Except that there may be one powerful motivating force that simply carries you along, and I think that was true of me. . . . When I was a very little girl I wrote a letter to my sister saying I wanted glory. I don't know quite what I meant by that now, but it was something different from fame or success or wealth. I know that I wanted to be a good writer, a good artist.

I: But weren't there certain specific events that crystallized that desire for you—something comparable to the experience of Miranda in "Pale Horse, Pale Rider"?

P: Yes, that was the plague of influenza, at the end of the First World War, in which I almost died. It just simply divided my life, cut across it like that. So that everything before that was just getting ready, and after that I was in some strange way altered, ready. It took me a long time to go out and live in the world again. I was really "alienated," in the pure sense. It was, I think, the fact that I really had participated in death, that I knew what death was, and had almost experienced it. I had what the Christians call the "beatific vision," and the Greeks called the "happy day," the happy vision just before death. Now if you have had that, and survived it, come back from it, you are no longer like other people, and there's no use deceiving yourself that you are. But you see, I did: I made the mistake of thinking I was quite like anybody else, of trying to live like other people. It took me a long time to realize that that simply wasn't true, that I had my own needs and that I had to live like me.

I: And that freed you?

P: I just got up and bolted. I went running off on that wild escapade to Mexico, where I attended, you might say, and assisted at, in my own modest way, a revolution.

I: That was the Obregon Revolution of 1921?

P: Yes—though actually I went to Mexico to study the Aztec and Mayan art designs. I had been in New York, and was getting ready to go to Europe. Now, New York was full of Mexican artists at that time, all talking about the renaissance, as they called it, in Mexico. And they said, "Don't go to Europe, go to Mexico. That's where the exciting things are going to happen." And they were right! I ran smack into the Obregon Revolution, and had, in the midst of it, the most marvelous, natural, spontaneous experience of my life. It was a terribly exciting time. It was alive, but death was in it. But nobody seemed to think of that: life was in it, too.

I: What do you think are the best conditions for a writer, then? Something like your Mexican experience, or—

P: Oh, I can't say what they are. It would be such an individual matter. Everyone needs something different. . . . But what I find most dreadful among the young artists is this tendency toward middle-classness—this idea that they have to get married and have lots of children and live just like everybody else, you know? Now, I am all for human life, and I am all for marriage and children and all that sort of thing, but quite often you can't have that and do what you were supposed to do, too. Art is a vocation, as much as anything in this world. For the real artist, it is the most natural thing in the world, not as necessary as air and water, perhaps, but as food and water. But we really do lead almost a monastic life, you know; to follow it you very often have to give up something.

I: But for the unproven artist that is a very great act of faith.

P: It *is* an act of faith. But one of the marks of a gift is to have the courage of it. If they haven't got the courage, it's just too bad. They'll fail, just as people with lack of courage in other vocations and walks of life fail. Courage is the first essential.

I: In choosing a pattern of life compatible with the vocation?

P: The thing is not to follow a pattern. Follow your own pattern of feeling and thought. The thing is, to accept your own life and not try to live someone else's life. Look, the thumbprint is not like any other, and the thumbprint is what you must go by.

I: In the current vernacular then, you think it's necessary for an artist to be a "loner"—not to belong to any literary movement?

P: I've never belonoged to any group or huddle of any kind. You cannot be an artist and work collectively. Even the fact that I went to Mexico when everybody else was going to Europe—I want to Mexico because I felt I had business there. And there I found friends and ideas that were sympathetic to me. That was my entire milieu. I don't think anyone even knew I was a writer. I didn't show my work to anybody or talk about it, because—well, no one was particularly interested in that. It was a time of revolution, and I was running with almost pure revolutionaries!

I: And you think that was a more wholesome environment for a writer than, say, the milieu of the expatriated artist in Europe at the same time?

P: Well, I know it was good for me. I would have been completely smothered—completely disgusted and revolted—by the goings-on in Europe. Even now when I think of the twenties and the legend that has grown up about them, I think it a horrible time: shallow and trivial and silly. The remarkable thing is that anybody survived in such an atmosphere—in a place where they could call F. Scott Fitzgerald a great writer!

I: You don't agree?

P: Of course I don't agree. I couldn't read him then and I can't read him now. There was just one passage in a book called *Tender Is the Night*—I read that and thought, "Now I will read this again," because I couldn't be sure. Not only didn't I like his writing, but I didn't like the people he wrote about. I thought they weren't worth thinking about, and I still think so. It seems to me that your human beings have to have some kind of meaning. I just can't be interested in those perfectly stupid meaningless lives. And I don't like the same thing going on now—the way the artist simply will not face up to the final reckoning of things.

I: In a philosophical sense?

P: I'm thinking of it now in just the artistic sense—in the sense of an artist facing up to his own end meanings. I suppose I shouldn't be mentioning names, but I read a story some time ago, I think it was in the *Paris Review,* called "The McCabes."* Now I think William Styron is an extremely gifted man: he's very ripe and lush and with a

*"The McCabes" was mistakenly not identified as a section from Styron's novel *Set This House on Fire.*

kind of Niagara Falls of energy, and a kind of power. But he depends so on violence and a kind of exaggerated heat—at least it looks like heat, but just turns out to be summer lightning. Because there is nothing in the world more meaningless than that whole escapade of this man going off and winding up in the gutter. You sit back and think, "Well, let's see, where are we now?" All right, it's possible that that's just what Styron meant—the whole wicked pointlessness of things. But I tell you, nothing is pointless, and nothing is meaningless if the artist will face it. And it's his business to face it. He hasn't got the right to sidestep it like that. Human life itself may be almost pure chaos, but the work of the artist—the only thing he's good for—is to take these handfuls of confusion and disparate things, things that seem to be irreconcilable, and put them together in a frame to give them some kind of shape and meaning. Even if it's only his view of a meaning. That's what he's for—to give his view of life. Surely, we understand very little of what is happening to us at any given moment. But by remembering, comparing, waiting to know the consequences, we can sometimes see what an event really meant, what it was trying to teach us.

I: You once said that every story begins with an ending, that until the end is known there is no story.

P: That is where the artist begins to work: with the consequences of acts, not the acts themselves. Or the events. The event is important only as it affects your life and the lives of those around you. The reverberations, you might say, the overtones: that is where the artist works. In that sense it has sometimes taken me ten years to understand even a little of some important event that had happened to me. Oh, I could have given a perfectly factual account of what had happened, but I didn't know what it meant until I knew the consequences. If I didn't know the ending of a story, I wouldn't begin. I always write my last lines, my last paragraph, my last page first, and then I go back and work towards it. I know where I'm going. I know what my goal is. And how I get there is God's grace.

I: That's a very classical view of the work of art—that it must end in resolution.

P: Any true work of art has got to give you the feeling of reconciliation—what the Greeks would call catharsis, the purification of your mind and imagination—through an ending that is endurable because it is right and true. Oh, not in any pawky individual idea of morality or some parochial idea of right and wrong. Sometimes the end is very tragic, because it needs to be. One of the most perfect and marvelous endings in literature—it raises my hair now—is the little boy at the end of *Wuthering Heights,* crying that he's afraid to go across the moor because there's a man and woman walking there.

And there are three novels that I reread with pleasure and delight—three almost perfect novels, if we're talking about form, you know. One is *A High Wind in Jamaica* by Richard Hughes, one is *A Passage to India* by E. M. Forster, and the other is *To the Lighthouse* by Virginia Woolf. Every one of them begins with an apparently insoluble problem, and every one of them works out of confusion into order. The material is all used so that you are going toward a goal. And that goal is the clearing up of disorder and confusion and wrong, to a logical and human end. I don't mean a happy ending, because after all at the end of *A High Wind in Jamaica* the pirates are all hanged and the children are all marked for life by their experience, but it comes out to an orderly end. The threads are all drawn up. I have had people object to Mr. Thompson's suicide at the end of "Noon Wine," and I'd say, "All right, where was he going? Given what he was, his own situation, what else could he do?" Every once in a while when I see a character of mine just going towards perdition, I think, "Stop, stop, you can always stop and choose, you know." But no, being what he was, he already *has* chosen, and he can't go back on it now. I suppose the first idea that man had was the idea of fate, of the servile will, of a deity who destroyed as he would, without regard for the creature. But I think the idea of free will was the second idea.

I: Has a story never surprised you in the writing? A character suddenly taken a different turn?

P: Well, in the vision of death at the end of "Flowering Judas" I knew the real ending—that she was not going to be able to face her life, what she'd done. And I knew that the vengeful spirit was going to come in a dream to tow her away into death, but I didn't know until I'd written it that she was going to wake up saying, "No!" and be afraid to go to sleep again.

I: That was, in a fairly literal sense, a "true" story, wasn't it?

P: The truth is, I have never written a story in my life that didn't have a very firm foundation in actual human experience—somebody else's experience quite often, but an experience that became my own by hearing the story, by witnessing the thing, by hearing just a word perhaps. It doesn't matter, it just takes a little—a tiny seed. Then it takes root, and it grows. It's an organic thing. That story had been on my mind for years, growing out of this one little thing that happened in Mexico. It was forming and forming in my mind, until one night I was quite desperate. People are always so sociable, and I'm sociable too, and if I live around friends. . . . Well, they were insisting that I come and play bridge. But I was very firm, because I knew the time had come to write that story, and I had to write it.

I: What was that "little thing" from which the story grew?

P: Something I saw as I passed a window one evening. A girl I knew had asked me to come and sit with her, because a man was coming to see her, and she was a little afraid of him. And as I went through the courtyard, past the flowering judas tree, I glanced in the window and there she was sitting with an open book in her lap, and there was this great big fat man sitting beside her. Now Mary and I were friends, both American girls living in this revolutionary situation. She was teaching at an Indian school, and I was teaching dancing at a girls' technical school in Mexico City. And we were having a very strange time of it. I was more skeptical, and so I had already begun to look with a skeptical eye on a great many of the revolutionary leaders. Oh, the idea was all right, but a lot of men were misapplying it.

And when I looked through that window that evening, I saw something in Mary's face, something in her pose, something in the whole situation, that set up a commotion in my mind. Because until that moment I hadn't really understood that she was not able to take care of herself, because she was not able to face her own nature and was afraid of everything. I don't know why I saw it. I don't believe in intuition. When you get sudden flashes of perception, it is just the brain working faster than usual. But you've been getting ready to know it for a long time, and when it comes, you feel you've known it always.

I: You speak of a story "forming" in your mind. Does it begin as a visual impression, growing to a narrative? Or how?

P: All my senses were very keen; things came to me through my

eyes, through all my pores. Everything hit me at once, you know.
That makes it very difficult to describe just exactly what is happening.
And then, I think the mind works in such a variety of ways.
Sometimes an idea starts completely inarticulately. You're not thinking in images or words or—well, it's exactly like a dark cloud moving
in your head. You keep wondering what will come out of this, and
then it will dissolve itself into a set of—well, not images exactly, but
really thoughts. You begin to think directly in words. Abstractly. Then
the words transform themselves into images. By the time I write the
story my people are up and alive and walking around and taking
things into their own hands. They exist as independently inside my
head as you do before me now. I have been criticized for not enough
detail in describing my characters, and not enough furniture in the
house. And the odd thing is that I see it all so clearly.

I: What about the technical problems a story presents—its formal
structure? How deliberate are you in matters of technique? For
example, the use of the historical present in "Flowering Judas"?

P: The first time someone said to me, "Why did you write
'Flowering Judas' in the historical present?" I thought for a moment
and said, "Did I?" I'd never noticed it. Because I didn't *plan* to write it
any way. A story forms in my mind and forms and forms, and when
it's ready to go, I strike it down—it takes just the time I sit at the
typewriter. I never think about form at all. In fact, I would say that
I've never been interested in anything about writing after having
learned, I hope, to write. That is, I mastered my craft as well as I
could. There is a technique, there is a craft, and you have to learn it.
Well, I did as well as I could with that, but now all in the world I am
interested in is telling a story. I have something to tell you that I, for
some reason, think is worth telling, and so I want to tell it as clearly
and purely and simply as I can. But I had spent fifteen years at least
learning to write. I practiced writing in every possible way that I
could. I wrote a pastiche of other people, imitating Dr. Johnson and
Laurence Sterne, and Petrarch and Shakespeare's sonnets, and then
I tried writing my own way. I spent fifteen years learning to trust
myself: that's what it comes to. Just as a pianist runs his scales for ten
years before he gives his concert: because when he gives that
concert, he can't be thinking of his fingering or of his hands; he has to
be thinking of his interpretation, of the music he's playing. He's

thinking of what he's trying to communicate. And if he hasn't got his technique perfected by then, he needn't give the concert at all.

I: From whom would you say you learned most during this period of apprenticeship?

P: The person who influenced me most, the real revelation in my life as a writer—though I don't write in the least like him—was Laurence Sterne, in *Tristram Shandy.* Why? Because, you know, I loved the grand style, and he made it look easy. The others, the great ones, really frightened me; they were so grand and magnificent they overawed me completely. But Laurence Sterne—well, it was just exactly as if he said, "Oh, come on, do it this way. It's so easy." So I tried to do it that way, and that taught me something, that taught me more than anybody else had. Because Laurence Sterne is a most complex and subtle man.

I: What about your contemporaries? Did any of them contribute significantly to your development as a writer?

P: I don't think I learned very much from my contemporaries. To begin with, we were all such individuals, and we were all so argumentative and so bent on our own courses that although I got a kind of support and personal friendship from my contemporaries, I didn't get very much help. I didn't show my work to anybody. I didn't hand it around among my friends for criticism, because, well, it just didn't occur to me to do it. Just as I didn't even try to publish anything until quite late because I didn't think I was ready. I published my first story in 1923. That was "María Concepción," the first story I ever finished. I rewrote "María Concepción" fifteen or sixteen times. That was a real battle, and I was thirty-three years old. I think it is the most curious lack of judgment to publish before you are ready. If there are echoes of other people in your work, you're not ready. If anybody has to help you rewrite your story, you're not ready. A story should be a finished work before it is shown. And after that, I will not allow anyone to change anything, and I will not change anything on anyone's advice. "Here is my story. It's a finished story. Take it or leave it!"

I: You are frequently spoken of as a stylist. Do you think a style can be cultivated, or at least refined?

P: I've been called a stylist until I really could tear my hair out. And I simply don't believe in style. The style is you. Oh, you can cultivate a style, I suppose, if you like. But I should say it remains a cultivated style. It remains artificial and imposed, and I don't think it deceives anyone. A cultivated style would be like a mask. Everybody knows it's a mask, and sooner or later you must show yourself—or at least, you show yourself as someone who could not afford to show himself, and so created something to hide behind. Style is the man. Aristotle said it first, as far as I know, and everybody has said it since, because it is one of those unarguable truths. You do not create a style. You work, and develop yourself; your style is an emanation from your own being. Symbolism is the same way. I never consciously took or adopted a symbol in my life. I certainly did not say, "This blooming tree upon which Judas is supposed to have hanged himself is going to be the center of my story." I named "Flowering Judas" after it was written, because when reading back over it I suddenly saw the whole symbolic plan and pattern of which I was totally unconscious while I was writing. There's a pox of symbolist theory going the rounds these days in American colleges in the writing courses. Miss Mary McCarthy, who is one of the wittiest and most acute and in some ways the worst-tempered woman in American letters, tells about a little girl who came to her with a story. Now Miss McCarthy is an extremely good critic, and she found this to be a good story, and she told the girl that it was—that she considered it a finished work, and that she could with a clear conscience go on to something else. And the little girl said, "But Miss McCarthy, my writing teacher said, 'Yes, it's a good piece of work, but now we must go back and put in the symbols!' " I think that's an amusing story, and it makes my blood run cold.

I: But certainly one's command of the language can be developed and refined?

P: I love the purity of language. I keep cautioning my students and anyone who will listen to me not to use the jargon of trades, not to use scientific language, because they're going to be out of date the day after tomorrow. The scientists change their vocabulary, their jargon, every day. So do the doctors, and the politicians, and the theologians—every body, every profession, every trade changes its vocabulary all of the time. But there is a basic pure human speech that exists in every language. And that is the language of the poet and the writer. So many words that had good meanings once upon a time have come to have meanings almost evil—certainly shabby, certainly inaccurate. And "psychology" is one of them. It has been so abused. This awful way a whole segment, not a generation but too many of the young writers, have got so soaked in the Freudian and post-Freudian vocabulary that they can't speak—not only can't speak English, but they can't speak *any* human language anymore. You can't write about people out of textbooks, and you can't use a jargon. You have to speak clearly and simply and purely in a language that a six-year-old child can understand; and yet have the meanings and the overtones of language, and the implications, that appeal to the highest intelligence—that is, the highest intelligence that one is able to reach. I'm not sure that I'm able to appeal to the highest intelligence, but I'm willing to try.

I: You speak of the necessity of writing out of your own under-standing rather than out of textbooks, and I'm sure any writer would agree. But what about the creation of masculine characters then? Most women writers, even the best of them like George Eliot, have run aground there. What about you? Was Mr. Thompson, say, a more difficult imaginative problem than Miranda?

P: I never did make a profession of understanding people, man or woman or child, and the only thing I know about people is exactly what I have learned from the people right next to me. I have always lived in my immediate circumstances, from day to day. And when men ask me how I know so much about men, I've got a simple answer: everything I know about men, I've learned from men. If there is such a thing as a man's mind and a woman's mind—and I'm sure there is—it isn't what most critics mean when they talk about the two. If I show wisdom, they say I have a masculine mind. If I am silly and irrelevant—and Edmund Wilson says I often am—why then they say I have a typically feminine mind! (That's one thing about reaching my age: you can always quote the authorities about what you are.) But I haven't ever found it unnatural to be a woman.

I: But haven't you found that being a woman presented to you, as an artist, certain special problems? It seems to me that a great deal of the upbringing of women encourages the dispersion of the self in many small bits, and that the practice of any kind of art demands a corralling and concentrating of that self and its always insufficient energies.

P: I think that's very true and very right. You're brought up with the notion of feminine chastity and inaccessibility, yet with the curious idea of feminine availability in all spiritual ways, and in giving service to anyone who demands it. And I suppose that's why it has taken me twenty years to write this novel; it's been interrupted by just anyone who could jimmy his way into my life.

I: Hemingway said once that a writer writes best when he's in love.

P: I don't know whether you write better, but you feel so good you *think* you're writing better! And certainly love does create a rising of the spirit that makes everything you do seem easier and happier. But there must come a time when you no longer depend upon it, when the mind—not the will, really, either—takes over.

I: In judging that the story is ready? You said a moment ago that the actual writing of a story is always done in a single spurt of energy—

P: I always write a story in one sitting. I started "Flowering Judas" at seven p.m. and at one-thirty I was standing on a snowy windy corner putting it in the mailbox. And when I wrote my short novels, two of them, I just simply took the manuscript, packed a suitcase and departed to an inn in Doylestown, Pennsylvania, without leaving any forwarding address! Fourteen days later I had finished "Old Mortality" and "Noon Wine."

I: But the new novel *Ship of Fools* has been in the writing since 1942. The regime for writing this must have been a good deal different.

P: Oh, it was. I went up and sat nearly three years in the country, and while I was writing it I worked every day, anywhere from three to five hours. Oh, it's true I used to do an awful lot of just sitting there thinking what comes next, because this is a great big unwieldy book with an enormous cast of characters—it's four hundred of my manuscript pages, and I get four hundred and fifty words on a page. But all that time in Connecticut, I kept myself free for work; no telephone, no visitors—oh, I really lived like a hermit, everything but being fed through a grate! But it is, as Yeats said, a "solitary sedentary trade." And I did a lot of gardening, and cooked my own food, and listened to music, and of course I would read. I was really very happy. I can live a solitary life for months at a time, and it does me good, because I'm working. I just get up bright and early—

sometimes at five o'clock—have my black coffee, and go to work.

I: You work best in the morning, then?

P: I work whenever I'm let. In the days when I was taken up with everything else, I used to do a day's work, or housework, or whatever I was doing, and then work at night. I worked when I could. But I prefer to get up very early in the morning and work. I don't want to speak to anybody or see anybody. Perfect silence. I work until the vein is out. There's something about the way you feel, you know when the well is dry, that you'll have to wait till tomorrow and it'll be full up again.

I: The important thing, then, is to avoid any breaks or distractions while you're writing?

P: To keep at a boiling point. So that I can get up in the morning with my mind still working where it was yesterday. Then I can stop in the middle of a paragraph and finish it the next day. I began writing *Ship of Fools* twenty years ago, and I've been away from it for several years at a time and stopped in the middle of a paragraph— but, you know, I can't tell where the crack is mended, and I hope nobody else can.

I: You find no change in style, or in attitudes, over the years?

P: It's astonishing how little I've changed: nothing in my point of view or my way of feeling. I'm going back now to finish some of the great many short stories that I have begun and not been able to finish for one reason or another. I've found one that I think I can finish. I have three versions of it: I started it in 1923, and it's based on an episode in my life that took place when I was twenty. Now here I am, seventy, and it's astonishing how much it's like me now. Oh, there are certain things, certain turns of sentence, certain phrases that I think I can sharpen and make more clear, more simple and direct, but my point of view, my being, is strangely unchanged. We change, of course, every day; we are not the same people who sat down at this table, yet there is a basic and innate being that is unchanged.

I: *Ship of Fools* too is based upon an event that took place ten years or more before the final writing, isn't it? A sea voyage just before the beginning of the European war.

P: It is the story of my first voyage to Europe in 1931. We embarked on an old German ship at Veracruz and we landed in

Bremerhaven twenty-eight days later. It was a crowded ship, a great mixture of nationalities, religions, political beliefs—all that sort of thing. I don't think I spoke a half-dozen words to anybody. I just sat there and watched—not deliberately, though. I kept a diary in the form of a letter to a friend, and after I got home the friend sent it back. And, you know, it is astonishing what happened on that boat, and what happened in my mind afterwards. Because it is fiction now.

I: The title—isn't it from a medieval emblem?—suggests that it might also be an allegory.

P: It's just exactly what it seems to be. It's an allegory if you like, though I don't think much of the allegorical as a standard. It's a parable, if you like, of the ship of this world on its voyage to eternity.

I: I remember your writing once—I think in the preface to *Flowering Judas*—of an effort to understand what you called the "majestic and terrible failure" of Western man. You were speaking then of the World War and what it signified of human folly. It seems to me that *Ship of Fools* properly belongs to that investigation of betrayal and self-delusion—

P: Betrayal and treachery, but also self-betrayal and self-deception—the way that all human beings deceive themselves about the way they operate. . . . There seems to be a kind of order in the universe, in the movement of the stars and the turning of the earth and the changing of the seasons, and even in the cycle of human life. But human life itself is almost pure chaos. Everyone takes his stance, asserts his own rights and feelings, mistaking the motives of others, and his own. . . . Now, nobody knows the end of the life he's living, and neither do I. Don't forget I am a passenger on that ship; it's not the other people altogether who are the fools! We don't really know what is going to happen to us, and we don't know why. Quite often the best we can do is to keep our heads, and try to keep at least one line unbroken and unobstructed. Misunderstanding and separation are the natural conditions of man. We come together only at these pre-arranged meeting grounds; we were all passengers on that ship, yet at this destination, each one was alone.

I: Did you find that the writing of *Ship of Fools* differed from the writing of shorter fiction?

P: It's just a longer voyage, that's all. It was the question of keeping

everything moving at once. There are about forty-five main characters, all taking part in each other's lives, and then there was a steerage
of sugar workers, deportees. It was all a matter of deciding which
should come first, in order to keep the harmonious moving forward.
A novel is really like a symphony, you know, where instrument after
instrument has to come in at its own time, and no other. I tried to
write it as a short novel, you know, but it just wouldn't confine itself. I
wrote notes and sketches. And finally I gave in. "Oh, no, this is simply
going to have to be a novel," I thought. That was a real horror. But it
needed a book to contain its full movement: of the sea, and the ship
on the sea, and the people going around the deck, and into the ship,
and up from it. That whole movement, felt as one forward motion: I
can feel it while I'm reading it. I didn't "intend" it, but it took hold of
me.

   I: As writing itself, perhaps, "took hold" of you—we began by your
saying that you had never intended to be a professional anything,
even a professional writer.

   P: I look upon literature as an art, and I practice it as an art. Of
course, it is also a vocation, and a trade, and a profession, and all
kinds of things; but first it's an art, and you should practice it as that, I
think. I know a great many people disagree, and they are welcome to
it. I think probably the important thing is to get your work done, in
the way you can—and we all have our different and separate ways.
But I look upon literature as an art, and I believe that if you misuse it
or abuse it, it will leave you. It is not a thing that you can nail down
and use as you want. You have to let it use you, too.

An Interview with
Katherine Anne Porter
Roy Newquist/1965

From *McCall's Magazine,* August 1965

Katherine Anne Porter, one of America's most distinguished writers, was seventy-two years old when her
first long novel, *Ship of Fools,* appeared in 1962. She
leads an extremely active life, writing, traveling and cop-
ing with the problems of being a celebrity. The following
interview, conducted by newspaper reporter and book
reviewer Roy Newquist, was tape-recorded at Miss Porter's home near Washington, D.C.

Katherine Anne Porter: Well, let's start, and I hope I don't ramble.
If I do, give me a chance to come back to the point.

I: The first question up is the standard query regarding birth and
education.

KAP: That tale is neither sad nor long. I was born on May 15,
1890, in Indian Creek, Texas, near Austin—I should say, sixty-five
miles away. This was in central Texas, black-land farming country;
but I didn't stay there long. Until I was eleven, I lived mostly in either
San Antonio or a small town named Kyle, that was about five miles
from my grandmother's farm. She had quite a large landholding
there; little by little, she dispersed it by giving it to her children, and
by the time she died, she had a very small farm, a few hundred acres.

After that, I was in San Antonio and in New Orleans. I went to
girls' schools and convents and had quite a classical, ornamental
education—the kind girls got then—and I don't think it took very
well. I seem to have spent most of my time "bootlegging" literature.
When they were trying to make us read Saint Thomas Aquinas, I was
reading *The Confessions of Saint Augustine.* I read and read and
read. I got most of my education from books. We had a good
collection at home; most old-fashioned literate families had. I think

mine was the very last generation with a certain sort of upbringing. After Grandmother died, everything was scattered, the books, furniture, the family life and all; and the next two generations were brought up on radio and records and cars—no books at all, nothing that we would have called education. It seemed an extraordinarily savage kind of upbringing, but they didn't seem to miss anything, so I suppose it was all right for them. It is very disappointing for me.

I remember once telling somebody who asked me about my education that by academic standards I was an illiterate. My father read this, and his feelings were hurt, and he said, "Well, we did our best to educate you, but you were proof against it." He was right. I really was proof against the kind of education they wanted to give me, and I never went to college.

I: How long *did* you go to school?

KAP: I left when I was about sixteen and never set foot in a university until I went there to teach. Since I came back from Europe, I have spent thirty-odd years traveling about this country, teaching and lecturing and running classes for would-be writers. The kind of class I liked best did not involve teaching them how to write—rather, it was how to read. In recent years, students have the idea that you don't have to know how to read in order to write. This kind of illiteracy hasn't appealed to me at all. In very large colleges, where I've gone as guest writer or lecturer, they have enormous classes of little people who were going to learn to write, and it turned out that they had never read a good book. Over and over, you would find them studying *Gone With the Wind* or Daphne du Maurier's romances. Some of them had never read anything but whodunits, and I used to look at them and think, I wonder where one begins. It was like being in a house with a whole set of very bright baboons. You expected them to burst into human speech at any minute, but they never did—not on the subject of writing, anyhow. It used to distress me a great deal. Yet was it always their fault? In a California university, where I spent a year persuading my class to read the work of masters, in order to know what the standard of excellence is, there was another teacher who ridiculed my work and my ideas to these same students, assuring them that there had been only two good short-story writers in this country—Bret Harte and O. Henry.

Well, you asked me about my education, and I can't draw a line, because I'm still picking up an education. You see and hear certain things and you want to know more, so you find out more.

I: Do you gather material for your books the same way?

KAP: I can't imagine deliberately going out to get material for a book. I suppose, if you were writing a travel book, you'd have to; but the writer doesn't really need to look for material for anything. It's there; you soak it up as you go along; it belongs to you, will come to you. Wasn't it Molière who said, "I take my own where I find it"? A great waste of energy. If you sit still, it comes to you.

I: You've done more traveling than "sitting still" though, haven't you?

KAP: I've been out of the country a great deal, yes. In Mexico and in Europe. I stayed in Mexico and Europe about seven years at one time, without returning, and when I came back, all sorts of things had changed. For example, there was a vogue for bus travel. And everybody was eating hamburgers and hot dogs. I was brought up in the South, where we had perfectly wonderful food; I think they're right when they say that our restaurants are bad; all the good food is at home. Anyway, I thought that getting things out of tins was perfectly savage and that bus travel was just plain hell, but I suppose it added to my education. I remember, in Europe, the way the American Embassy people would celebrate the Fourth of July by sending back here for canned pork and beans; they'd buy hot dogs, which are Vienna sausages—Austrian origin—and, of course, hamburger—German. All of these things are European, you know—not particularly American. It's just that Americans pick up all the worst things from Europe, just as the Europeans pick up all the worst things from us. This cultural exchange starts in the basement; it may work its way up to the ground floor someday, but it doesn't seem to be going there very fast. We exchange everything frightful. The yeh-yeh, the jazz, the hoodlum manners, the tight jeans, all the dreadful little girls who go about looking like Cinderella ten minutes before she was hauled out of the ashes. They were all over France and Italy when I was there in 1963, with boys to match. You want to tell them: "For God's sake, go comb your hair."

I: You certainly don't sound hopeful about the young people you meet.

KAP: I probably sound like an old fuddy-duddy. I know how bright they are, really, and how good-looking—taller, in better health, in every way better off than we were—and I don't understand how they consent to be so ugly and, worse than that, like tramps. But this is not only of today I am speaking; I'm referring to things I began to notice thirty-five years ago, when I gave up wearing slacks because of the kind of woman I saw wearing them. It isn't any newer than this pornographic-literature thing. And heaven knows pornography isn't new. The first person I knew personally who wrote that kind of thing was Henry Miller. He gave me a copy of his *Tropic of Cancer* the day it came off the press. That was in Paris. I have it yet, dated 1934, and the funny thing is, nobody has ever gone further in plain and fancy nastiness than he did. Several years go, I was called upon to go over to Maryland to testify for Henry—I've done this several times—and I thought, I wonder if I'm ever going to be called upon to testify in defense of a good book? Why must it always be a bad book, with a few little dirty words and scenes that don't interest me?

I: You don't think that "pornographic" books are ever good books?

KAP: When you write like a green boy just being broken into the Army, you're not even pretending to turn out literature. You're forgetting your language. And anyway, this verbal riot of mud, blood, latrine smells and sex has about run its course. It's high time writers got their minds above their belly buttons. Some very exciting and entertaining things happen from there up, too!

There is a natural human speech which is the speech of literature, of human beings, of poetry. It isn't from the gutter, and it isn't exalted. It isn't Pentagonese, or Madison Avenue, or Freudian jargon, or any dialect, or the steerage-bilge school of criticism—it is the daily human speech of those who love and respect their mother tongue and learn to speak it clearly.

I can't understand why people think they can get through life on a vocabulary of three hundred and fifty words—we have such a marvelous, rich language, and I don't know why we are so tolerant of the dull minds who try to destroy it. Hearing this ugly patois, this language that isn't my language, is a fairly unpleasant part of my recent education.

I: What do you think is responsible for the deterioration of vocabulary and pronunciation?

KAP: I think it comes from the popular lowering in standards of education. We have the mistaken notion that everybody in the world has to go to college. If he doesn't go to college, he won't be able to get a job.

The colleges are already crowded with people who never in this world will absorb more than a rudimentary education, and we dilute everything to meet this low standard, instead of giving the ten per cent of students who can take higher education a chance to use all their powers.

Picasso—he's an awful bore, but he does know another painter when he sees one—said about Matisse that when Matisse put three colors together, the viewer would see a fourth. It's the same with language and poetry; it's the artists who hear the overtones that say something with layers and layers of meaning and shades of feeling and sound. Matisse said, in effect, "You must be very careful to keep your colors on your palette separate and pure, put them side by side carefully; if you mix all the colors on your palette, you'll have mud." And this is exactly what we're getting, apparently what the great common world wants—the mud where they feel at home. They want mud, they are mud, they're at home in mud, and they will have mud and refuse everything beautiful that grows out of it.

This nature totally lacks the faculty of respect for excellence. There is a homely old saying that everyone must eat a peck of dirt in his lifetime. Maybe, but the important thing is to know what you are eating and call it by its right name. So often in Europe, I would feel humiliated by the awful things, the parodies of our national character we sent to represent American culture.

I would think, I don't know who you're representing, but I know you're not representing me, and I don't think you're really representing my country, either. They would have these international festivals, where every country in the world sent something, presumably the best it had; whether the art was theater, dance, music, painting, the beautiful things would come. I'm thinking most about Paris in 1952, because I was there and took a great interest; I was one of our delegates.

What did we send? *Four Saints in Three Acts*—or are the numbers the other way around?—with a Negro company. Can you imagine this as representing the American arts? I think Virgil Thompson is a very good composer, but this strange little trifle appalled me. And Gertrude Stein was American-born but got back to Europe as fast as she could and stayed there. She was an interesting phenomenon in her own right, but representative of anything American? I think not. The Negroes were extremely good singers and dancers, and it was an amusing little show; but was that the best we could send? And I thought, Oh, this is terrible; let me live to get away.

I: In painting it's worse, isn't it?

KAP: Painting doesn't exist any more. The gang has taken over. I never knew Jackson Pollock, but I've seen pictures of him dribbling paint, you know, like a little boy building very sloppy mud pies, and recently he came to a full and deserved cycle: I saw a jigsaw puzzle of a Jackson Pollock painting. This is beyond comment.

I've always been a hopeful person, though, and I'm hopeful now. We've had dark times before, times that seemed just as dark to previous generations as our age seems to us. But we'll come through. Even if we have to fight for every breath, forever, we do not have to be destroyed. What we do need is endless courage.

I: And intelligence.

KAP: Yes, because courage without intelligence is brute nonsense. But I have to be hopeful—we have artists in every medium, at present, who possess very high degrees of talent. We can't have them too clearly, because we have to let our age recede into some measure of the past before the great figures really stand out.

I was brought up in the generation that Miss Stein described as "lost," but I'll be damned if ever I was lost. I always knew where I was. I sometimes wondered how I was going to get out of it, but I knew where I was and how I had got there. I don't think we were lost, straying off somewhere like witless children in the woods; we merely had to work at finding our right way.

Perhaps we represented the real break with the nineteenth century. That century, in very important ways, was an appalling fraud, and we were nurtured on the Victorians, and it took us a while to realize what stuffed shirts they were on the whole—with what strange giant geniuses, like civic monuments!—and to recognize our own world and our own talents.

Look back, now, at the giants of our age, starting with Henry James and Hardy, then Yeats and Joyce and T. S. Eliot, then our whole group of wonderful poets, like Robert Penn Warren and John Crowe Ransom, Wallace Stevens, Allen Tate, Marianne Moore—oh, many! People like that were very grand, and I see some others coming up, now, who are going to last. But we're not the future; we can't judge. We'll have to judge as well as we can, however, to see that the splendid talents of our day aren't neglected or crushed or driven to the wall.

I: When did you start writing? How did it all begin?

KAP: I suppose that is a question that has to be asked—about how you started to write—but there isn't any answer. I don't think any writer knows. A child can't be told to start walking, you know. He crawls till he's ready; then he just gets up and starts.

I began writing when I was a child. All children, if you leave them in a room with crayon and paper and books, blocks and letters on them, will start making things. I started to write, and I also illustrated what I wrote. This was when I was about six years old.

You see, we had this old-fashioned home education—the place was full of books and music and very literate grown-ups, who tried to bring us out, to teach us; and a young governess, who lived with us for several years. I don't remember learning to read and write—it seemed I could always sing the scales and count to ten and read "The Cat is on the Mat," or something similarly profound.

When I was six, I wrote what I called a novel—I spelled it "nobble," but I knew what I was talking about. The title was *The Hermit of Halifax Cave*. The cave itself was about ten miles out in the country near a roaring river; we used to go there for picnics and summer holidays. I don't know where I invented the hermit—perhaps it came from Peter the Hermit, who got up the Children's Crusade. At any rate, I wrote my "nobble" very carefully, and illustrated it with crayon, and sewed it together like a book. Then I passed it around to the family, and far from cradling and coddling me and looking upon me as a prodigy or budding genius, they just laughed their heads off and passed it around to the neighbors, and the neighbors laughed *their* heads off.

I got to be such a laughing stock that I learned something: to keep things to myself. No child had less encouragement; but I suppose the "nobble" was funny, and I wish I had the thing now. So that was my start in literature. Oddly enough, I went right on with it—I couldn't help writing, and they couldn't teach me anything in school. I couldn't learn arithmetic, for one thing. They dragged me through all stages of mathematics by the hair, and I don't know to this day what they were talking about. I was mad about history, grammar, world geography, music, poetry, painting; I'd put books on subjects that enchanted me inside textbooks and read, read, read.

At home, I found all the things I really needed to learn. We had all of the classics—we started with Homer and came all the way to the moderns, like Thackeray and Dickens, of whom my grandmother didn't quite approve. She thought that Dickens was a bit coarse and Thackeray frivolous. But I was allowed to read *Wuthering Heights*. She didn't stop me from reading anything I wanted to read, but she made her disapproval very obvious. Perhaps she was right about Thackeray; he bores me to this day. As years went by, it became obvious that I really was trying to write. My family's attitude was: "What do you expect to add to Homer and Dante and Chaucer and Shakespeare, to say nothing of Henry James?" They didn't realize that if young people felt that way, they wouldn't turn a hand to anything; they'd vegetate. Those literary heroes gave me a foundation.

I: With so much discouragement, I wonder what made you stick to it.

KAP: I don't know why I kept writing. I didn't particularly want to, and I said a hundred times that I would never write another line. Yet I wrote all the time. I kept notebooks, and I'd write things down on pieces of paper and throw the paper into a basket. I've got all the baskets, and they haven't been opened for years.

I think that a real bent, a genuine vocation, comes so naturally that one simply performs. I've been kept from writing for long stretches, making tours and lecturing for a living, and all my energy went into these secondary things; but nothing could stop me for good. I always went back to writing—or, more precisely, I had never really left it.

I: How did you first come to be published?

KAP: Oddly enough a professional career of "getting published" never occurred to me. I felt I wasn't good enough, didn't know enough, and didn't have any business trying to get published. I was literally trying to learn to write, as a pianist runs scales. I practiced, I imitated, I parodied—wasn't it Stevenson who said he played the sedulous ape? Incidentally, I can write very good parodies of Doctor Johnson, Montaigne and Gertrude Stein. But for a long time, I did nothing of my own. When I did branch out to try to see if I couldn't do more than imitate. I discovered I had acquired a very good vocabulary, a feel for the language. I wrote a couple of novels and had the sense to throw them away, but I have most of my early stuff around somewhere—every once in a while, I run into some of it, and I'm astonished at how good two lines will be and how horrible the rest of it is. Evidently, I was the world's worst when I started, and I don't know what kept me at it.

And then, once—I don't know why—I decided that I had to finish a story. My life was going along, and I had been writing, and there I was—twenty-eight, as I recall—just doing magazine stuff; editing, not writing, with all sorts of jobs behind me. I think my first trip to Mexico by myself set me off. I ran into things, heard things, saw people. One might think my New York experiences would have been the catalyst; but New York never impressed me particularly. I went back to Mexico and began to be really interested in motives and to make stories. When I came again to New York, I used to tell these stories, and by then I'd met all kinds of writers and editors and publishers, who would say, "Why don't you write these things?" One evening, I was talking to a man who said, "Oh, I wish you would stop telling your stories and letting them go into the air. Why don't you put them down?" I told him I *was* putting them down. He said, "I want you to finish *this* story and let me see it."

I thought it was a good idea, and I actually did finish the story. I didn't have very much money—I lived at the edge of starvation for the next fifteen years, in fact—but I thought that was part of the business. But after I got started, I never thought that having or lacking money had anything to do with me particularly, except when I was really hungry.

But I finished this story. I worked on it for seeenteen days and nights. I had paid for my room and breakfast—cups of wonderful black coffee and a bunch of grapes and a big, crusty roll with butter went with the room. It was run by a French-Swiss woman, on Washington Square South. The house is gone now, and the land is now part of New York University. I lived on peanuts and bananas, in addition to the food my landlady furnished, and at night I'd go around the corner to a little place that had sawdust on the floor, to buy one hamburger. With onion. That was my supper. Then I would go back to my room and keep working.

Oh, I wanted to quit writing it; but I finished it, finally, and called it "María Concepción." The next day, I called my editor friend, the one who'd goaded me into doing it, and said, "I've got the story." He didn't wait for me to bring it down—he came over and took it away with him. Three days later, his magazine sent me a check for six hundred dollars. It was the old *Century* magazine, and the editor, of course, the literary editor, was Carl Van Doren. My friend—the one who got me to write the story—was the art editor. I had never thought of him as anything in the world except a good dancing partner and someone who could be totally depended upon to take me out occasionally for a very nice dinner in some very nice place. It was this casually friendly young man who took my story to Carl Van Doren.

I: I'm not trying to be gossipy, but I vaguely remember the fact that you've been married, but have really read nothing about your marriage.

KAP: I have no *hidden* marriages. They just sort of escape my mind, and I think other people forget about them, too. They caused me great trouble, but they are over. I've never had any secrets— there's always somebody somewhere still living who knows all there is to know about me. I mean, many people, each of whom knows a part, at whatever time of my life I was near them. As for marriage, there's probably nothing more public than getting a license and going before a notary public. Now, I won't say I was unlucky; but with the best will in the world, I didn't make a success of any marriage. I've been divorced three times, and that's enough. I don't know whether the subject is worth talking about—there was nothing scandalous about any of it. I was just a little ahead of my time. After the first divorce, they all said, "Well, go right ahead; be cast into outer darkness." It was a very disreputable thing to do at the time.

I: You were Roman Catholic—

KAP: It wasn't exactly that. I suppose Catholicism was part of it, but the whole society took a dim view of divorce. It was just as disgraceful for a Presbyterian to get a divorce as for a Catholic. So I did break with my family and with my part of the country; I'm sure they all thought I was just leaving home to lead a disreputable life. I did, of course, after years, reconcile with my family, and we became good friends.

I: But to be divorced, and to be writing—

KAP: My father once said, "If you want to write, you can write just as well here at home. Besides, what business has a lady writing? Why not write letters to your friends? Look at Madame de Sévigné!"

I had no intention of sitting in my little two-by-four bedroom in the old family house writing letters to people. I had to get out to see the world, and my idea of seeing the world was really rather innocent. I realize, now, how extraordinarily innocent a generation we were. We were guarded and cared for and watched, and we had about as much chance of being seduced as learning to fly by flapping our arms. I never got nearer than arm's length to a boy until I ran away and got married when I was just past sixteen. Mrs. Treadwell's instructions from her dancing teacher in *Ship of Fools* are a literal transcript of the instructions we were given for dancing. You put your arm like this and kept your young man this far away, and if he tried to impinge—well, you lengthened your separateness again, and if he was a gentleman, he took the hint. If he didn't take the hint, he didn't get back in the group. The innocence and credulity were astonishing.

I: Today's generation at least doesn't have *that* problem.

KAP: Today's youngsters know far too *much* about sex far too early, and it has destroyed something that was rather nice. God knows I'm not for all moonlight and roses—though youngsters naturally have a lot of this in their makeup. But when I was a girl, a girl and a boy together at a party didn't take their minds off each other for one split second, yet all we could do was look at each other. But oh, what a lot we got from those looks. Then, too, the fact that I was instructed to hold off this wild man gave him such importance. He was *dangerous,* don't you see, and it set him up no end.

But they have destroyed something that ought to exist in sex. God knows it's an animal instinct; but we are not four-footed creatures, and when it's debased, we're destroying something profound in human nature. Today's children know so much about sex they can dance without touching each other—narcissistically by themselves, a ritual that has nothing to do with real dancing. Dancing should provide great pleasure, based on sexual attraction, not on boredom;

on attention to one another, not preoccupation with self. But let's get back to my marriages.

My first one was a plain disaster. I was so terribly young, and it took all my resources to get me out of the scrape; but I got out of it, and I've forgotten about it, really. He went off and married somebody else and seems to have done very nicely—he was several years older than I, and he'd be a very old man by now. He is dead. He was from the Deep South. There was nothing wrong with him—he just wasn't the man for me, and I had no business bolting off with him. He was rather a nice man—I know that, now—but I didn't like him, and that's no foundation for marriage.

He wasn't the most composed of men, come to think of it; but it was a typical thing on my part, because I've always loved men like that, high-strung, moody, fickle—in a word, impossible. Once a doctor told me, when I was in a very bad state, having great trouble with life, just trying to exist, to survive—I had said to him, "Do you know I attract insane people?"—and I do, the hysterical, lost people often quite clinically mad, who come to fasten themselves around my neck, and I have to deal with them; so I said to the doctor, "Do you suppose that it's deep calling to deep? That they know I'm just as crazy as they are if I would only break down and admit it?" And he said, "No, on the contrary. They're looking for sanity, a stable sort of relation, a person who stands firm." So I've been certified as hopelessly sane, and I can't get out of anything.

I used to get fits and leap up and down and tear my hair and say to my second husband, when we were traveling about in Europe and we'd have to pull up stakes and go somewhere else—he was with the foreign service—I'm going to wind up in Bellevue if this goes on!" And he'd say, "Don't be silly. You're never going to enjoy the advantages of Bellevue." Sure enough, I never have, and I've sometimes longed for it.

At any rate, I've been married to three very passable men and couldn't make any of the marriages work. I suppose the contrary demands of career—my husbands' and mine—got in the way. But we're kaffeklatsching now; interviews always degenerate into this sort of thing.

I: All right, let's change the subject. What about the letters you get?

Quite a few writers I've met complain about the tremendous number they get from students and would-be writers.

KAP: Well, I think we should complain. Teachers, apparently, are bored stiff with literature—especially the teachers who teach literature and English. They can't or don't want to answer the questions their students ask, so they sic the student onto the poor, hapless author. "We have been assigned a topic," you know, or: "We were to choose an author, and I chose you," and they never have my name spelled correctly, and they never, even by accident, mention a book I wrote. They don't seem to know a thing, yet the questions they ask are wonderful.

I've now got into the habit of writing back, "Ask your teacher about how one goes about researching an author or any public figure you want to learn about. If your teacher doesn't know or is unwilling to tell you, follow these instructions. Go to the library and look up my card. Just do that, and you'll know how to spell my name, at least."

I: We haven't talked about *Ship of Fools* yet. Recently, Mark Van Doren told me that the success of that novel "proves there's a God in His Heaven."

KAP: He's one of the sweetest men who ever lived. I haven't seen him for years, but we used now and then to be on a radio program together. I met him when he was young—he was one of the most delightfully good-looking men you could hope to see. He's a good poet and has such a gentle and beautiful mind. Of course, Carl was the one I knew first—Carl was sort of a hearty, hefty person, totally outgoing. He was really the one who thought of introducing Gypsy Rose Lee into social and literary circles, for example. He gave a party for her and invited his highbrow friends, who wondered what they'd been missing all those years. He helped her write her book, and somebody asked her what she was doing, and she said, "I'm making with the book words." Gypsy talked like that, naturally; she had never learned English and did not really need it.

I've had some strange things happen with *Ship of Fools*. The half-young set, the set the old ones of my time helped establish, helped them get their Guggenheims, got their first stories published, have grabbed up the literary quarterlies and are now slashing up poor old Granny and Gaffer with pruning hooks. One of them—a man I've always been so friendly to, and helped—has gone back to take in even my short stories and is trying to undermine them, to bulldoze me out of the landscape from the beginning.

I don't blame them if they don't like *Ship of Fools*. But isn't it odd that they can read Burroughs' *Naked Lunch,* they can read Hawkes' scene in *The Lime Twig,* about that man in the dark cellar beating a woman to death with a sandbag; they can read and applaud all the horrors in the world, from Norman Mailer to James Bond; but they hate *Ship of Fools.* Nobody's going to identify with that man in the cellar—that's all sexual daydreaming. They know it doesn't apply to them. However, *Ship of Fools* is about live people, and if they don't take care, they're going to see themselves.

About *Ship of Fools* they say, "No nobility." Of course, there's nobility and there's goodness and love and tenderness and feeling and emotion, but with the instability of the human heart and the uneasiness of the human mind and the terrible stress and strain of human relations—these qualities are tempered and strained and frayed and aborted.

They can't stand *Ship of Fools,* because the people in it are alive and real. Not one of them would beat anybody to death in a dark cellar with a sandbag, with the double meaning of a beastly sexual act. But in the most civilized houses, the best people in the world do the most horrible things to each other, sometimes not knowing what they're doing, and when they find their lives approaching some sort of disaster, they don't know what happened. This is the true human predicament, and it's there, on *every* page of *Ship of Fools.* It's life as it's lived, not detached insanity, though we must recognize insanity for what it is.

Nor are all of my people commonplace. There are two painters and some dancers, a doctor who is really a good man of noble intention—

I: And that unfortunate dog.

KAP: Yes, that unhappy dog, and they said, "That revolting dog." What's revolting about the poor darling? He was seasick. I think Jenny was rather a good girl—wayward, misled.

I: Sometimes she irritated me.

KAP: And sometimes she annoyed David, remember? David could irritate a reader, too, and very rightly, and he was quite annoying at times. Yet David had his qualities. I don't understand why people can't see that people are all very much like the people in *Ship of Fools.*

We're all capable of doing virtually anything. We hurt each other and injure each other and are cruel to each other in small, cowardly ways. Just like my people. The only real crime is when the children throw the dog overboard. The Spanish people beat up their children, but only once; come to think of it, I've known one of the most talented writers of our time to beat his small daughter with a razor strop.

I can't know this absolutely, of course, because I can't go all the way into their minds; but I do think the critics and the writers, the enemies and the friends who disliked *Ship of Fools* the most, and protested so much, were really protesting the glimpses they caught of themselves.

I: In *Ship of Fools* and in so many other writings, you seem to have such a wonderful affinity with Mexico and all things Mexican. How did this come about?

KAP: Being born in Texas, of course, had something to do with it. Some of my very earliest memories—pleasant and unpleasant, but vivid memories—are of San Antonio, which was a Mexican town.

And then my father took me to Mexico when I was about ten years old. Díaz was still the president, and I was impressed with those wonderful, wide streets and the painted carriages and the horses with silver bridle reins and silver shells on the harnesses, and the music was really quite unforgettable.

Do you remember, in "Old Mortality," when Harry takes a shot at Raymond, who came over and danced with his sister? Well, my father was the one who took that shot, and he had to go to Mexico while the thing blew over. Most of his letters, while he was courting my mother—they were already engaged, and why she didn't break it off I'll never know; but she was a patient woman, I imagine—came from Mexico. He stayed there almost a year. I still have the packs of love letters he wrote, in which he described his life down there. He tried to make her jealous by telling her about the dances he went to, and the beautiful, dark-eyed señoritas he danced with, and so on. At any rate, I had a true feeling for Mexico. I was there, you know, during most of the 'twenties, when everybody was hauling off for

Greenwich Village or Europe. So I missed more than half of the
'twenties in Greenwich Village; I missed the Hemingway epoch in
Paris; and I think these are two of the luckiest misses I ever made.
Paris in the 'twenties, I suppose, was Hemingway's time and place;
but that had nothing to do with me. I have never been drawn into a
group; I cannot join a circle, a crowd, the thing I call a "huddle."

Mexico was wonderful—a crowd of us were there, perfectly free of
each other, yet happily knit together by our interest in Mexican art.
The one person who tried to make a thing out of us was Diego
Rivera; but he came later. I was there before his time, and he was the
fraud of frauds, with his syndication of painters, and his false
Communisim, and his totally shameless pursuit of publicity.

Mexico has meant something else to me, and I can't explain it any
more than I can explain how you fall in love. I hear all the analyses
and theories, and I can rationalize and give you a dozen reasons; but
not one of them would be right, because there are no reasons. If
there are, they're so hidden in my experience, so much a part of
imagination and feeling, that they can't be isolated. So *my* nineteen
twenties were spent in Mexico, not in Paris, not really in New York,
and I didn't miss a thing.

I: And why did it take you so long to write *Ship of Fools?*

KAP: In the first place, I didn't know how to write it. I looked upon
myself as a short-story writer. I started with short stories and
gradually expanded them—whatever a story took, I gave it its own
head, so to speak, and gradually went from little things like "Magic,"
all of fourteen hundred words, to "Flowering Judas," to five or six
thousand words, to "The Cracked Looking Glass," which is thirteen
thousand. As I became more practiced, and worked easier with
length, they—the publishers—kept shouting for a novel. When I took
The Leaning Tower, the third collection of short stories, to Donald
Brace, he said, "Oh, we can't publish any more short stories." I
somehow emerged with three short novels. They are not *novellas;*
they are not *novelettes;* they are short novels.

Every time I see the word "novella," my hair stands on end. I have
tried so hard to keep that pretentious, slack, boneless word out of the
language. I say we have four classifications, and they're good
enough: short story, long story, short novel and novel. Who needs
something cute and tricky and horrid like "novella"?

But back to *Ship of Fools*. While I was living in Basel, after my first trip to Europe, I made some notes. Then there was a sort of log, or long letter, that I'd kept on my first trip, sailing from Vera Cruz to Bremerhaven. I sent it to Caroline Gordon, and she sent it back, saying she thought I'd need it someday. I read it over, began thinking, and what I believed would be a short novel began forming in my mind. So when I came back to the United States in 1936, I had several things all ready to go. I went to a publisher and made a contract for four short novels, the titles to be "Noon Wine"; "Old Mortality"; "Pale Horse, Pale Rider"; and *Ship of Fools*.

I wrote "Noon Wine" in one week, from Saturday to Saturday, and that very evening, I started *Old Mortality* and wrote that in a week. Then I got interrupted, somehow; I'd gone up into the country and had taken a room in an inn and in fourteen days wrote those two short novels; but the interruption finished that. The thing that is death to me is to have my time frittered away; I must have absolute concentration, no breaks until the vein is worked out, so I went to New Orleans and found another hidey-hole—an old Scotch word. It took me nine days to produce "Pale Horse, Pale Rider," and I rolled up my sleeves and said, "Here goes the big voyage," because I knew it couldn't be a short novel. I worked and worked, month after month, and the notes piled up incredibly.

Oddly enough, everything you see in the book was there at the start, except that the novel itself is five or six times as long as I'd intended it to be. Not a character has been taken out. But as I tried to write it, I realized that I was up against something I probably couldn't handle, so I wrote to the publisher and asked him if he'd let me off this fourth one. He was happy to have the three and let me off, so I kept working on *Ship of Fools*. There were interruptions. I had to go to Reno to get a divorce; I broke up a household in Louisiana; and I had to take to the road, though perhaps I never left the road; I always lectured when I came back to the United States, and took jobs in universities. That may have been one reason why the marriages didn't last; but I had to work at these things to make a living.

There came a reprieve when I could sit down, and in six weeks, I wrote the first forty-eight pages, and the novel was started. I realized, from the slow pace it had started with, that it was going to be a very long novel and I didn't want to write it. But I had painted myself into a corner, committed myself to it, and I had to go on. I'd work on it and push it away. I separated myself from it for two or three years at a time; I'd quit in the middle of a paragraph and start again months or years later, and I thought it was going to look like a piece of restored pottery dug out of a prehistoric midden. Yet I would come back and finish the dangling sentence where I'd left it, and little by little, I decided that I was just being obstinate, cutting off my nose to spite my face, and that I was going to write a long book no matter what it might take.

For the deepest truth is that I loved the book, and the times I worked on it were the happiest, most exciting days I have ever known. At last I relaxed, but I still went along, thinking, You don't *have* to write it, you know. My professional pride was at stake—I wanted those publishers to admit my *right* to be a short-story writer. I was like the poor donkey; they put carrots in front of my nose, they beat me with sticks, they lit a fire under my belly, they walked ahead of me playing flutes—and nothing worked. They offered me a fortune—goodness, how they gave me money. Year after year, they poured money into it; but even this didn't spur me, because I have no respect for money as such. Money is only to spend, as far as I'm concerned, and I spend quite a lot. I spend all I can get my hands on, as a matter of fact. I enjoy the things I buy with my money.

Now I've made a small fortune, but they've got it stashed away in a big lump in the bank, and I can't get my hands on it. I suspect it's just as well that I can't. I have a yearly income until I die, and unless I live to be a hundred and twenty years old, my family will receive some good sums. So I get by on my measly little income—I shouldn't say that, it's really very good, and I'm glad to have it. Until *Ship of Fools,* I couldn't see any future for me except sleeping under bridges. I certainly wasn't going to any old ladies' home, and I figured that as soon as I wasn't able to totter about on platforms any more, I was finished. And boy, at that point, I was tottering. I was so tired I thought I would die.

But back to *Ship of Fools.* I was determined to finish that book, so I went into the country and leased a house, an inexpensive country house on a hill, and I lived there for three years, and every single blessed day I worked on that murderous, entrancing book. Then the lease ran out, so I had to do something else. I went to the University of Virginia, then to the University of Washington and Lee, and tried to write in the hours I didn't face amiable, shiny faces; but I couldn't. To me, the situation was getting ridiculous—they'd started advertising the book and had set up a false clamor.

Somebody told me that when the book came out, I'd get a *Time* magazine cover. I had always heard that a *Time* cover is the kiss of death; but by the time the book came out, they were so crashingly bored with the whole subject, they hardly mentioned it at first. I got what they called a "takeout," but it was the most casual, superficial treatment imaginable.

In the meantime, I had left Harcourt, Brace; they were tired of me, and I was certainly good and tired of them. Seymour Lawrence came along and said he was going to Atlantic Monthly and Little, Brown, and asked me to come with him, so I went along. Little, Brown took me on with magnificence. They bailed me out of Harcourt, Brace, gave me an advance, and I was thirty-five thousand dollars in debt to them by the time *Ship of Fools* was published. Very few publishers will do all that. But Book-of-the-Month Club, in turn, bailed me out and erased all the deficits.

At any rate, with all the clamor about the book going on, I decided I couldn't put off finishing it any longer, so I went to an expensive—I didn't know how expensive, at the time—place on Cape Ann, overlooking the sea. I had a great glass wall, a stunning view, and I sat there for three months. They'd send me my breakfast on a tray, and when I didn't skip lunch, I'd walk a few steps for it. Nobody came near me, and when the girls came to sweep the room, I'd just move into a corner and let them work around me. No telephone calls, no visitors, no telegrams, nothing.

And I finished the thing; but I think I sprained my soul. I got rid of that large problem, but other troubles began.

Ship of Fools was like Mark Twain's tight shoes. He was having an argument with a friend—I think it was William Dean Howells—who said, "Say something in favor of tight shoes." And Mark Twain replied, "Well, they make you forget all your other troubles." This was my book, you know. As long as I had it to worry over, I couldn't have other troubles; but now a sea full of other things has washed up to haunt me.

I: Where did you get the title?

KAP: It's explained in the book, but nobody looks at it. "Ship of Fools" is a satiric poem by Sebastian Brant, with wood-block cuts, published in Basel in, I think, 1494. I spent a great deal of time in Basel; my husband was in Geneva at what they used to call a "peace conference," and I hated Geneva, so I stayed in Basel, and he came down on weekends, and we walked in the Black Forest. I spent most of my time in the great Basel library or walking about with my camera or making notes. This was when I made most of the notes on the short novels and began piling up the preliminary work of *Ship of Fools*, though I didn't call the novel that at the time. Because Donald Brace, my editor and publisher, objected deeply to it—he said it was "stacking the cards"—I didn't agree then, and I still don't. When Atlantic Monthly Press asked for the title, I said firmly, "Ship of Fools," and so it was.

At any rate, I ran into the book, this delightful book, written, I believe, first in German, then translated into Latin. I read it in both languages. The day I found "Ship of Fools," I decided that my book was to be the story of a ship setting out for eternity, stopping at all the ports where people leave—the deaths, you know. Very few of us arrive at the last port, the far port of very old age.

I'm one of them. It looks as if I'm going to live forever, a chilling prospect. No, it's not that bad; I enjoy living, and I intend to do so as long as I can; but I do not accept silently some of the conditions of living and wonder why I should put up with them.

Anyway, *that's* where I found the title.

I: A final question. If you were to give advice to the young writer, just starting the voyage, what would that advice be?

KAP: Art is not a religion; it's not a substitute for religion; and though it can be a friend of religion, or an enemy, it's strictly of this world. But you have to be sure of your vocation. You can't just say, "I'm going to be a painter," or "I'm going to be a writer," without being so sure of yourself you can't be thrown off. You've got to have a certainty beyond rationalization or question. Nobody can help you, and nobody can promise you anything. You've got to take your life in your own hands, and you can't go showing manuscripts to other people and asking advice. You've got to work on your own, without letting anyone else touch your work.

I suppose, like all advice, this is not to be taken. I told a friend not long ago that I will never again attempt to tell any young person what to do, because the really gifted don't need advice and the others can't take it.

I remember Robert Lowell. I knew him when he was very young, nineteen, more or less, when he came to a writers' conference in his blessed innocence. I was there, along with John Peale Bishop, Allen Tate and Caroline Gordon, Sherwood Anderson, who knows who else? We were all enjoying a vacation, showing off a bit, having fun, and this solitary, strange, gifted child came among us, so we all took turns reading poetry and talking to him. Finally I said, "I'm not a poet and I'm not a critic, but I think your poetry is wonderful and you are going to be a poet, so why not go to Allen Tate?"

Well, he followed the Tates, went to their country place in Tennessee in a battered little jeep. The Tates didn't have any room—people were always streaming in and out of their lives—so Lowell erected a little tent of some sort on their lawn and lived out there a whole summer—sitting at Allen Tate's feet, so to speak. Allen was wonderful in instructing him in techniques, shifts and strategems. This is what a good poet can do for one who is *going* to be good. But the funny thing is that there's not one echo of Tate in Lowell now, yet what he needed was to see that the life of the artist can be real. Life is short, and art is long, and what is needed is a living touch with reality, a tangible proof, in a way, which an older artist can sometimes give to a young one.

But I'm the last person who should give advice—I'm anywhere from fifteen to twenty years older than my contemporaries, because I was a late starter. The others started out to go their way; they knew something of what they wanted; they saw writing as an active way of life, in which you advance from one point to another—and I never saw it that way at all. I still don't, even when it seems as if I've lived forever. I've stayed with the ship, and heaven only knows what glorious islands I'd have found if I'd got off somewhere along the route.

But perhaps every young artist has to do it one way, his way, and the hell with patterns. Remember who you are and where you are and what you're doing. Nobody else can do anything for you, and you really wouldn't want them to, anyway. And never take advice, including this.

A Country and Some People I Love
Hank Lopez/1965

Katherine Anne Porter, whose "Ship of Fools" and many other stories have ensured her place as one of the great American writers of this century, talked with Mr. Lopez in Mexico City last December. This summer, at home in Washington, she reviewed and filled in the text of their tape-recorded conversation. Mr. Lopez, director of the Inter-American Cultural Institute, describes Miss Porter as a "fascinating conversationalist—volatile, pensive, profoundly humorous, and almost disturbingly speculative."

I: Miss Porter, since our magazine, *Dialogos,* is based here in Mexico, we're especially interested in your Mexican experiences. You once stated that "I went to Mexico because I felt I had business there, and there I found friends and ideas that were sympathetic to me. That was my milieu." Could you expand on that?

KAP: Yes, of course. But let me approach it this way: I've had a great deal of difficulty persuading young people who want a beginning in what they call a literary career, that we don't begin it as a literary career. We begin as a vocation, and you don't go looking for material. They're always looking for material. And that was the reason why at this time in my generation all the young people were heading off for Europe. It was all this going into exile and being so romantic about it and turning their backs on this "crass American civilization" and so on. Well, I am an old North American. My people came to Virginia in 1648, so we have had time to become acclimatized. I can leave it when I please and go back when I please. Everybody was hastening off for Europe, at that time, and going into exile. It seemed so provincial and so ignorant, and they were ignorant and provincial.

120

I: You're talking about those younger writers that went to Europe?

KAP: I'm talking about that whole gang that headed out and made Jimmy's Bar famous, you remember. The so-called Hemingway period in Paris. Well, I had no business in Paris. I was born in Texas, brought up there partly, and my father brought me to Mexico when I was ten years old. We were not rich people, we were Southern people who had many losses in that famous war and we didn't travel to Europe because we weren't able to. Our foreign travel was Mexico, which we loved, and so when the time came for me to travel and get out in the great world a bit, I just came back to Mexico.

I: Had you met some Mexicans in New York? Were they your entrée?

KAP: I was brought up in San Antonio, which was always full of Mexicans really in exile—since Diaz was overthrown. It was a revolutionary city, so, we kind of kept up with things in Mexico. But in New York almost the first people I ran into were all these charming young Mexican artists, and Adolfo Best-Maugard was among them. He died a few days ago; was a lifelong friend of mine from that day to this. And there was a wonderful lad—he called himself Tatá Nacho. He's still living—he was at Adolfo's funeral the other day. He was playing the piano in a Greenwich Village cabaret to make his living, and he was a great revolutionary. I was living in Greenwich Village, too, and we got to be friends. I was thinking of going to Spain. But they told me, "Don't go to Spain. Nothing has happened there for four hundred years. In Mexico something wonderful is going to happen. Why don't you go to Mexico?" We talked it over and I finally decided I would. I headed down for Mexico in December 1920.

I: Just about the time of the Obregon Revolution.

KAP: Yes, just a few days, just a little while after he came into the City.

I: How did you come down here then? Train? Boat?

KAP: Very simple. Train. I went out all by myself, and this crowd of Obregon revolutionists stayed in Greenwich Village.

I: I call that courage.

KAP: When you're young you don't know that you have courage. It never occurred to me I was doing anything unusual at all. When I got on the Mexican train, the whole roof was covered with soldiers and rifles and young women with charcoal braziers and babies, you know. So I said to this man who spoke to me, "What's going on, what's happening?" And he said, "Well, we're having a little revolution down here." I thought this was interesting, kind of exhilarating, you know.

I: Were there many other Americans on the train with you?

KAP: Two others, two men. They didn't seem to think it was so strange for a young American girl to be traveling by herself. The worst thing was that the coffee gave out. But we did get to Mexico City perfectly safely.

I: Did you have trouble adjusting to the revolutionary turbulence of Mexico?

KAP: Not at all. I went and looked for a room, and I got a very nice one on 20 Calle Eliseo. I had the ballroom on the third floor, absolutely open, no glass in the windows, no furniture, and I went to the National Pawnshop and bought furniture, an old desk, a bed, and a couple of chairs. I was absolutely comfortable with that. Then Adolfo Best-Maugard sent me to Manuel Gamio and Jorge Enciso, who were then young, extremely learned, attractive young men.

I: Were they engaged in the Revolution?

KAP: No, they were sympathetic, but they were not active. They were, after all, already in the National Museum, in archaeology and that sort of thing. They were altogether pleasant to me, gave me all kinds of advice, introduced me to a few revolutionaries, and sort of handed me around.

I: When one reads "Flowering Judas" one can't escape the conclusion that you yourself were rather actively engaged in the Revolution.

KAP: Yes, I was.

I: Can you tell us about that?

KAP: I didn't do it on purpose. I just got drawn in because I was interested, I always used to say that if I were English I would be the Loyal Opposition. I am always the Loyal Opposition. *I'm the dissenting party, by nature.* My father was a real old-fashioned conservative stubborn Jeffersonian Democrat in the most absolute tradition that you can imagine, and he rejoiced when the Russian Empire fell because he said that nothing could be worse—it must be a change for the better. Well, that's the way he felt about Mexico at that time.

I: So you had a predisposition yourself in favor of the Revolution?

KAP: Yes, I did. I was involved in that atmosphere. I was drawn into it like the girl who took messages to people living in dark alleys. I was really like that girl.

I: I rather suspected.

KAP: But I'm not the girl entirely. I'm not the girl the young Zapata captain tried to take off of the horse one day. That was Mary Doherty. She's still here.

I: Now that you mention some specific characters, was "María Concepción" based on some actual event or some specific person?

KAP: I would tell you as an absolute rule that has never been broken yet, that *everything I ever wrote in the way of fiction is based very securely on something real in life.* In the case of "Flowering Judas" it was just exactly this: There was a man (you would know his name if I mentioned it, but I rolled four or five objectionable characters into that one man) who was showing Mary a little attention. Now Mary was one of those virtuous, intact, straitlaced Irish Catholic girls. Paul Rosenfeld once said that the Irish were born with the fear of sex even before Christianity. Well, this fat revolutionist got in the habit of dropping by with his guitar and singing to Mary. Goodness knows, nothing could be more innocent. But you know, she wasn't sure of him; so one day she asked me to come over and sit with her because so-and-so was going to come in the evening and sing a little bit and talk. She lived alone in a small apartment. The way I described the place was exactly as it was. There was the little round fountain, and what we call a flowering judas tree in full bloom over it. As I passed the open window, I saw this girl sitting like this, you see, and a man over there singing. Well, all of a sudden, I thought, "That girl doesn't know how to take care of herself."

I: And so you undertook to help her.

KAP: I decided I could stand guard or something. Baby-sit, you might say. As I came in this fellow gave me a kind of sidelong look, but I sat down and sat and sat and finally outsat him. I think that's a universal international situation, don't you? But it just had its special flavor and color for being where it was and the time it was and the kind of man he was. You know this thing stuck in my mind and stuck in my mind, the whole situation. So that story is made of a great complex of things that really happened. But not all at once or to the same people. I had come in all fresh and wide-eyed and taking in everything, and suddenly I began separating the villains from the heroes, don't you see.

I: I gather from the story that there were some presumed heroes who weren't all that heroic.

KAP: They certainly were not. The fighting heroes nearly all went out when their war was won. You know the trouble with every movement, every revolution, is that the people who do the work and do the fighting and bloodshedding and the dying, quite simply are not the people who run the thing afterwards. It's a phenomenon that exists everywhere. And it was happening here in Mexico, but you know they didn't quite get away with it. I never heard of a revolution more successful than this one was.

I: The Mexicans would say is . . .

KAP: Yes, is, is. But I saw things as they were, *then,* and everybody said, "You mustn't say this, you mustn't say that because, you know, it's . . ." And I said, "It's absurd to pretend that all these people are good and brave, when this man is distinctly trying to undercut his own people." This wicked sort of man had got his own intrigues, and I couldn't see where I was obliged to say that he was a hero when he wasn't. Even as "propaganda" this was no good. You know it's not true that wickedness is more interesting than goodness. I don't find it so, but I do find it compelling because it is so often unrecognized, it so often gets away with its murder for the reason that no one has had the courage to oppose it; or perhaps they sympathize with it secretly.

I: I am just wondering if the Mexico of that time offered a more authentic reason for writing than Europe?

KAP: In retrospect? Why yes, of course. But it would depend so much on the person. It certainly offered more to *me* because I was not running from anything. I wasn't living in exile. I just came to Mexico because it seemed the natural place for me to come after meeting my young friends in New York. When I got here, a little *chamaco* (is that a nice word now?)—named Covarrubias, Miguel Covarrubias—was a great favorite of mine. I have caricatures he made of me when he was fifteen. I took his first caricatures to New York and showed them to Frank Crowninshield and editors on *Vanity Fair* and places like that. And they brought him to New York and he had a tremendous career there. By the time he was nineteen years old he was the most famous caricaturist in the United States.

I: Now that you've mentioned Covarrubias, you said the other day at the North American-Mexican Institute that you had some role in arranging for that Mexican exhibit that first went to the United States. Would you tell us about that?

KAP: We, myself and the Mexican artists and archaeologists in Mexico, were all passionately interested in the Indian and Mexican popular arts, not the bourgeois arts of the mid-nineteenth century which I find very interesting now. Of course, the Pre-Columbian things hadn't been discovered—what we were interested in was the whole history of the Indian art from the beginning, things they had dug out of the earth in buried cities. It was Adolfo Best-Maugard who headed the whole thing. He was in a way the intellect of the crowd, the really conscious person who had a plan. It was he who suggested to the President that he needed me as the North American representative and organizer and subsequently appointed me formally. I was to go back to the United States and get the galleries lined up for the show. The plan was to have an enormous traveling show, the first that had ever been sent out of Mexico.

I: What went into this Exhibit?

KAP: It was a grand idea. It had eighty thousand objects of the most beautiful work that was ever made in Mexico. We had the most beautiful statues. We even hauled this enormous Chac Mool around—then known as the Mayan Bacchus. It was a tremendous idea and the whole thing was done by very young people—I was almost the oldest person in the crowd. I was twenty-seven. Adolfo Best-Maugard was twenty-eight. But Covarrubias, who developed into a perfect genius of discrimination and selection, was about fifteen; and Lozano and Merida, the young painters, they ran around twenty-one or twenty-two. All of us taking advice from Jorge Enciso and Manuel Gambio in the National Museum. We collected it in about six months, and I did the monograph in about the same time.

Then I went on back to the United States to see if I couldn't get galleries, and I couldn't get any. I tried the Corcoran in Washington, the Anderson in New York, and in St. Louis and Chicago, and in all cases they wouldn't let us have the gallery—because the political pressure had been put on. The U.S. government did not allow the show to come into the country because it was "political propaganda" and the government hadn't recognized Obregon's government. I could tell you one of the most appalling stories about our active enemies who really stopped us.

You can't imagine the number of powerful men who were determined that the government was not going to be recognized. And they attacked that show, they wouldn't let us take it into the country. Finally somebody said if we'd bring it to California they would see that we got it going. So we took it up there, a great trainload of specimens, but we were stopped at the border. They said we couldn't go through unless we declared it as a commercial enterprise and paid duty.

I: That must have been heartbreaking.

KAP: Yes, this is what we were up against. It was the hardest thing that ever happened to us. They kept us on a siding for nearly two months. We tried everything in the world. But you know you can't fight international politics, at least we couldn't. So there was a dealer who came and said that he would buy the whole show.

I: A Los Angeles merchant?

KAP: Yes, he bought it. And so we had this great show that made the most enormous hit. All the tremendous interest in Mexican art in the United States stemmed from that. People poured into that place from all over the country and they bought all of these beautiful things. It was scattered all over the world. And so we were all in simple despair. I just threw up my hands and quit. Xavier Guerrero, Covarrubias, Best-Maugard, Tito Turnbull the photographer (the working team), we were all separated and scattered by that time, off in different places, trying to salvage the pieces. All of us really heartbroken. Honestly we were emotional about it.

I: Did you ever write about this incident?

KAP: Not immediately. I just put it aside, and thought, "That's a defeat if ever I saw one."

I: You saw parts of the Exhibition later?

KAP: Yes, in 1952, which was exactly thirty years after our disaster in Los Angeles. I was one of the representatives of North American literature to the International Festival of the Arts in Paris in 1952. Just after the exhibit began, my good friend and French

translator, Marcelle Sibon, said to me, "Do you know that the
Mexican exhibit here is the best thing in the show? Why don't you go
to see it?" And I said, "I've seen a Mexican show, Marcelle, I don't
want to see another." I was still as bitter as gall that politicians could
have been allowed to do so much destruction, so much damage; that
internal politics, and oil and finance could ruin art . . . was just to me
horrible. Then she said to me one day, "I never saw you behave like
this before; I don't understand it. You're just missing something."

I did finally go by myself; and oh, they had it laid out in the most
marvelous way. I walked into that great hall with the great dome over
it, and there was our show. Re-collected from all over the world. It's
incredible, isn't it? And this is the strange thing—everybody on the
committee was still alive then and everybody had worked on it again
except me. They hadn't invited me again because I had gone into
such a rampage the first time.

I: Had anything been added?

KAP: Yes, they had gone into the Pre-Columbian things, brought
us right up to the Diego Rivera thing which happened immediately
after. And I must say it was the least interesting of all the things there,
because I never (after sort of being hoodwinked by that particular
school of art) appraised Diego quite the same way. Before I was
finished I didn't like his character—he was a treacherous man and a
dishonest artist. When I was there I used to go and grind paints for
Rivera over at his place. Everybody did—it was the thing to do—go
and grind paint for Rivera. I knew all of the people around Rivera—
Siqueiros, Tina Modotti, and Dr. Atl—all the young artists and would-
be artists.

I: You have visited Mexico many times since your first visit here in
the twenties. How do you feel about the intellectual and cultural
climate of Mexico today?

KAP: I always thought it was good and do now. You know I am an
artist and I am really not an intellectual, but I feel the atmosphere of
the living arts, and I think I know intellect when I meet it; I've always
had a very comfortable feeling here. I like the way people talk, the
way they are not afraid of talking about the serious things of life, at
least the things that appear serious to me. There are certain at-
mospheres in the United States where there seem to be airless little
ghettos, full of people who live in tight knots trying to run things,

making a cartel of the arts. There doesn't seem to be that kind of competition here in Mexcio, as if the arts and literature were an arena or a gladiatorial contest or something of the sort.

I: Recently here in Mexico there was a conference at Chichén Itźa of writers and artists. What do you think of that kind of conference?

KAP: I think it's just nonsense.

I: For what reason?

KAP: Because—when I left to go to Europe in 1931 they had established in the United States a dreadful thing called writers' conferences, in which they were trying to teach young people to write. They'd have these cut-and-dried sessions, and I just think they are death-dealing. The French writers used to have a summer session in the abbey of Pontigny, in Burgundy, where they used to meet once a year—the men of letters. They would simply spend a season together in which they talked, discussed, associated, reminisced . . .

I: Without any formal structure?

KAP: Without much formal structure, just enough to hold the thing together. I think that artists and such people associate by nature, they're birds of a feather. But these conferences to "teach" writers to write—absurd.

I: You know, we haven't had a chance yet to talk about *Ship of Fools* at any great length. I've wondered how you decided upon the structure.

KAP: I didn't really. Do you remember the little set of three short novels, "Noon Wine," "Old Mortality," and "Pale Horse, Pale Rider"? When I signed a contract for those stories I had had them in mind for years. Then all of a sudden, it's like an egg forming, they were ready to go. So I went to see my publisher and said I'm ready now to make those stories that we were talking about. They gave me a contract for four short novels and so I took my little notes and papers and went up to the country and sat down in a little inn and wrote the first one in seven days—"Old Mortality." I wrote the second one, "Noon Wine," in another seven days. And then I was inter-rupted, as usual, you know. People came and caught up with me and I had to jump up and run to another place. I went to New Orleans and sat down and wrote "Pale Horse, Pale Rider" in nine days. It was nearly six months later.

And then I came to the really tough one, which I called *Ship of*

Fools, based on my voyage from Veracruz to Bremerhaven, my first voyage to Europe. Would you believe it wouldn't accommodate itself? I couldn't do it in 25,000 words. And I said I'm not going to do anything more. This is my limit. I'm a short-story writer, and if I can't say what I've got to say in 25,000 words, I won't begin. And this kept haunting me and bedeviled me and I kept writing and taking notes and thinking about it—how to get this into 25,000 words. And it would not. It just obstinately would not. I finally just kept writing and writing. Years passed and I'd go back and add some more and then I'd worry about this thing. I couldn't get rid of it. It had to be written and I had to find a way to write it. And I couldn't because I was obstinate, you see. I would not write a novel. They'd been after me to write a novel for years. I kept telling them, "I will not—you have to leave me alone. This is my way of working and I am not going to do anything to change it." It was partly obstinacy, partly professional pride, partly the fact that I thought I knew what I could do and what I couldn't do. And I had to work it out. It took me years and years. I'd go back and add again, and I'd go back over it, and little by little it shaped itself in my mind. But I was doing so many things, you see, I was teaching and lecturing and I published three other books. I also did some translating and was very tired most of my time. And finally I thought I must begin and it's going to be maybe not a novel, but a long, long story. I simply sat down in the middle of July or August. I think it was 1942.

I recall writing "Flowering Judas" in that same frame of mind. It was a cold Janaury evening about seven o'clock when I started. And I was out on the corner just after midnight dropping it in the mailbox to send it to Lincoln Kirstein, who was running the *Hound and Horn.* And he published it.

I: You wrote that story in five hours, then.

KAP: Five hours. And just corrected a little with a pen. And that's the way with this novel. I just sat down and started it. And all of a sudden my mind cleared. In about six weeks I wrote the first forty-eight pages of that novel. And then I was interrupted. A terrible domestic crisis—I had something practical in my life I had to do, and I stopped writing for a little while. From then on, and for years and years, I was separated from that book sometimes as much as five years. And sometimes I was interrupted in the middle of a paragraph with all kinds of things. You know how life is. I've never had any protection or margin, nor any buffer between me and the economic grimness of life. So I would leave it in the middle of a paragraph and maybe not get back to it for months. I said once upon a time, "This story has been cracked and mended in a hundred places. And does it show?" And someone said, "If you hadn't told me I wouldn't have known it wasn't one piece." Well, it was one piece in my mind. But getting it down on paper was the hardest thing I ever did in my life.

Finally I said I'm going to finish this if I die for it. And I did finish. I took three months off and went up to Cape Ann and sat there just the way I sat in the inn when I was doing the short novels. I said to the people, "Now, don't let anybody come near that door. Give me my breakfast at eight o'clock in the morning. I will leave the room for an hour for the maid to do it up, and otherwise I'll come out when I get hungry." Well, they left me alone, and I finished it. It took me three months. It took me another month to do the proofreading, but it was over. I think it was from '42 to '62, just twenty years almost to the month. They keep saying, "Why did you take so long?" They stand over you in the United States, and breathe down your collar while you are working. They say, "Why don't you finish that book," as if you had promised to turn one out every year. And I just say to them, "Look here, this is my life and my work and you keep out of it. When I have a book I will be glad to have it published." You know, they don't understand anything. They invade. They have as much right to do that as they have to break into other peoples' houses, but they don't understand that either.

I: There's talk of the movie version they are going to do. Have they started on this?

KAP: Oh, they've done it. They're going to bring it out, I think in January or February. And they tell me they've absolutely changed it; you couldn't recognize it to save your life. Everything I did—the whole point of my book—has been completely put aside, I am told by friends who saw a preview.

I: Speaking about movies, you had a movie experience yourself, didn't you?

KAP: Oh, dear Lord, do you know about that? It's the funniest thing—the most curious thing. Oh, dear, I cannot say it. Well, they used to think I had good legs and feet! I never could see it myself, but I couldn't help but be pleased. There was a little man here. His name was Roberto Turnbull, and he came and asked me if I would pose for the legs and feet in a little comedy he was going to make about a young man who was working in a half-cellar and fell in love with the legs and feet of a girl passing by the narrow window above. The whole story was his pursuit of the upper part of this girl.

It was just about as silly as anything could get, I expect. But, you know, it was fun. They made me seventeen pairs of the most beautiful shoes you ever saw, everything from red and gold brocade to the most exquisite black satins and colored shoes and beautiful suede—oh, lovely shoes. And these beautiful thin stockings. I said, "Oh, I'll settle for that." Of course, I wore them in the picture, you see. That was what they were made for. I went to see it later. It was really very funny. From the knees up was played by an extremely beautiful girl and I felt that her feet and legs were quite as good as mine and certainly her hands were just perfect, exquisite. I never had good hands. And so they finally got us together. But there was some embarrassment. The camera wasn't quite good enough at that time and they never did get my legs matched to that Mexican actress. But where did you hear of it?

I: I don't remember, I heard this years ago.

KAP: Yes, and do you know something? Several years later I met a Mexican artist who gave me that dead-fish-eye look in the face and then his gaze wandered down past my knees to my feet and he said, "Oh, I know you. I know you, I remember you now." I never did ask him why.

I: You make those Revolutionary days sound amusing as well as exciting.

KAP: Yes, they were lovely. But we also knew what the tragedies were. Many of my friends died in that time, and some of them just threw their lives away as if they were throwing off an old hat. They did it so well though. After all, Felipe Carillo was lined up against a cemetery wall with fifteen of his cabinet members, three of his brothers, I believe. Death was there among us all the time. Every kind of tragedy, and the most incredible criminality, international criminality. But the young can't be crushed by it. They have to live. Even with all those problems, it was a very good time. I remember saying this to poor Hart Crane. He came down here a long time after, and I tried to take care of him. He said once he wished he had come to Mexico in the first place, when I first told him about it, that he would have done better than to go to Paris. "Here I feel that life is real, people really live and die here. In Paris," he said, "they were just cutting paper dollies."

I: I believe you yourself said that you felt Scott Fitzgerald was writing about people who were of no importance.

KAP: I did. And I still think so. Somebody said I shouldn't feel like that, that everybody was important. Well, that's just one of the fallacies of the world. That's one of the things we say when we think we're being democratic. Eighty percent of the people of this world, as Ford Madox Ford said, are stuff to fill graves with. The rest are the ones that make it go round. We might as well face that I was in New York at the time they were having those tea dances and Scott Fitzgerald's romantic dreams about all the collegiate boys and girls dancing in the afternoons of false romance and luxury, and the low sweet fever of love. That sort of thing. And I simply couldn't stand it because I couldn't stand the society of those people. I ran like a deer every time I got near them. And poor Hart, he came here and said they were just cutting paper dollies. Poor man, what a terrible time we had with him. He was doomed I think. His parasites let him commit suicide. He made such a good show and they had no lives of their own, so they lived vicariously by his, you know. And that of course is the unpardonable sin.

I: Who of this newer generation of writers do you like most?

KAP: I never got the habit of thinking in generations of writers: my living favorites are of all ages, and degrees of reputation. We have always with us the professional promoters of the trade of writing, who appear to choose their candidates by lot, who drum up a new school of writing every five years or so, and while raising their new groups they try to destroy the older ones. This is not necessary at all, there is room for all, but just the same I too have my choices, every one very dear to me—all ages, sorts, and sizes. I leave out the spectacularly famous (except Eudora Welty), but here are the names of writers whom I found for myself and chose from the first work of theirs I read, with no advice from anybody, and disregarding then as I do now the commercial reviewers. I want to tell you there are some good ones in this list, and I'll bet you never heard of some of them; we have some big-time rotters who are getting all the foreign and most of the national publicity.

Peter Taylor is one of the best writers we have—do you know him?

He has published three books, and the latest one, *Miss Leonora When Last Seen,* is a collection of splendid short stories. Then Eudora . . .

I: I remember *The Ponder Heart* . . .

KAP: Yes, but *A Curtain of Green, The Wide Net,* and *The Golden Apples* have her finest stories. Do you know J. F. Powers, a great short-story writer whose latest book is a fine novel, *Morte d'Urban?* He has been for a good while a superb artist, so at last one of our prize-giving organizations got round to giving Mr. Powers an award, and high time, too. Flannery O'Connor, who died lately, was greatly gifted, a dreadful loss to us all. Glenway Wescott and Caroline Gordon are two such different kinds of writers it seems strange to put their names in one sentence. But they are both quietly geniuses, good working artists who have yet to publish a bad piece of work; as with all the writers I admire so much, I read everything they publish with pleasure, and I have my favorite works, too. Wescott's *The Pilgrim Hawk,* a masterpiece; and Caroline Gordon's *None Shall Look Back*—the best novel I know set in the South during the Civil War. It is a grand book, and I am amazed to learn that it has been allowed to go out of print. . . .

It's that kind of neglect that sometimes disheartens me about—not American writing, that is safe and sound in some good hands—but American publishing and debasement of American taste. I don't suppose I could like an artist—not only writers, any kind of artist—if I didn't like and respect his work. In fact, I can't separate anybody from his words and acts, but especially this is true with artists.

I: You know, when I read "Noon Wine" I had a feeling that Flannery O'Connor was very heavily influenced by you.

KAP: She said she was. But I cannot see it. William Humphrey, who has just published a brilliant novel, *The Ordways,* is the only writer I know who ever said in print that his writing and his style and his feeling about writing have been influenced by me. I have read carefully everything he has published, and I cannot see a trace of my influence to save my neck. But if he wants to say I influenced him, I'm very flattered, for I do so like what he writes. There is young Walter Clemons, who has a first book of short stories, *The Poison Tree*—he is not well known, but he will be. You watch him. Another good beginner is George Garrett.

It is probably my own personal preference in forms, but all these writers are also first-rate short-story writers; in fact, with one or two exceptions, I prefer their short stories to their novels, but their novels are among the best being written too. We are being sluiced at present with a plague of filth in words and in acts, almost unbelievable abominations, a love of foulness for its own sake, with not a trace of wit or low comedy to clear the fetid air. There is a crowd with headquarters in New York that is gulping down the wretched stuff spilled by William Burroughs and Norman Mailer and John Hawkes—the sort of revolting upchuck that makes the old or Paris-days Henry Miller's work look like plain, rather tepid, but clean and well-boiled tripe. There is a stylish sort of mob promoting these writers, a clique apparently determined to have an Establishment such as their colleagues run in London. It's perfect nonsense, but it can be sinister nonsense, too.

Also it is very hostile to the West and, above all, to the South. They read us out of the party every so often; they never tire of trying to prove that we don't really exist, but they haven't been able to make it stick, so far. New, gifted, unclobbered heads keep bobbing up from all points of the distant horizons, and they can never know from what direction they may come. Truly, the South and the West and other faraway places have made and are making American literature. We are in the direct, legitimate line; we are people based in English as our mother tongue, and we do not abuse it or misuse it, and when we speak a word, we know what it means. These others haven fallen into a curious kind of argot, more or less originating in New York, a deadly mixture of academic, guttersnipe, gangster, fake-Yiddish, and dull old wornout dirty words—an appalling bankruptcy in language, as if they hate English and are trying to destroy it along with all other living things they touch.

But I have named my candidates for a living American literature, only a prime few of many whose work I love and treasure; they cannot be destroyed and they will keep coming on, decade by decade, one at a time—never in a group, never with a school, never the fashionable pet of a little cartel, never in fact anyone but himself, an artist—no two alike.

We can afford to be patient.

Katherine Anne Porter
Makes a Feast of Life
Josephine Novak/1969

From *The Evening Sun,* Women's Section, Baltimore, 26 February 1969. Reprinted by permission of *The Baltimore Sun.*

This is the first of a two-part series on Pulitzer-prize winning author, Katherine Anne Porter, and the rooms which have been established in her honor at the University of Maryland.

In 1963, when Katherine Anne Porter was told her novel, *Ship of Fools,* was going to be a hit, she purchased a 22-carat emerald ring set with two rows of diamonds and a matching necklace and bracelet.

"Katherine Anne," said an old friend, "Didn't you need something other than these emeralds?" Miss Porter replied, "Perhaps I do need a new dress, but first things first."

A portrait of Miss Porter, who is regarded as one of the most distinguished writers in the world today, has just been completed by John Spencer Churchill. In it she is wearing her jewels and a white crepe-silk gown designed by Geoffrey Beene.

The painting will hang in the "Katherine Anne Porter Room" at the University of Maryland.

Miss Porter was at home last week in her English-style mansion in Washington, taking a respite from a new flurry of pre-publication activities.

She was in an emerald-green dressing gown with lace collar and cuffs and, as she poured French champagne into exquisite long-stemmed Austrian goblets, she said:

"I like to make everything into a party. People should be happy when they eat or have dinner or anything, even if it is just a cup of coffee. I have done that all my life.

"Somehow I feel that food should always be a feast. To me dinner

135

isn't dinner without a good wine, and I consider the preparation a
kind of sacred aspect—especially bread. I bake my own bread,
always—and very reverentially."

Her thick, wavy, white hair framed her finely chiseled face softly,
and her gray-blue eyes flecked with orange, were merry.

Some years ago her lifelong friend, Glenway Wescott, wrote of her:
"She has in fact a lovely face of utmost distinction in the Southern
way, moonflower pale, never sun-burned."

"There was a time," she continued, "when my favorite breakfast
was champagne and snails. I love life, and I've enjoyed it and lived a
great deal. I can't somehow regret anything except that life is going,
but I think that is a difficult thing to accept no matter how well-
prepared for it you thought you were.

"Things were not easy. When I got out into the world to try to be a
writer, I wasn't writing the kind of thing that sold, and I really didn't
expect it to. But I had no means of support, and I had decided I had
only one thing that was really mine—this art I was attempting to learn
and to practice. If I betrayed that, I would betray my whole life."

"I've always lived by that decision, so I had to find some other way
to support myself. At first, I did newspaper reviews and articles, and
then I found that I had a knack for speaking and reading poetry, and
I have spent—oh, heavens, 35 years, I think, traveling around this
country to more than 200 universities and colleges, reading poetry
and speaking about literature.

"A friend once said to me "the kind of life you've lived would have
killed two dock workers in a week." "Well, it took 35 years to put me
out of the running. At present I'm not able to work."

"I never wanted a great deal, but when I want something, I want it.
I've always been a little extravagant, and I suppose if it came to a
showdown in which I had to choose between food and some
probably useless thing—but not useless to me—I would do without
the food.

"Back in the days when I had to struggle and someone pointed out
to me that I was living beyond my means, my answer was: 'How can
you accuse me of living beyond my means when I haven't any means
to live beyond?'

"My first book was brought out in 1930 when I was 40. I had been
writing short stories since 1923.

"I have been three times married and three times divorced. I've never been angry with them. Really, they couldn't live with me because I was a writer and, now and then, writing took first place.

"If I can't work, I'm as good as dead, and sometimes the only way I could write was to go away for a while. Everything I have ever written was written in that way—I had to leave home and disappear for a while, and when I came back I would have quite a lot of husband trouble. They felt neglected. I don't blame them.

"To be an artist—No marriage was worth giving up what I had. I am so glad I was really strong enough to make those decisions.

"So many things have happened to me and almost everything I wrote, when I did write, was based on real experience, either mine or someone else's.

"Well, I had meant to use life; I had meant to live it. That turned out to be a good deal more than I could ever possibly record or use."

Glenway Wescott, she said, had spent the previous weekend at her home discussing and organizing a soon-to-be-published book of Miss Porter's personal letters written to him and to a few other friends over a 35-year period.

A collection of essays and critical analyses concerning her work is also scheduled for publication.

And "Dayas Before," her book of occasional writings published in 1952 will be reissued this year under a different title. The new collection will include works published since 1952 and is expected to be double its original size.

"One thing is happening," Miss Porter said, "which is really quite lovely." She walked into the next room to her library, and returned with a slender volume titled "Katherine Anne Porter's French Song Book."

Not long ago, a rare leather-bound copy of this book brought $2,600 at auction. It was published in France in a limited edition, on Miss Porter's 43rd birthday by Harrison Press founded by Glenway Wescott, Monroe Wheeler and Barbara Wescott then Barbara Harrison.

"This is a book of translations of old French songs and poetry which dates from my Paris days. After 36 years it's going to be fun and happiness and joy again to hear these songs arranged for voices and old instruments and given in a concert.

"Miss Rose Marie Grentzer, who directs the University of Maryland's 'Madrigal Singers,' brought her little group here during the holidays to serenade me with Elizabethan or Sixteenth-Century music.

"That is my favorite period in music. I invited several friends, of course, and we had good old champagne with homemade bread and sweet butter. Oh, it was perfectly lovely.

"Then I remembered this little book of old French songs. I gave a copy to Miss Grentzer and she called me later and said her husband, Mr. Harold Spivak, who is head of the music division of the Library of Congress, would like to plan a concert using these songs.

"We're hoping all four people who were originally involved in this book in Paris will be able to attend."

Now Katherine Anne Porter opened the book and began to read aloud in a soft, expressive voice, a song by the Chatelain de Coucy (1157–1192)—first in flawless French, then in English. "Now that is a good translation; I'll die at the stake for it.

"It covers about 600 years, up to about 1650. But there is one poem which I wrote in the back of the book in longhand because I discovered it too late to have it included.

"Listen. It was written by Clement Marot—
Oh I am no more than what once I was;
And what I was no more shall be;
My jolly summer and my spring
Have taken thieves' farewell of me.
Oh love how I have worshipped thee,
Above all gods I thee adore,
And were I twice-born, I should be
But born again to serve thee more.

Miss Porter arose from an elegant Napolean III sofa upholstered in deep lavender velvet. "It's getting dark," she said. "I have to feed my little birds."

Walking to a small summer room, she scooped up a container of wild bird seed from a 100 pound sack and sallied forth into the chill night air in her emerald green dressing gown, to feed her birds.

Katherine Anne Porter On:

John Dorsey/1969

From *The Sun Magazine*, Baltimore, 26 October 1969. Reprinted by permission of *The Baltimore Sun*.

It was about this time of year, 50 years ago, that Katherine Anne Porter arrived in New York to become a writer. She was within a few months of 30, but though she had been writing things since she was 6 she had never quite managed to finish any of them. She had been married and divorced already, a fact that no doubt raised more eyebrows in 1919 than it would in 1969. That first marriage she now passes over as "most unfortunate." She had been raised in Texas and Louisiana; she had lived in Chicago, where she worked as a movie extra, whence came the apocryphal story that she was a Mack Sennett bathing beauty; and she had worked on a newspaper in Denver, whence came the story "Pale Horse, Pale Rider," the most famous and most directly autobiographical of all her stories.

The story begins with Miranda having a dream that she is riding a horse and beside her rides a ghostly figure, the figure of Pestilence, one of the Four Horsemen of the Apocalypse. When she awakens she feels unwell, but goes to her job on the newspaper, where among other things she is the theater critic. Later she goes out with the handsome young man, Alexander, who lives in her boarding house and with whom she is in love.

She falls ill, and he takes care of her for three days because the hospitals are full—it is the influenza epidemic of 1918. Finally he finds an ambulance and sends her to the hospital. After many months she recovers, but never sees Alexander again. He has meanwhile died of the same disease.

"And except for the fact that it didn't happen quite as fast as I say, it was just like that, the dream and everything," Miss Porter remembers now, still—two husbands, a career and half a century later—still in love with him. "I always thought it was so funny that he should have died and I should have lived, because I was small and not

139

particularly strong, and he was big and magnificent looking. And I trusted him so. I had absolute faith in him. I remember saying to a Spaniard in Mexico once that Alexander was the only man I could ever have spent my life with. And he replied, 'Just think, now he can never disappoint you.' And I suppose if there is anything at all good about it, that's it, but it does seem an awfully high price to pay to keep one's illusions, doesn't it?"

"We were so shy. One of the criticisms I had of that story was from a printer on the *Southern Review* who was setting the story in type, and my husband of the time, Albert Erskine, who was an editor of the *Review,* was in the composing room and heard the printer say, 'Oh, why doesn't this couple go to bed and get it over with?' And Albert said he was shocked for a minute, but then he reflected that the printer couldn't know anything about me, so he just said, 'Well, they were not that kind of people.' And we weren't, you see.

"He was so patient with me, those nights when I was sick and delirious, getting me things and always just sitting there. Whenever I would wake up he would be there, sometimes with his foot propped up. And after I went to the hospital he sent me two dozen roses and a note. They took the roses away from me because they said flowers used up oxygen. And the nurse read me the note, and I could hear that she was reading but couldn't make out the words. And that was all. He died. And no one seems to think that was important, and it was one of the most important and terrible things that ever happened to me. And who gives a damn?"

Then she went to New York and became a writer, or perhaps, since some people think writers are born, not made, fulfilled her potential. And the central mystery of her life is: if Alexander had lived, would she have become a writer or would she have spent her creative passion in love? If the latter, then Alexander did not die in vain, for we should be immeasurably poorer without "Old Mortality" and "Noon Wine" and *Ship of Fools* and the others.

Despite her depressing production record—one thickish book of stories, one novel, one book of "occasional writings," a Christmas story and a French song book are not much for a writer 79 years old—Katherine Anne Porter, partly because she has never done anything less than first-rate, has a place among the best writers of that great American flowering of the Twenties, and she is almost its last remaining bloom.

Strange that she should have survived so long, for she was a late-blooming flower even 45 years ago. Hemingway produced his first book at 25, Fitzgerald at 24, Eliot at 29; but Katherine Anne Porter was 32 before her first story appeared in a magazine in 1922, 40 before her first book was published. The stories that went into the book came out of the long, hard years between 1919 and 1931, when she divided her time between New York and Mexico.

"I had to go to New York. I needed literary people whom I respected. I needed conversations. But I hated it and could barely live there. I spent about half the time in Mexico. When I was in New York I lived in Greenwich Village, and I wrote a lot but I never tried to get anything published because I thought it wasn't good enough. I would start things and not finish them. I did that with 35 or 40 things. I met a lot of people, and one of them was George Sill, who was the art editor of *Century* magazine.

"He was my dancing beau. In those days the girls all had their beaux identified. There was the flower beau and the bookish beau and the candy beau. George and I spent a lot of time dancing. 'Twas lovely.

"And finally after one of my trips to Mexico I was determined that I was going to finish a story. I said I'm going to finish or die. And I almost did. I hadn't got any money and I was very hungry all the time. I was living in an old house in Washington square, where I had a room and I got a big, crusty roll with butter and a cup of coffee and sometimes an orange in the morning, so I could start the day, and then I'd hold out as long as I could and then go down to the corner and get myself a hot dog or a hamburger, and a banana. I always had a banana because I'd been told that was nourishing.

"I wrote the story 'María Concepción.' It took me 17 days and 17 nights. When I was finished with it I didn't know what to do with it. But I mentioned it to George Sill and he said, 'Why, you come down to the *Century* magazine and I'll introduce you to Carl Van Doren, who was the editor. And so I did and Carl took it and looked it over right before me and said, 'I think you're a real writer,' and I just went out walking on air. I never said anything about money at all.

"And the next day George Sill himself came down in person, on the bus, to Washington square and handed me a check for $600. I was launched!

"I said to George, "I didn't realize there was money in this,' and he said 'You might have hurried up a little if you had.' "

But she has never been a hurrying kind of person. It took her 20 years to write *Ship of Fools,* only partly because she had to give up writing every so often and go to colleges and universities as lecturer or writer in residence to support herself. "But it doesn't actually take me a long time to write. I write at top speed, but there are long intervals because things form slowly, slowly, and I don't write until it's absolutely ready to go."

This deliberate speed is one of the most southern things about her. Her family, which is connected to the Philadelphia Rittenhouses and has had a number of writers in it, including O. Henry (William Sidney Porter), a second cousin of her father, went west "just on the heels of Daniel Boone" and settled in Texas. She was born in Indian Creek, Texas, on May 15, 1890, was brought up in southern girls' schools and with tutors at home, and still has a southern accent which reposes behind her careful enunciation. She has always loved to wear white and still does, and the implication is not lost. There is a certain genteel virginity about her, which is probably due to the fact that her eyes are always open wide, and her speech has a girlish, breathless quality. Little and beautiful are her favorite words, and she talks, sitting in her velvet living room in her College Park apartment, incessantly. "I don't ever stop. Someone leaned over once and said please excuse me for interrupting you and I said honey I don't know how you'll ever get a word in if you don't." She is frail, bedridden much of the time now, and tough at the same time, and always has been. She is a lady, but with a past. "I'm tottering on the brink, but I don't mind. I've had about all the life anybody could want."

At 6 she wrote her first work. "I called it a 'nobble.' I wrote it in seven or eight different crayon colors, and illustrated it and it was called 'The Hermit of Halifax Cave.' That was a place we used to go in the summer sometimes for camping trips. We'd live in tents and sleep in those wide Mexican hammocks, and fish, and oh, the water was so beautiful and brilliant and green, there was a vast river there, and it had great potholes in it in which you would fall and have to be pulled out.

"And so I put an old man there and drew long whiskers on him and had him sitting at the entrance to this cave, you know, and I had him go down and catch a fish, and fry his fish and eat his fish, and then I couldn't think of another thing to do with him. So I had to stop, and I put 'to be continued,' and I sewed it together like a book and then I went and handed it with all confidence to my sweet, beautiful grandmother—she was bringing me up, my mother died when I was about 2—and she just laughed and laughed, and she showed it to the household and everybody laughed, and they handed it about and the friends and neighbors laughed, and I was so unhappy, because I thought I was going to be praised, you know, and told how good my book was. One thing it taught me: I didn't think of it then, but I got the message. Never show around anything you write before it's published. And I never have.

"But Halifax Cave reminds me, there are a couple of things I would like to set straight. Some awful man wrote a book and in it he had two slanders about my family on one page. I don't understand how these stories come about, because I've lived my life as if I were in a goldfish bowl, there have always been clouds of witneses around, and it wasn't as if I tried to have secrets.

"Anyway, this man wrote that my grandmother drove her matched pair of horses to death. My grandmother never even had a matched pair of horses. She was a fine horsewoman and rode every day, even when she was in her 70s; but she loved animals and was gentle to them all. When we would go to Halifax Cave there was a place where it was steep and rocky, and she would not only make us all get out of the surreys, she would make the boys and men help the horses up.

And then he wrote that I was a Mack Sennett bathing beauty, and of course that wasn't true. I was in the movies, though. That was in Chicago in the teens, before Denver and Alexander, after the southern girls' schools.

"I tried to get a job on a newspaper in Chicago, and the editor asked me if I had any experience and of course I hadn't, but he was willing to try me anyway. In those days, you know, the movies didn't have any advance agents, or any of that. They were news, and the papers would send reporters and interviewers out to beg them for stories.

"So I was sent out to this movie studio, and I had on this rather bright blue suit affair, oh it was very pretty, with a little hat to match it, and I had my hair cut very short." Her genius for detail has always enlightened her stories, as it still does her memories of 50-odd years ago.

"There was a long line of people when I got there, and a man at the head of it telling some people to go one way and some to go the other. And I went up to him, and he said, 'Here, little boy blue, you go over and get in that line.' And I said, 'But I'm from the newspaper.' And he said, 'Oh, go on, get in that line and go to the dressing room.'

"And so I did, and found myself in a huge dressing room with just plank seats all around and bald lights and sheets of mirror and more planks to put your makeup on. I didn't know what I was supposed to do, and the girl next to me said, 'Well, go on and put your makeup on.' And I said 'I didn't bring any make-up.' And she said, rather kindly, I thought, "Well, you can use mine today, but don't make a habit of it.' And then I followed them all out when they went. And all we were supposed to do was be an audience at some trial scene and then get up and leave when it was over.

"And afterward the director came up to me and said 'Little boy blue, you take this slip of paper over to the cashier and get your five dollars.' The paper was going to pay me $15 a week, and I could tell the difference between that and $5 a day, so I stayed with the movies, as an extra. Whenever there was a scene where the mother had to come crawling out of a burning building with a baby strapped to her back, that was the scene I got.

"And then one day the director came up to me and said, 'Little boy blue, pack up your suitcase.' And I asked why and he said we were going to Los Angeles to open a new studio there. And I said 'But I'm not going.' He had started to walk away, and he turned around and just stared at me for a moment and said 'Do you mean you don't want to be a movie actress?' And I said 'No." And he said, 'Well then, you must be a fool.' Hee hee haha ha ha."

Her laugh, which is sometimes almost raucous, punctuates everything she says and everything anyone else says. She seems to try and
squeeze every drop of enjoyment out of each hour. As her story
unfolds in jerks and starts, going from the past to the present and
back again with hardly a breath between, you are amazed at the
people and places this sweet little old lady has known. Rich now, for
the first time in her life, she indulges herself almost vulgarly with
emeralds: a necklace with 5 large ones totaling 50 carats and a ring
with a single, squarecut 22-carat emerald that overwhelms her left
hand.

"I never cared much about diamonds or anything of that sort, but I
always wanted an emerald, my birthstone. I had three husbands and
every one of them asked what kind of engagement ring I wanted and
I said an emerald and they all said nonsense.

"So when *Ship of Fools* was published, and I knew it was going to
be a best seller and I was out of debt and a little ahead of the game I
said to the jeweler you get me the biggest emerald you can find. And
he thought I meant something as big as my fingernail and brought
one or two over and I said no. I don't mean that at all. So then he
found this.

"I haven't stopped working, you know. I'm collecting what I call my
'occasional' writings" which will appear in a new edition shortly 'and
I'm trying to get together a book of short stories that I like, written by
other people. Ones that no one else remembers or knows about. I
think of them as little violets and anemones, and I want to get some
of them out in the air.

"There's a perfectly beautiful one translated from the Russian
called 'Living Water.' It's just this story of three peasant women jolting
along in their little cart, to market you know, taking their vegetables
and things, and they find a man full of bullet holes in the ditch.

"This was at the time of the empire, and this lad was caught by the
oppposition, and they plugged him full of bullets and left him in the
ditch, thinking he was dead. Well, the three women put him in the
cart and take him to the hospital and leave him there for dead.

"And a month later, when they're coming back to the market
again, they buy a wreath and go into the graveyard to find the grave
of the young man and they can't. And then they see him rolling along

in a wheelchair, and they say, "God's grace, it's our man,' and fall down on their knees. I could just cry thinking about it. It's the story of the most pure and lovely charity. And nobody knows it but me.

"There's one by A. E. Copard, called 'A Field of Mustard.' He's a very well-known writer, but no one remembers that one. It's from the oldest kind of *Dial,* you know. Forty years ago, I tried to get some of these younger writers, too, like Roth, you know. I believe his name is Philip, is that right? Well I don't think he's writing well at all now, for the simple reason that he got too ambitious, and spoiled himself. But he wrote the most delicious story, called 'The Conversion of the Jews.'

"It's about a little boy who gets in an argument with a rabbi, and the little boy is holding out for the Virgin birth, that he's just heard of. And everyone says nonsense! You know that's terrible. You can't say such things. And he says, 'Well, if God could make the world I guess he could do that.' So momma just slaps him good and hard, right across the face, while he's enjoying his chicken soup, and he goes up on the roof and threatens to jump off. And a crowd gathers and he says 'I'm not coming down until you admit that God can do anything He wants to.'

"It's a heavenly story, and when I saw it I thought, here's the next one. But—and he won't let me have the story for my collection, either. I don't know why. Maybe he doesn't like me.

"And then there's a story about the man who betrayed Joan of Arc—but I don't think I'll tell you that, I don't want anything printed about it yet. I remember once Jean Cocteau saying to Edith Sitwell, 'The French people really don't like Joan of Arc' (which wasn't true, they love and revere her) and Edith said, 'Oh, I'm so glad to hear you say that, because it was one of my ancestors that put her to death.'

"I loved Edith. I used to say there was no one in the world cozier over a cup of tea with rum in it than Edith Sitwell. We became friends when I wrote a glowing review of some of her poetry. I thought she was a great poet.

"I used to have a little half basement in New York—they called it a garden apartment, but I said I know a basement when I see one— and this gigantic, lumbering woman (over 6 feet tall, you know) would come down those little steps and sit and have tea with me. And Seymour Lawrence walked in one time, unexpectedly, and found Edith sitting there cozily, and went out and reported that we were taking the hide off every literary person in the world, and it wasn't true. We never said one unkind word about anybody. We were just being pleased with each other.

"I learned a lesson from Edith's oversensitivity, too. I don't like criticism either, but I will die before I will answer a critic, I don't care what they say short of actionable slander. But Edith just fired in all directions at once. She was like a fortress defending itself constantly."

Miss Porter has known or at least met most of the people from her generation and later, Eliot and Pound and Hemingway and the rest, and has kept as friends Eudora Welty and Robert Penn Warren and Allen Tate and Glenway Westcott and some more. "You never had the feeling in New York in the Twenties, that you get there now, that there's nothing but a bunch of literary gangs up there, always trying to keep people out.

"The *New York Review* is a good idea, but all they have are a lot of hatchet men. That Elizabeth Hardwick, she ought to be called a hatchet man, too. Hatchet woman sounds too gentle for her.

"Did you know that I was the first person Robert Lowell ever brought his poems to? Yes, he was 18. And I knew Truman Capote, too, I used to dance with him at Yaddo 20 years ago before his first book came out, and he looked like a little freshly hatched duckling, the hair just that downy color, and the innocence of his face, you know. I liked his early things very much, and that Christmas story. But then he's just got to keep his name in the papers and he's got to know all the right people and that kind of life is such a crashing *bore* that I couldn't put up with it for a week, and I can't understand it in him. Back in the Twenties. . . ."

Back in the Twenties, when she was dividing her time between New York and Mexico, she also managed to take up a few causes. She picketed for Sacco and Vanzetti, and got herself arrested on purpose ("and this nice Irish policeman came up, he was a tall, beautiful looking man and had immaculate white gloves on, and he just took my arm very gently and led me away so politely to the patrol wagon"—confrontation isn't new, but it's changed some).

"There was a time, almost, when if I hadn't been in Mexico I might really have gone left. But I was inoculated against communism down there. I saw the way they worked, the way they behaved to each other, to say nothing of the way they behaved to me! They would not only steal all of my things, they would steal from each other.

"But I knew them all, including Obregon, who became president and was later assassinated, and Felipe Carillo, the governor of Yucatan, who was also assassinated. He was as civil and gentle a man as I ever saw, and a notorious killer. I used to go dancing with him, and boating on Lake Chapultepec. And I organized the first large-scale traveling exhibition of Mexican art, did the catalogue and everything, and brought it to this country in about 1924, I think."

Her early stories were published in book form as *Flowering Judas* in 1930 and she was immediately praised by the critics for her style and her subtle delineation of character and psychology. The following year she got her first Guggenheim fellowship, about the time she was playing hostess in Mexico to Hart Crane, the poet, who shortly afterward killed himself.

"Poor boy. He stayed with me for five months, and he was so desperate. And that horrible woman, Peggy Cowley, was pursuing him and trying to get him to marry her and Hart was to say the least not the marrying kind.

"And when he got on that ship to go back to New York he was just trying to get away from her. He didn't want her to know which ship he was taking, but she found out anyway and followed him. And one morning on the ship she burned herself trying to light a cigarette, and someone came to wrap up her hand and Hart, who was in his dressing gown, just looked at this operation for a few minutes and went out and jumped off the ship. And then she tried to claim that she was his wife so that she could get all his papers."

Ships pass in the night. The Guggenheim came ("Edmund Wilson was one of my sponsors, that was one of the two favors he has done me") and she sailed from Vera Cruz for Europe in 1931, that same Vera Cruz that opens *Ship of Fools*. It was that trip that was the basis for her novel of 31 years later.

The brilliant six-page passage that opens the novel, the scene in the town square, with the people and animals in it, contains in briefest form a synopsis of the thematic structure of the novel, she is now willing to say for publication. All the themes of interacting good and evil, all the emotions from lust to hatred to contempt that are to be developed in the next 500 pages, and most particularly that perverted psychology that makes the inferior arrogant—everything to come is there, and what amazes her is that none of the critics, nor anyone else, has ever mentioned it or given any indication of having perceived what the passage was about.

"They all say they don't understand the purpose of that strange scene in the square. You know I get an idea sometimes that people don't know very much about each other, and sometimes that they don't know very much about themselves, because that's the whole point of that thing. I thought at the time it was almost too obvious to use, and they can't see it."

On that trip she kept a diary and out of the diary grew the novel. "They said I didn't know enough to write that book, but I did. I knew the political situation very well. So much of the book is pure reportage. The condesa, do you remember her, she was a Spanish woman aboard. And the 700 or 800 people they drove into steerage? They were driven aboard when we stopped at Cuba because they were laborers and the bottom had dropped out of the sugar market and they were burning the cane in the fields.

"They said I was being sentimental about Mrs. Treadwell. I said good God! She was being sentimental about herself. She was brought up in Murray Hill in New York, you know, and she went to the most exclusive schools and led the most sheltered life, and then she married the wrong man and it ruined her life. She didn't have the slightest idea what to do with it.

"I'm not in the book—I keep telling people I suppose I'm the last of that old and I guess vanishing race, the omniscient but absent author—but my life is in that book. Not all that I know in the world, but an awful lot."

That was much later, though. In Europe she went to Paris, "and I parlayed that into 6½ years by marrying a man in the foreign service, Eugene Pressley. We were married on the 11th of March, and I remember it well because Ford Madox Ford was the best man, and his daughter Julie was a little girl then, and the bridegroom insisted on buying the bridal bouquet but Ford wouldn't have it.

"He made me give my bouquet to Julie and he gave me a bunch of purple and white heather, which he said is the bridal bouquet of Scotland, and is supposed to bring just awfully good fortune. Well, I carried it, and it lasted well for about seven years and then the marriage hit the rocks like a ton of ha ha ha bricks. But still it was a good marriage while it lasted.

"He had a silence that was really almost unnatural and it scared everybody but me, because I didn't ever stop talking. People would say why doesn't he speak, and I would say he doesn't speak because he doesn't want to.

She became friends, as virtually every good writer in Paris did, with Sylvia Beach. "She was a dear love, and the most faithful and devoted friend, and she wanted everybody she loved to love each other. She just adored talented people, and she was witty and shrewd as anything herself, but she only wanted to help other people. She wanted to have a bookshop, and she did have it, Shakespeare & Co. She had a good life, too.

"When she died in 1962 I was in Paris a few days later and I went to see the house. And there was her little cup and saucer on the table, and her little flimsy panties and stockings hanging on a string in the window to dry, and a sort of dusty grayness around in the air. Some places I used to get very strongly the feeling of the presence of the person who had lived there. In Keats's house in Rome I kept looking around. But at Sylvia's I thought, she's really gone, and she's taken her books with her.

"I remember once years before, when I was living in Paris, dropping into her shop on a rainy cold day, evening, getting dark, and I was on my way home, and I passed by Sylvia's little shop and the light was on. She stayed there sometimes all night, because that's where she liked to be. And I thought I would go in and browse around and get something to read.

"And so I was standing there, she had an enormous round table—mine is 6 feet, but I think Sylvia's must have been 8 or 10 feet, it was the biggest round table I've ever seen except the one at Michigan University. And it was all piled up with books and I was standing there looking them over and in bursts the door, like that, and in barges this huge man with a raincoat and a little drippy hat, you know, just pouring water.

"And Sylvia gave a little squeal, like a little bird, and leaped into his arms, and he hugged her, wet as he was, and then let her plop down on the floor and she grabbed his hand and she reached over to grab mine and she said 'I want to introduce the two best short story writers in America.' And he just froze.

Well, she never did get our hands together, because just then the telephone rang in the next room and she went to answer it, saying 'make friends now, I'll be right back,' says she gaily, and I thought isn't it funny. She's known Ernest Hemingway for years, and just loves him, and has read all of his books, and she doesn't know a darn thing about him. Because she has done the one thing in the world that would utterly prevent us ever being friends.

"We stood there just staring at each other with perfect poker faces, not moving, and then all of a sudden he simply turned around and dashed out into the rain. I never saw him again.

"And years later I met Mary Hemingway at a dinner somewhere. She came over to me and said 'I recognize you because I've seen your picture at Sylvia's and other places and tell me something: Why is it that you're the only woman in this room with any sex appeal?' And I said, 'Mary, I didn't have it for your husband.' "

When later in New York she met T. S. Eliot, the meeting was just as brief but the occasion was memorable. "You know I was the first person in America to write a word against him, but he was very charming. It was when his play *The Cocktail Party* was in New York, and the publishers were having a whole, ghastly day for him, beginning with breakfast and running right through to a big party at night. I was invited to the whole thing, but I hadn't been well and could only go at night.

I had to see *The Cocktail Party* on opening night, and I had sat right in back of the Prince of Wales—or you know, the Duke of Windsor and his wife, that—little woman—and at the intermission the Duke turned to the person next to him with his face just sparkling and said, 'Why it *seems* to be some sort of blank verse, doesn't it?' That was worth the evening.

"At the party, though, there was every literary person that could cram into the house, and I just knew the poor martyr was being massacred, don't you know, with everybody dying to meet the celebrity. But I thought well, I didn't come to see Djuna Barnes, or even Marianne Moore, so I'd better find him and I did, he was sitting over in the corner on a little stool with about six people around him.

And when I went up he got up and said, 'Why Miss Porter how kind of you to come. Please sit down.' And I did, but it was no use. In a moment or two they surged in on me, honey they were like ravening wolves, I think they would have torn me in pieces if I'd stayed there.

"After a minute I got out, and the thing I remember about that night was that Allen Tate was there, behaving like he always does, getting drunk and just rolling around. I've met some of the worst behaved people when they're drunk. But I like them. I just stay away from them when they're drunk. Allen was making a perfect show of himself and the woman he was with, who was not his wife at the time, finally got him up off the floor and there stood Marianne Moore with her little glass of fruit juice in her hand, she never takes a drop of anything you know, and she said to me, 'That man is just speckled all over, like a trout, with impropriety.' ha ha ha ha. Isn't that a lovely line?

Marianne is such a funny woman. I love her. A great many people do. She lives like a hermit almost, but she *will* do anything anyone wants her to, and so you see her in the papers more than any poet I ever heard of. She even joined a parade in her three-cornered hat.

"Did you know she has two hats? A three-cornered hat, and a little straw hat that she wears sometimes in the summer. And she's had those same two hats for 40 years. Well, she doesn't wear them very much.

"But you know she has a great many friends and acquaintances but no strong emotional ties, and never has had. How old is Marianne now, 80 or 82? And someone said to me, 'Do you believe that Marianne really has never been in love, and is really a virgin?' And I said 'If there is one virgo intacta in the human race it's Marianne Moore, you can bet on that!' ha ha ha. No man could ever have got near enough to her. She would have stuck him with a hatpin. She wears hatpins around her waist."

The only famous meeting, the one with Dylan Thomas that was put into the play "Dylan" was misrepresented there, according to Miss Porter. "He was most objectionable, trying to get his hands under my dress, and picking me up, until finally I just had to get out. But they sent me tickets to the play and when I saw it I said I wished they had asked me about it first. Because the woman they had playing me was about 15 years too young and about 20 pounds too heavy, and I never was a blonde, you know. My hair was black, until I got the plague in 1918 when it all fell out and came back in again all white.

"But the worst thing was that they had me sitting alone at a bar, which is something I've never done and never would. That made me most annoyed. I suppose even if you didn't know my age you could tell my generation by the fact that that upset me so."

Her generation was almost fading away, but she had yet to begin her largest work, when in the late Thirties she divorced her second husband and married Albert Erskine and went to live with him in Louisiana. "We were married only 10 days after the divorce came through—do you suppose that was all right? I called Eugene my Paris husband and Albert my New Orleans husband, but I don't know why because we lived in Baton Rouge.

"And when we were breaking up four years later I said to him, 'I guess I'm just no good as a wife.' And he said, 'You just have a permanent engagement with a higher power.' Don't you think that was a charming way to put it?"

After that she was married only to the higher power. From 1942 to 1962 she worked on *Ship of Fools* in a little house here and a little apartment there, between money-making trips to colleges and universities—"I've been to over 250." When *Ship of Fools* appeared some of the critics, particularly the American ones, were hard on it. "But several of the really good critics in England, V. S. Pritchett and Sybil Bedford and Cyril Connolly and one or two others, praised it. And I thought, I can do with that.

"But you know people started calling me and saying filthy things over the telephone. They thought the book was dirty, you see. And it got so bad that I had to close up the house here in Washington and go to Paris for a while, and when I got back I had to get an unlisted telephone and a new house."

Which is where she lived until early this year, when she moved to College Park. She has a batch of honorary degrees, the gold medal of the National Institute of Arts and Letters, the Pulitzer Prize, the National Book Award and a clatter of other prizes, the opinion of Edmund Wilson, in print, that she is a fine writer ("that was the

second favor he did me"), her collection of books, papers and
memorabilia securely ensconced at the University of Maryland library
not far away, and her reputation seemingly secure, too.

She works some, and sees people, when she is well enough, and
talks and laughs and talks and laughs. Sometimes she helps young
writers, or helps young people to discover that they aren't writers.
"One of my nicest friends, whom I like so much, I spent seven years
struggling with that girl, and finally I said, 'You're just wasting your
time. You're such a young girl and so pretty, and you've got such a
nice husband and good life, why don't you just enjoy it? Writing is a
dog's life.' And do you know she took it very sensibly, and we're still
good friends. I think I saved her marriage, too."

Writing is a dog's life. But then life, according to Katherine Anne
Porter, is a dog's life. "One time after *Ship of Fools* was published I
went to a Jesuit college and there were a lot of nuns there, and one
of the sisters came over to me and said 'You look like such a nice
woman, how could you have written that dreadful book?' And I said,
'Sister, this is a perfectly dreadful world, don't you know that?' And
she just looked at me and stalked away.

"It is a horrible world. But it's a funny thing. Sometimes I have
found little pockets and little corners and little bits of time when you
couldn't believe that everything could be so nice. I have had very
good luck, and very good friends."

It is late. The afternoon has crept into its shadows. Miss Porter has
finished her drink and is tired, and it is time to go. But there is one
more thing, the most important thing, that she wants us to know: She
has been, it has turned out, like so few, the master of her fate.

"And you know, in the very strangest kind of way, I can't explain
this, but I have come as near as anybody I know in the world to
getting just where I wanted. I wanted to be a good artist, and I
wanted to be known as an honest artist, and they can say anything
they want, but they can't say that I ever compromised on that one
point. It took everything I had. It took a lifetime, and it took an
enormous amount of suffering. But it was worth it. It was what I
wanted."

Don't Scare the Horses, Miss Porter Tells Liberation Women

Josephine Novak and Elise Chisholm/1970

From *The Evening Sun,* Baltimore, 25 March 1970. Reprinted by permission of *The Baltimore Sun.*

Katherine Anne Porter, America's grande dame of letters, was given a reception by her publishers Monday afternoon in the Theodore R. McKeldin Library, University of Maryland, College Park.

The champagne party, was held by Seymour Lawrence and the library to celebrate the publication of *The Collected Stories and Occasional Writings of Katherine Anne Porter,* in the Katherine Anne Porter Room, which houses her books, manuscripts, papers, library furnishings and mementoes.

Miss Porter was wearing her Geoffrey Beene emerald green shirt dress ("my old firehorse outfit"), double strand of pearls with diamond and emerald clasp, diamond and emerald spray pin, and her 22-carat emerald ring set with two rows of diamonds. She carried a bouquet of American Beauty roses and small white flowers given to her by Jerome Weinstein, husband of Cyrilly Abels, her literary agent.

Wan and still weak, after her convalescence from a serious arm injury suffered in a fall in her home several months ago when a kitten stepped under her feet on a staircase, Miss Porter was nevertheless in high spirits on this occasion.

She paused for photographs, flanked by her lawyer, E. Barrett Prettyman, Mr Lawrence, and Howard Rovelstad of the University's library.

Someone asked if she were ready to join the Women's Liberation Movement and she laughed uproariously.

"Certainly not. . . . I don't agree with them. I told them, 'I will not sit down with you and hear you tell me men have abused you.'

Any man who ever did wrong to me got back better than he gave."

"And I don't care about my rights. Rights never did me any good. I want my privileges. (I haven't always gotten those)."

"There is something lacking there. I just can't read any more about them. I don't care what they do just so they don't do it in the streets and scare the horses."

"I felt that way, too, about Betty Friedan's book when it was sent me to read. While I was going through it, I thought, "Oh, Betty, why don't you go and mix a good cocktail for your husband and yourself and forget about this business."

The highlight of the party was a short concert given by the University's Madrigal Singers under the direction of Rose Marie Grentzer.

A chorus of mixed voices sang "Now is the Month of Maying" by Thomas Morley, which was followed by four Elizabethan selections (Miss Porter's favorite music) played on the recorder and harpsichord.

The program concluded with four songs from "Katherine Anne Porter's French Song Book": Manon's Song, Full Moon, Three Sailors, and Marlborough.

After the concert Miss Porter shook hands with each member of the group.

Among the guests at the reception were William J. Smith, poet-in-residence at the Library of Congress, and his wife, Sonje; Harold Spivacke, head of the music division of the Library of Congress and Miss Grentzer's husband; Libby Cator (Miss Porter's neighbor when she lived on 49th street in Washington); and Rhea Johnson of Washington.

Mr Johnson said he met Miss Porter in 1959 when she moved to a house in Georgetown.

"I was living in the basement of that house when she moved in," he explained, "and she didn't know I was there. She was rather non-plussed when she went out into the garden one day and I was sitting there minding my own business."

"Since then, we've both moved to different places but we've remained friends. We brought up a cat together in that house, I still have the cat."

To the author he jokingly said: "Miss Porter, I told this lady we lived together once; that wasn't quite the right way to say it, I know."

Katherine Anne Porter's eyes twinkled: "If all the men I'm supposed to have lived with were crammed into this room, we couldn't turn around."

Following the reception, Miss Porter's publishers gave a dinner for her in the University College Center for Adult Education.

Glimpses of San Antonio
at Turn of the Century
Mildred Whiteaker/1973

From *The San Antonio Express-News*, 21st January 1973, p. 2-A—PART II—Family Section. Reprinted by permission of Mildred Whiteaker and *The San Antonio Express-News*.

Novelist Katherine Anne Porter was born in the Indian Creek community south of Brownwood 13 years before the Wright brothers flew the first aircraft.

"On May 15, 1890, at 3:30 a.m.," she said, the voice firm, ladylike and still Southern.

Last month she was a passenger on the S. S. Statendam's "Voyage Beyond Apollo," a ship of scientists which anchored off Cape Kennedy for the first night moon launch and last scheduled U.S. moon landing in this century.

"The only sad thing in that beautiful sight," she sighed, "was that I wasn't in the capsule."

"Twenty-five years ago I wrote a piece saying I was certain they were going to get to the moon in my lifetime, and I planned to stow away."

Now "going on 83," the author of *Ship of Fools* was aboard the cruise ship to record her impressions of the moonshot and the daily space seminars for *Playboy* magazine!

Katherine Anne Porter could never be called a senior citizen. She's a free spirit. A young writer assigned by *Playboy* to escort her on the nine-day cruise found her "the most stimulating conversationalist" he had ever met.

Sailing on the Statendam with a dozen other fashion writers, I ran into Miss Porter the first day at sea. She, too, was exploring the decks and getting acquainted with the ship.

"San Antonio," she repeated after introduction. "That's where I spent my childhood."

From then on, we chatted frequently. The renowned writer, who

158

now lives in College Park, Md., is a book of vignettes on San Antonio before and after the turn of the century.

"Trying to keep dates and places straight isn't easy," she said. "I've moved around so much. And I never thought anyone would be interested. I must have lived in 45 places."

"But there was always that one steady and unbroken thread in my life. My writing."

Her mother died in 1892 and her grandmother took care of the family (Katherine, her dad, brother and sister).

"My sister and I went to school at Our Lady of the Lake convent in San Antonio, and would go back to the farm in the summer. But for some reason, when I was about 11½ we enrolled in the Thomas School for young ladies out on West End Lake (now Woodlawn Lake)."

"Maybe it was because we lived nearby and we could walk to school. It was a boarding school, but we were day students. We had moved to San Antonio by then."

"We wore mortar board caps at the Thomas School as if we were little doctors of philosophy, and navy pleated skirts and white collars with bands on them just like a sailor."

"I don't remember too much except that we went to all the shows and operas and plays. All the important actors and actresses came to San Antonio. Any theater in town would take us for 25 cents each for the finest events. There weren't any ballet companies at that time, but every opera had a ballet."

"There was even a ladies' musical club which had a concert every Tuesday morning. Everybody was invited—all 35 or 40 of us—and it was beautiful. They had nothing but violins. Violas, cellos, second violins, every kind of fiddle there was, those ladies played. About half of them played and half sang. And, oh, how I loved those Tuesday musicals."

Turning to her young companion, she added, "We would have picnics in the old Alamo, which was a ruin in those days. Of course, it has been restored. I liked it better the other way . . ."

"And I almost forget to tell you," she smiled, "that San Antonio was filled with dirty, muddy streets with three saloons on each side of every block. We were always being marched back and forth across those streets to keep us from walking in front of the saloons."

Katherine Anne was 13 when the family moved to New Orleans. "My grandmother (also named Catherine Anne Porter) died when I was 11, and we sold the farm and all of her land. The whole family got together and broke up the land holdings and divided them, you know. My best memories of San Antonio are up until the time my grandmother died. She was really somebody and I'm glad I knew her. If I hadn't, I don't know what would have become of me."

"Well, I married real early, and the marriage was a disaster, of course. It couldn't have been anything else. I stayed on in New Orleans until I decided to make the break for freedom."

And almost in a whisper. . . . "Oh, that narrow-minded family I stumbled into. . . ."

On a happier note, she mentioned that she began writing at age 6 and taking it seriously at 16 or 17.

Reminded that she sometimes talked like an original "women's liberationist," she said, "I was born free. And I've always stayed free. I have nothing against women's lib, except that lunatic fringe that's making us all look ridiculous. But I don't feel ridiculous about it. I think it is very serious business."

"There's no use, however, in saying you can give women the same treatment as a man because you can't, and it would be murder to try it. I remember back in school, girls of 12 to 16 doing pole vaulting— enough to render every one of us infertile for life."

Although she didn't bring them into the conversation, a biographical sketch in the Brownwood library states that she worked as a newspaper reporter in Dallas and Denver, that her father was a first cousin to O. Henry (William Sidney Porter), and that her mother (Mrs. Alice Jones Harrison Boone Porter) was a descendant of Jonathan Boone, Daniel's younger brother.

She was past 70 when she completed *Ship of Fools,* later made into a motion picture. Some of her earlier works, such as the novelette "Pale Horse, Pale Rider," gained even more critical acclaim. Critics rate Miss Porter as one of this century's major American writers.

A running joke on the cruise was whether we comprised a second *Ship of Fools.* Miss Porter had an answer. "But remember, just as I wrote in the book, I, too, am on this ship. I am one of you."

Is she currently working on a novel?

"Oh, yes. And I have been working on this one for 43 years! It's a story of witchcraft in Salem."

Writing is an art, she said, and it has basic principles. "I'm disgusted with the current trend of using any dirty word that comes to mind. I call it pop pornography."

She lives close to the University of Maryland and spends a lot of time with the students. She also lectures, and would like to come to San Antonio on her lecture circuit.

We said good-bye in the Promenade Lounge an hour or so before the Statendam docked in New York. She was wearing a China blue silk suit which matched her blue eyes. A silver initialed KAP pin was on the shoulder. Her white curls were tied in a white silk scarf.

When I mentioned the suit, this slender, shapely women's lib champion who is every inch the Southern lady grinned impishly.

"It's a Christian Dior, you know."

Katherine Anne Porter:
The Vanity of Excellence
Henry Allen/1974

From *Potomac* magazine, *The Washington Post,* © 31 March
1974. Reprinted by permission of *The Washington Post.*

Four or five months ago, Katherine Anne Porter, at 83, bought her
own coffin from a mail-order carpenter shop in Arizona that does
very nice work. The coffin has long brass hinges, and joints all
sanded smooth. It is six feet of pine box, ready to be painted up
Mexican style, like the kind of coffin she asked her nephew to buy for
her in Mexico, except that he wouldn't do it so she had to order it
herself by mail, from Arizona.

Lord knows what the neighbors thought when the coffin was
delivered. It's not that kind of apartment building. It's the kind of
apartment building that jolts up from a bulldozed plot by a highway
in Prince George's county, with the wind howling through the
balconies. There are lobbies with acres of wall-to-wall carpeting, and
couches marooned like shrubs on an IBM lawn.

It's not what you'd expect of a lioness of letters, author of the
Pulitzer Prize-winning *Ship of Fools* and three books of short stories,
among the most widely praised in American literature. What you'd
expect would be something nobly cozy, with lots of cats and fire-
places, but anybody who expects anything from Katherine Anne
Porter is in for a lot of surprises.

"Can you keep a secret?" she asks, in the briefest of indecisions.
She is not a woman who hesitates very long in conversation,
although it took her 20 years to write her sole novel—and sole big
moneymaker—*Ship of Fools.*

"Gentleman's agreement? You won't say a word? Well, you can
hang your coat in there, then." In there is the hall closet, and leaning
against a wall like a bridge table in anybody else's hall closet, is the
coffin, casually and benevolently provident, like the packing crates
that Army families store in their closets, waiting for their next move.

Having startled the visitor into splutters of curiosity, she has to cool him off, which she does, promising to explain about the coffin in just a few minutes, after a few other things get said, and after she settles into one of eight or nine chairs in the spare, pastel luxury of her living room, where the wind slams against the big plate glass windows, in back of all the potted plants.

Miss Porter is tiny, powerful and charming. She wears an aqua hostess gown, with half a dozen buttons open at the throat, where a small emerald links two strands of pearls. A big emerald floats on her left hand. Her eyes swim behind thick glasses, and they are fierce and violet. Her hair is the pure white it turned on the day she came close enough to dying to see heaven, she says, during the great influenza epidemic of 1918—"the plague," as she likes to call it, in a tone that suggests she would not like to have survived 83 years, three marriages and divorces, a Pulitzer Prize, lectures or writing-in-residence at 135 colleges, the deprivations of reality suffered in a Southern and Victorian girlhood, the deprivations of luxuries suffered in a Bohemian womanhood, untold loves and despairs, two administerings of the last rites during two of the more severe of her many and varied illnesses, a revolution in Mexico, the critics and literati who had only reverence for her work until *Ship of Fools,* when some of them turned on her with an iconoclastic delight . . . she would not want to have survived all this without a plague thrown in there, too.

"I told my nephew I've seen everything. The things I see happening now I saw happening 60 years ago. You can't surprise me."

She likes to do the surprising herself, coffin-style as she reminisces and rambles in her terrific, lilty rush of words. Her accent rings more Southern than Western, though she grew up just outside San Antonio. She may have acquired it from her fiercely unreconstructed Southern-belle grandmother whose defense of the Ante-bellum prides in the face of conspicuous reality provided a life model. In true Southern style, Miss Porter has managed to carry on unreconciled to what she has called "grotesque dislocations in a whole society when the whole world was heaving in the sickness of millenial change."

Anyhow, she rushes on to explain just how she learned what she knows, and survived it all.

"I was brought up in such ignorance, you see. Although that had more to do with the time, which was the Victorian age, than the fact

that it was the South. Such ignorance. All the boys were in military
schools and all the girls were in the convent, and that's all you need
to say about it. I was brought up in this quite curious way of knowing
exactly who you were and what you were."

"I cannot find any fault with those people, though. They had the
best in literature and music. When I was little, I would sit on the arm
of my father's chair at the theater. I saw "Mary, Queen of Scots" and I
was so disappointed to learn that it wasn't really the queen up there
on the stage, being beheaded. All we had to read in the convent
school was St. Thomas Aquinas, except that I'd hide a copy of St.
Augustine in my room for secret reading . . . of course, anyone could
walk right into the San Antonio public library and take out Voltaire,
and I did. But I knew nothing, so when I tried to break away, it was
terribly difficult. I lived like an outcast. I nearly starved to death for
years and years, I didn't know how to boil an egg properly. I
addressed envelopes by hand for $2.50 a day, you see, I did that. I
sold neckwear for the wonderful salary of $15 a week. But you see, if
all this had not happened to me, I wouldn't have known anything
about the world."

She knots and folds a handkerchief with her left hand. She fondles
her pearls with her right. She watches the note-taking for reactions,
responds to the smallest murmur, even if by ignoring it. She misses
nothing. It is clear that words about the coffin will have to wait until
she is sure of persuading her audience of the perils and prides of her
youth. She regales. She cajoles.

Miss Porter was born in 1890 in Indian Creek, Texas. She was the
third of five children whose mother died in 1892. A year later, her
father moved the family back to Kyle, Texas, to be raised by Miss
Porter's grandmother, in a house full of books, on land worked by the
family's ex-slaves and in defiant gentility:

"My elders all remained nobly unreconstructed to their last moments, and my feet rest firmly on this rock of their strength to this
day," she has written. An elderly resident of Indian Creek, a Miss
McAden, told a researcher that "at the age of four she was still a big
baby. I wouldn't say she was spoiled, but when she wanted something she wouldn't give an inch until she got it."

After the grandmother died in 1901, the father and children moved
from place to place, with one family friend reporting that Miss Porter

had a great interest in the stage. "She got high marks in history, literature and composition, and "D" in everything else except deportment, in which she often did worse," according to one biographer.

At 16 she ran away from her convent school to get married to "a rich man who shut me up," she recalls now. She left him three years later. A year after that she left Texas. "I didn't want to be regarded as a freak. That was how they regarded a woman who tried to write. I had to make a revolt, a rebellion . . . so you see, I am the great-grandmother of these bombers, and students beating each other up with bicycle chains."

So she embarked on the vibrantly motley career that genteel rebels fall into, if they're lucky.

She reported for a Chicago newspaper, acted as an extra in the movies, came down with tuberculosis or perhaps bronchitis, wrote drama criticism and gossip in 1917 for *The Critic* in Fort Worth, moved to the *Rocky Mountain News* in Denver in 1918, nearly died of the influenza plague she described in "Pale Horse, Pale Rider," moved to New York where she lived in Greenwich Village and supported herself by ghost writing until she left for Mexico to build a revolutionary tomorrow with organizers of the labor movement, and on and on through constant travel; book reviewing; arranging a Mexican folk art exhibition; winning a Guggenheim award; publishing *Flowering Judas* in a limited edition in 1930; quarreling with poet Hart Crane; embarking for Germany in 1931, a sea voyage that would provide the setting for *Ship of Fools;* filling trunks with unfinished short stories; meeting Hitler, Goebbels and Goering and thinking them "detestable and dangerous;" marrying Eugene Pressly, a member of the American Foreign Service; divorcing, marrying Albert Erskine, Jr. of the Louisiana State University staff; divorcing again.

"It is a disaster to have a man fall in love with me," she has said: "They aren't content to take what I can give; they want everything from me." Finally she wrote movie scripts in Hollywood, where she was "like a fox with its leg in a trap," then started her long circuit-rider trek from campus to campus; she published *Pale Horse, Pale Rider* (1939); *The Leaning Tower* (1944); and made her enormous critical reputation—and very little money.

So sitting in the cool, rich isolation of her living room, all paid for by the bonanza of *Ship of Fools*—the old rolltop desk, the gilt ormolu mirror with two gilt cherubs flying up the wall toward it, a spinet, an oriental rug—in the middle of this luxury she frowns at the floor, remembers and says: "I nearly ruined my health with hardships, but if that was what it took, that's what it took." And half an hour later she'll tell you: "I can't tell you how good it was. We were so happy. there was never enough to eat, never a decent place to live, but there was a sort of ferocious pleasure, a sense of fighting a good war, it was *joyful,* I tell you."

If she could not live by writing, however, she could live by being a writer, being savvy and martyred at the cocktail parties of college English departments, marketing both her privacy and her fame, playing the writer in the days when the myth of the writer won its greatest devotion, and publishers enshrined authors on dustjackets as veterans of everything from gun-running off Mauritania to editing a literary gazette in Paris—that same huge range of life Miss Porter lived.

All of it would be printed under the sort of photograph Miss Porter has on her livingroom wall. It shows her seated at her spinet, a number of years ago, glancing up at the camera with the flat, tough, vulnerable look that photographers have found on the faces of a lot of 20th-century artists, Jean Genet or Jackson Pollock, for instance; the look of fatigue which implies the terrible burden of integrity in an ersatz world.

Like her grandmother, Miss Porter has been in this world, but not of it, as the Sufis say. She has wrapped herself in what she calls her "vanity of excellence." If the South she fled had watched its impossible feudal niceties dwindle—and with someone, the Yankees, to blame—Miss Porter has watched propaganda and political messianism and the economics of the lowest common denominator bloat and corrupt the civilization of the whole West. And if anyone is not to blame, it may be she. She has stayed aloof.

'My life is so strange," she says. "It's something I have in common with Madame DuBarry, who said on the way to her execution, 'My life is incredible. I don't believe a word of it.' But things just happen to me, I don't turn a hand. One time, in Berlin, I was probably the only American woman around, so I got invited to dinner by the correspondent for the Chicago Tribune, and the guests were Hitler,

Goering and Goebbels. They all arrived late, about halfway through dinner, each with his beautiful blond Aryan bodyguard with a totally blank face, and each of them crippled. Goering always walked with a cane, and Goebbels had a club foot, and Hitler had sprained his foot I believe. I thought he was the most awful, insignificant, underbred, unhealthy-looking creature I had ever seen."

"I simply could not believe he would do the things he said he would do. No one took him seriously, the same way nobody listens to these people now, the black revolutionaries and all of them. We are in one hell of a world, my dear. I met all those half-wits who came back from Russia in the '20s, poor old Lincoln Steffens saying, 'I have seen the future and it works.' And that parading John Reed . . . God, they were a sickening lot. I used to listen to all their yammer over bad beer in Greenwich Village. Of course I had seen all that in Mexico, the revolutionaries, good ones and bad ones. Zapata and Villa, they tore Mexico apart. The poor stayed poor. They redistributed the land and it's all back in the hands of the rich landowners. We don't learn anything. I have seen it all. Everything is promised and nothing is fulfilled."

"I used to go to see Emma Goldman, the anarchist, in Paris, and sit with her, an awfully sweet old woman, in the cafe, in her carpet slippers. I said one day, 'You've had such a hard life. You'd have been happier married with children, living under a good government.' And she said, 'There's never been a good government,' and she's right, you see. But the good things survive somehow, and last."

So Miss Porter can install her manuscripts and furniture and artifacts of gentility and sensibility inside the bureaucratic grossness of a Westchester Park apartment, because she's been doing it all her life, staying pristine in a sullied world.

"Every piece of furniture is fine," she says with the kind of finality the world demands of its lionesses. "The lovely, the beautiful, the grand are so rare, and I treasure them. And I tell you this: evil puts up a terrible fight. And it always wins in the end."

"I do not understand the world, but I watch its progress. I am not reconciled. I will not forgive it."

Her books of short stories, *Flowering Judas, Pale Horse, Pale Rider, The Leaning Tower,* are set in an atmosphere of airless inevitability—chronicles of the autobiographical Miranda, who is constantly and fiercely negotiating for her total, solitary integrity in a world of cloying families and the hearty menace of World War I patriots; or the story of an American artist being tugged into the fester of European fatigue; or "Noon Wine," the saga of a Texas farmer doomed to suicide: "He lay down flat on the earth on his side, drew the barrel under his chin and fumbled for the trigger with his great toe. That way he would work it." The ironies of that sort of desolate realism lit a lot of American short stories, like a truck flare, between the world wars, the stories of Hemingway or Ring Lardner, for instance, or the brutal "Big Blonde" by Dorothy Parker.

Howard Moss said in the *New Yorker* in 1962: "We are impressed not by what Miss Porter says but by what she knows." But there's abundant grace, a lot of humor, and omnivorous reportage and seamless skill. She has authority, describing the morbid honor of a duel-scared Heidelberg student or the comparative tobacco chewing habits of two men in South Texas. Her ease is seductive and artistic. The "millenial sickness" is present, not in raging but in an atmosphere of implication or imminence, like a day of heat lightning.

Despite the lights going out all over Europe and so on, Miss Porter has made herself famous with scores and scores of friends for her parties, letters, conversation and cooking.

"She's brilliant, all charm and loyalty," says Peter Taylor, the short story writer and writer in residence at the University of Virginia. He has known her for 25 years, including the year she succeeded Faulkner as the university's writer in residence. "She gives the best parties, her Twelfth-Night parties in particular. And she writes the best letters of anybody."

One friend told Paul Crume, author of a critical article in the *Southwest Review* in 1940, that "every now and then she stops being what she is and becomes something else. She leaves her old life . . . dry and forgotten and dead, something she has put forever behind her."

This might explain the store of contradictions in her own accounts of her life, telling one person she worked on the *Dallas News,* and another that she didn't; claiming in one interview that she never, never quarreled or competed as a little girl, then detailing exactly the opposite in an essay, "Portrait: Old South." Or, she publishes a letter

to her from Donald Sutherland, and a response which assures
Sutherland that neither his nor any of her correspondence will ever
be published. The years and names and places swap around in the
various accounts of her life "with all the elements of mystery and
shadow which Miss Porter uses to surround her non-fictional presentation of the past," one biographer has said.

But these are the peccadilloes of an artist, of someone who has
said: "No man can be explained by his personal history, least of all a
poet." These are also, perhaps, the fibs of a Southern belle, born and
bred to be forgiven things like that, and to be capable too of Miss
Porter's extraordinary charm.

"Can you imagine that I held my own and survived with people
like Gertrude Stein and James Joyce and Hemingway and that
crowd?" she asks sweetly, with a little cough that punctuates things
now and then. One can imagine she held her own very well,
especially after reading her description of Miss Stein, in her celebrated Paris salon, as "extremely like a handsome old Jewish
patriarch who had backslid and shaved off his beard." Stein's nature,
Miss Porter said, was sluggish; "like something eating its way through
a leaf."

She met Hemingway once, she says, in Shakespeare and Co., the
Paris bookstore owned by Sylvia Beach. Miss Beach grasped the
hand of each—Hemingway imposing and dramatic in rainy
trenchcoat—and said: "I want the two best modern American writers
to know each other." The phone rang, Miss Beach ducked out for a
moment. "Hemingway and I stood and gazed unwinkingly at each
other with poker faces for all of ten seconds, in silence. Hemingway
then turned in one wide swing and hurled himself into the rainy
darkness as he had hurled himself out of it, and that was all. I am
sorry if you are disappointed. All personal lack of sympathy and
attraction aside, and they were real in us both, it must have been
galling to this most famous young man to have his name pronounced
in the same breath as a writer with someone he had never heard of,
and a woman at that. I nearly felt sorry for him," Miss Porter recalls in
"A Little Incident in the Rue de l'Odéon." She said Miss Beach
"continued to think this very strange; I didn't and I don't."

Like Hemingway, she dedicated her life to writing, and to being a writer. But she has survived it. "This is all a drastic change in my life," she says. "When I was starting out, I never said goodbye to anyone. Nobody missed me. It was wonderful.

"Now I get 5-600 requests a year to write an analysis for somebody's term paper, write letters . . . my letters are worth something now, you see. They all make me feel like I've got things in my veins." Her hands flutter at her throat. "Bloodsuckers. I wouldn't have dared send a letter to Yeats or Hardy or James. I wouldn't have had the impudence."

So she is happiest, she says, at night, alone, patrolling the long white hallways and shiny parquet floors of her apartment—two apartments, actually, connected across the hall.

"At night, the place is quiet, quiet, quiet. I ramble around, making notes. I read. I am absolutely happy alone, working. If I weren't working I might be one of those pests who call people and ask them to come see me. I suppose life would be perfect if there were just someone to leave the mail on the table, you see, and not tell me."

It's a solitude reminiscent of the "beatific" vision she glimpsed when she came close enough to death to have her hair turn white that day in 1918. The autobiographical and dying Miranda in "Pale Horse, Pale Rider" comes to a place where "there remained of her only a minute fiercely burning particle of being that knew itself alone, that relied upon nothing beyond itself for its strength; not susceptible to any appeal or inducement, being itself composed entirely of one single motive, the stubborn will to live."

That stubborn will drags Miranda back to the bleak, breathy pawings of the world, on Armistice day, to the sound of "ragged, tuneless old women, sitting up waiting for their evening bowl of cocoa singing 'Sweet Land of Liberty.' "

So, 15 floors above the crawl of rush-hour traffic on Kenilworth Avenue, in the slow burn of a February sunset, the sunlight snagging in the lenses of her thick glasses, she lifts a hand for shade, flashing the large, cool emerald. "I have nothing to complain of in my life. It was hell on earth, earlier, but I am glad I lived it."

"Now I have this other thing, and I hope I die before it overtakes me." Gravely, she points to her head. "Arteriosclerosis," she says. "Of course they finally discovered that I'd had emphysema too, for years.

And my eyesight is going and I fell and broke a hip a few years ago. I am a cripple. I am incurable."

If so, she is the fastest moving cripple in Prince George's County, and the survivor of an untold array of other illnesses throughout her life, mystifying her friends with a very Porterish contradiction of weak health and strong constitution. Glenway Wescott, the critic, has told of a doctor who said Miss Porter's health was a matter of allergies. He explained: "You're allergic to the air you breathe."

The only truly mournful augury of the afternoon has been the coffin in the closet, which she finally gets around to discussing, with more than her usual vigor. "I bought it by mail from Arizona, for $160, which is far less than they would try to make you pay in these funeral homes. I deeply resent this ghastly show and expense. When I die, I have told my executors that I will have the coffin and a linen sheet ready for them. I brought the linen back from Liége. I forbid the undertaker to touch me. Simply take me to the crematory, then scatter my ashes anywhere at all."

In that blithe meander which is apt to lead her conversation anywhere at all she states that when she really wants to go, she'll do it herself, shoot herself, she's a very good shot, and not that anyone should follow her example . . . But later, the talk turns back to more sweeping things, God and corruption, and she murmurs darkly that ultimately she knows "nothing, nothing, nothing."

She recalls her friend Ford Madox Ford "who had a heart condition and took these digitalis tablets I take. And one day in his hotel room, in the south of France, he had an attack. His wife came running in and put the tablet under his tongue—you put it under your tongue—but she didn't get there in time, you see, and all she could do was hold him while he died. Thank God . . . thank God he did not die alone."

She shakes her head. "I would not like to die by myself. At nights, alone, when I feel the attacks come on, I take that little thing and put it under my tongue and I go on reading." Then her eyebrows lift back toward their usual blithe station. "I just go on reading and taking my notes, you see."

"I have had to spend so much of my time in bed the last six months that I have gotten no writing done. My Cotton Mather biography is in good enough shape now that somebody else could finish it. Now, I am working on a medieval mystery story, but that's absolutely all I will say about it."

We ramble on through Miss Porter's apartment in a guest tour, finally, admiring the Franklin clock, all the potted plants—Chinese jade, orchids, ferns, pines—and a poster of a kitten apparently attempting a chin-up over a caption reading "Hang in There Baby."

At the front door, in Southern style, she makes one feel splendidly guilty for leaving so soon, and she inquires: "You won't talk about my coffin?"

She hesitates again, just a blink or two before saying: "Oh, go ahead then. Let's break the news."

She brushes past, into the closet, to say yes, it is well made, and to swing it open and point to the white cloth folded at the foot. "And that's the Belgian linen I told you about, that I bought in Liége." There is a tangy morbidity about the whole thing, an electricity she generates with fine ease. With dancing school grace she executes a little turn, and steps back into the coffin, two white mesh slippers perched on the linen.

"You see, it's a bit big for me," she says, floating a measuring hand above her head. "Would you like to take my picture in it?"

She laughs a very big laugh.

"No," she says. "That would be too much."

Katherine Anne Porter Reigns for Students

Carl Schoettler/1974

From *The Evening Sun*, Baltimore, 15 April 1974. Reprinted by permission of *The Baltimore Sun*.

Katherine Anne Porter is conjuring up magical images like a high priestess of some private cult to which very few are admitted.

Her voice is high and firm as she speaks unembarrassed of the art of her writing, but also oddly metallic as if created by a toymaker to a Byzantine emperor.

Her hands move through incantations while she speaks to the young women from the College of Notre Dame who have come to her home as if for an audience at the court of an exiled queen. The famous emerald on her left hand gleams like the fulfillment of long-deferred desire.

Miss Porter is recalling the distress caused by the screenwriter who transformed her novel, *Ship of Fools,* into a movie script.

She had gone to Rome to recuperate from the publication of the novel, which was an instant bestseller in 1962, but which had taken her roughly twenty years on and off to write. The screenwriter asked to come to call and hung around three weeks.

"I saw that man every day either for luncheon, cocktails or dinner," she says with a great show of indignation.

"And he was the dullest man I've ever met in my life."

Miss Porter is a small woman sitting very tall in her chair as Sister Maura said she would.

Sister Maura Elchner and Sister Kathleen Feeley, president of Notre Dame, teach the course in women writers that has brought the students to Miss Porter's apartment.

"He wore black glasses. I never saw his eyes. He asked me silly questions like 'Who did Mrs. Treadwell sit with at the dinner table?'

"It's in the book," Miss Porter says, snipping off the sentence like a loose thread in a needlework pattern. "She sat alone."

Then she remembered one day they sat in a café as the sun died over the Via Veneto.

"And a streak of sunlight hit the back of his glasses and I could see his eyes like licorice behind his glasses like that man Faulkner describes . . ."

"Popeye?" someone recalling *Sanctuary* suggests.

She agrees. And after that when asked a question about her novel she said "Look it up."

The movie people gave her $400,000 for the rights to her novel, which was pleasant even if the screenwriter's eyes weren't.

"As long as I was going to be disgraced," she says. "I was glad I wasn't going to have to sleep under bridges, as I thought I would have to when I got too old to totter around (lecture) platforms. I never made a living from my writing."

Miss Porter is 83 now and far from tottering. In some ways she seems as youthful as the college seniors sitting at her feet, and perhaps, even now, less set in her ways.

She is dressed all in white, openwork shoes, slacks, ribbed sweater, all white. The window behind her lights her white hair with a regal corona that one suspects she is not unaware of.

"I've got to the point in my life," she says, "when I cannot write except in my own way."

She was given an advance for a book of letters and she sent it back when the publisher wanted something more like a memoir.

"I haven't got a contract and I haven't got a debt. It's exactly like when you start out. You have got absolute independence."

She has always jealously guarded her independence and her privacy.

Only one of her stories was ever rejected by a publisher (she doesn't say which one), and she resisted any effort to change them: "I'd say it's finished."

"I wasn't so very good at punctuation," she confesses. "I'm not so very good yet. But I wouldn't even let them change that."

Sister Kathleen and Sister Maura have brought Miss Porter the honorary doctor of humane letters degree the college conferred on her last spring.

Sister Maura sits at her side to read the citation and Miss Porter claps the nun's hand in her own.

"It was written with great love," says Sister Maura, who is a poet and who wrote the citation.

"Please don't make me cry," Miss Porter says. "Please."

"Titles like 'Flowering Judas,' "Pale Horse, Pale Rider,' 'Noon Wine' and *Ship of Fools*, linger in the mind like bell sounds in quiet sunlight," Sister Maura reads.

"Her fiction—exploring man's enduring themes—links her with the great company of classic story tellers."

Miss Porter listens with great concentration, her eyes downcast.

"She believes in the young. Because she is young. Because she is young of heart, she invites us all to timelessness in God. She is our flowering branch, our spring renewal."

Miss Porter does not cry. She is quite pleased: "I feel I ought to make a little bow."

"I've been talking to your people for 40 years," she says. "There is a new generation every four years in college."

"You are new as can be," she tells the students before her, in a voice as intense as the stories she is famous for.

"Each one of you is an individual unlike anyone else in the world."

Graduation from college is only the beginning of education, she says. Learning continues throughout life.

"You learn something the day you die," she says, with the flash of brave truth that illuminates her stories. "You learn how to die."

"It's all before you," Miss Porter says. "I could almost envy you. But I couldn't do it again. Once around is enough."

And she remembers her own early education in an Ursuline convent in New Orleans where the walls were 8 feet high and you couldn't stand within 6 feet of an open window when dressing.

"About eight or ten of us wanted to stay there and be nuns. They had to throw us out."

Miss Porter says she was glad for the strict education: "I was naturally wild, naturally obstinate."

And later on she serves a punch of tea and ginger ale and whatever other juice is available with cookies and recalls that once—40 years ago, in Mexico—she smoked a marijuana cigarette.

People's heads seemed all transparent and the workings of their brains like clockwork and she thought it unpleasant and she wrapped a kerchief around her own head in case anyone should think her brain unpleasant.

And she thought it might be a good time to start flying but was saved from plunging over a 60-foot balcony by two friends. And she hasn't smoked any since.

"So I don't know anything about it except it's not something to make a habit of."

"Right," Sister Kathleen says, by way of punctuation.

"There's nothing to it except you see inside of heads like the works of clocks. And you don't have to see that because I've described it to you."

"Right," Sister Kathleen says.

And everyone is shown around Miss Porter's apartment and admires the prints and books and the plants that crowd each window and the table at which she works within her "office."

Then it is time to go and Miss Porter is left standing at the end of a long hall, dressed all in white, quiet and alone, with one arm folded behind her, the other resting at her side.

Almost Since Chaucer
with Miss Porter
Mary Anne Dolan/1975

From *The Washington Star,* © 11 May 1975. Reprinted by
permission of *The Washington Post.*

Katherine Anne Porter, born May 15, 1890, has, through
her novel *Ship of Fools* and her volumes of short stories
and essays, become one of the country's most treasured
writers. She spends her days now in the plant-filled seclu-
sion of a four-bedroom high rise apartment in College
Park, finishing up her work on the life of Cotton Mather
and, currently, writing an article for *Esquire* magazine.

Question: As a writer who has always cared for the precise usage of
words, what's your opinion of the state of language in America today?
   Miss Porter: There are so many things I abhor in what they're
doing to the language now. I say to myself, "Well, be sufferable, it has
changed a good deal since Chaucer." I think it's changed even a little
more since Shakespeare and a good deal since Dr. Johnson. They all
spoke language very purely and remarkably. Of course, the changes
come in gradually, but you have to be very careful about what you
allow. Now they have brought in so much peculiar abstraction.
   Q: Who do you think is responsible?
   A: The politicians, of course. They are taking words that have no
meaning whatsoever and using them, making whole speeches out of
them. I really don't know what they are talking about most of the
time. The thing that makes me so angry with them is that it is
indecent. It's like the criminal argot. It's meant to deceive. It's meant
so that you can talk in the presence of people and say anything and
they can't understand you. This is what the politicians have been
doing now for several generations in an effort to keep everything
secret. That is really decay.

177

Q: Did you feel it particularly during the unfolding of the Watergate story?

A: Yes. But you know it really started a long time ago. The whole thing began, I think, around World War I. You must remember that I'm of very great age. I've been here a long time and I was observant from the beginning. We have never been the peace-loving country or the freedom-loving country that we have been taught to believe we were. I have seen so many wars and they increased in horror and terror and wickedness, cruelty and falseness as they came. Everything that the government takes on, it either turns rotten or destroys. We've had it that way now roughly since President McKinley.

Q: You've known Zapata in Mexico, worked for years with revolutionary labor organizations. You've dined with Hitler. Back in 1927, you were out on the streets in Boston demanding a stay of execution for Sacco and Vanzetti. Why then, in your writing, have you remained so detached?

A: I have stayed detached in a way, yes, because I had stories that I wanted to tell that were just about plain human beings. I thought somehow if you presented the story of the poor people with the little idiot boy—do you remember that, the story called "He"—well, it seems to me that I make pretty plain what my attitude is. When I was in Berlin, I did have experiences and I wrote to places like the *Nation* and *New Republic* and I tried to tell them what was happening. You see, I knew instantly, the minute I put my face in the place and saw Hitler going along in that great six-wheel wagon of his down the street, standing in the middle while people went right up to him throwing rose petals and violets and confetti and screaming at him with hysterical joy. I stood there and I knew—I went through five revolutions in Mexico—what was happening. But I couldn't get any editors in this country to take anything from me. I was not a newspaper reporter. I was not a woman known for her political views. Even if I knew what I was saying and even if I had proof, it was hard to make anyone listen.

Q: Do you think that kind of experience was a product of your being female?

A: Oh, I suppose everything in my life had to do with being female. But, you know, I never thought about it. I was a little person to begin with and I was young at that time and nobody had ever heard of me and I never liked publicity. I always took it for granted that if a person had a certain point of view and was a certain kind of person, you'd be accepted. But it's not true. I just had to claw my way through things like that. Even in Berlin, when I met all those people . . . The one I talked to most was Goering. It was at this little party and we just sat by the fire and discussed Germany and he explained to me what they were going to do to the Jews and I said, "Well, you know, I wonder how you dare to do it because it's never done any good and it doesn't suppress them. It does do great damage to the country. Look what happened to Spain. Nobody has ever prospered harassing the Jews. They are rooted and they are going to stay and I don't see what you have against them." He said the time had come to clear out the degenerate forces in the country. "We've got to restore that good clean German blood," he said. I argued with him a little bit that nobody had pure blood at this time. I could say with confidence that I was a mixture of British, Scotch, Irish and Welsh. We're all the whole white race. Well, no one ever listens to me except in conversation. It makes me so furious. I was in a place—in Germany—and I knew what was going on and I couldn't get anybody to let me tell it. I just stopped trying.

Q: What is the process of your writing like? Do you polish and repolish your words? Is that why it took you 20 years to write *Ship of Fools?*

A: I write straight off and then I correct with a pen. Even that novel was not rewritten. People get the idea I sat there mildewing over a desk writing *Ship of Fools* for 20 years. They don't seem to realize that at that time I brought out three other books and I spent most of my life traipsing around the country speaking. And I lived year in and year out in a dozen different universities carrying as many as three classes. I studied music, lived in Europe, was married three times. I went to the Cordon Bleu. I never lived anywhere near or with anybody who had the faintest idea that I was meant to write. And I never met anybody in the world who didn't want the use of me.

Q: So you were actually a part-time writer.

A: I could only write when I could grab a minute. Then sometimes, I could disappear and leave no address. My friends would get so furious at me and I'd say, "I'm just doing like the American Indian woman, when her tribe was on the trail and she had to have a baby.

She just stopped and went in the thicket and stayed there by herself until she had the baby and then she caught up a little later carrying the child." I said, "I always come back with a baby, don't I?"

Q: Have you had problems over the years with editors trying to change your words?

A: They can't change my work. They have got to send it back. You know, I write when I can. And the point is that I have waves when I feel the time is ready. Stories roost around in my mind for years and become and become and I live with them without doing anything at all about it. Then one day, and I cannot in the least explain why it is that day, I realize it's ready to be written. I sit down and smack it off in just the time it takes to get it on paper. That happened with "Flowering Judas." I was stopping with some dear friends in Brooklyn. They loved things like playing bridge. I like poker, a good game of poker. Anything else in the way of cards I consider a waste of time. We had a nice pleasant supper but I'd been thinking about this story and I went and sat down at the typewriter and began to work. This friend said, "Please come and take a hand, won't you?' And I said, 'I have something to do now. I have to work.' I got up and shut the door and between 7 o'clock and 1 o'clock, I wrote that story. A little bit before 1, I was up to my ankles in snow out at the corner putting it into the postbox.

Q: Is there nobody who has come along in the public spotlight during the last 10 or 20 years who has been a good force on the language?

A: I know a great many people who speak beautifully and properly. I say 'properly,' of course that now is a word that is a little bit out of date. But I was thinking that some of my best friends, some of the best writers in this country, speak well.

Q: Who are they?

A: Allen Tate. Robert Penn Warren. There's a young woman, Eleanor Clark, who is simply marvelous. Hers is imaginative language. She can pick up the snappy things they are saying now and it becomes perfectly right and good. She never takes up anything that is, as we used to say in the South, 'tacky.' Almost everybody I know as writers has beautiful language except I think almost nobody reads them. In the high schools, did you know that they've thrown me out? Guess what they took, "The Jilting of Granny Weatherall." And do you know why they did it? Because she takes the name of God in vain. She's an old woman dying. She was an old-fashioned lady who used that kind of strong but perfectly solid language. I know because I had a grandmother and I was surrounded by old ladies and gentlemen who talked like that. And she says, "God, give a sign." And they said that was blasphemy. Can you imagine? That story has been in the textbooks for 25 years. There were 11 authors banned in one list I saw and of all of them I would say two of them were second rate and shouldn't have been there in the first place. I just don't know what they are going to replace it with. As for me, I feel amused in a way because that particular story has brought more letters from students and teachers. Hundreds of them in the last 25 years.

Q: Is that kind of reaction due to the influence of bad fiction, do you think?

A: Of course, and the stuff they hear on TV and the radio. The horrible viciousness of the new kind of fiction that you read. It's obscenity and indecency, dirty filthy stuff. Who'd want that in a school?

Q: Have you read any of the new feminist fiction? Erica Jong, for instance?

A: Yes and I think it's perfectly disgusting. The point of the matter is those awful creatures like her have been presumptuous enough to say they represent woman. They represent the lowest kind of woman there is. And the strange thing is that instead of making themselves equal with men, they have descended to the level of the vilest men we have. I know so many men that just simply aren't like that. Most of those women shouldn't be let in the back door of a decent house. I resent it immensely. Sex to me has always been one of the dullest things to read about in the world. I've always said there is only one sexual experience I am interested in and that is my own. But my experience is truly and forever and absolutely private.

Q: Did books and reading encourage you?

A: Oh, goodness, I lived on books. By the time I was 16 years old, I had read what Allen Tate himself said real intellectuals didn't read their whole life long: Homer, Dante, Chaucer and Shakespeare and the 18th century people, that sort of thing. I was a Catholic and I loved the saints. Joan of Arc, I knew her history by heart by the time I was 10 years old. I remember I read *Wuthering Heights* four or five

times over before I was 20 years old because I loved it so much. I
was mad about it.

Q: Is it a sign that we are not reading enough that our language is
so poor?

A: I think that TV and radio have been the twin curse because it
does not require anyone to think. There are good things about two or
three times a year.

Q: Do you watch television yourself?

A: Oh God no! Excuse me, I'll be thrown out of the school if they
hear me say that.

Q: I ask you that because I wonder if you think intellectuals in
America have ignored the role they could play on the television by
comparison with, say, the British. Where are the American intellectuals while Alistair Cooke and Kenneth Clarke are on the tube
interpreting history for the public?

A: The point is that I have always wanted to do that and they
won't have me. I was on three or four programs years ago but they
only lasted a few weeks or a few months. Like "Invitation to
Learning," which was a pretty bumptious title for people like me and
Mark Van Doren and Allen Tate. But we did one time discuss *Alice in
Wonderland* with Bertrand Russell. Later, they just closed up the
show.

Q: Then it's the fault of the commercial television networks that we
don't see more things like that?

A: Yes, it's that and the fault of the people just not listening. We
were talking pretty good sense. Another time, for several years, I was
on a really good program called "Camera Three." Then I wasn't
invited anymore. Also, I've been talking to audiences since my first
speech in Paris in 1934. I never could make a penny on writing. My
publishers thought I was something that would never really be
popular and they were right. I never was, but I had to make a living. I
had to do something. And I talked. I was a Fulbright speaker. I was
all over Europe. I talked freely, said exactly what I thought. But I was
never quoted in a newspaper. When they came to interview me, they
wanted to know something trivial or frivolous, wanted to make a
Southern belle of me.

Q: Then you would argue against the point of view that American
intellectuals prefer to remain isolated?

A: That's right. I don't think they do. People just won't listen to what they say. The only chance we have is speaking on what we mean, what we believe in. But nobody listens. Robert Penn Warren is an extraordinarily fine speaker. They give him prizes and buy his books and make horrible movies of them. But they don't really pay attention to him.

Q: Why were you never part of the *New Yorker* crowd?

A: I received the first copies of the *New Yorker* ever put out and I just thought it looked like some kind of country boys bowled over by New York. That silly-looking man on the cover. I thought, "That is the most naive thing." But that was 50 years ago. Later, I received letters from them asking me to write them a story. But I heard that they practically rewrote everything there in the office, that no story ever pleased them. That settled it for me. I have always told my students the first thing they have to do is to fight that battle with the editors. They'll destroy your work and you can't let them do it. My work is the only thing in the world that I have that is absolutely my own and nobody can touch it.

Q: But didn't you once submit a piece to the *New Yorker?*

A: Well, Harold Ross and that lovely Mrs. White took me to the Algonquin and asked me why I didn't have anything for them. Then that nice William Maxwell and dear Frank O'Connor kept trying to persuade me. One day I found a whole packet of unpublished manuscripts I had written and in it was "The Fig Tree." That was only 5 or 6 years ago. I sent it off to Maxwell and didn't hear anything and didn't hear for two or three weeks. I didn't like this and besides I had my suspicions. Finally, he wrote me a letter and sent the story back and said, 'Everybody loved the story and we did want to publish it. You know, it was nearly perfect and we thought if we could just get you to change some points it would be more perfect.' Well, to me, people who say something can be "more perfect" I can do without.

Q: So that was the end of the *New Yorker* for you.

A: That's right. I had to live by my rules. My writing was the only thing that made life worth living and having it made everything. It's very hard to be as poor as I was, with real suffering, real hunger, real cold, real loneliness. All right, if that's what it took, that's what it took. But I didn't want anything to do with a world that couldn't see those things the way I did.

The Katherine Anne Porter Watch: After Sacco and Vanzetti, What? 'The Devil and Cotton Mather'?

Doris Grumbach/1976

From *The Village Voice*, 26 January 1976. Reprinted by permission of Doris Grumbach.

In 1926, just 50 years ago, Horace Liveright, president of the then flourishing firm of Boni & Liveright, was delighted with a prospective book he had been offered by an unknown 33-three-year-old Texas writer named Katherine Anne Porter. In his fall catalogue he described her forthcoming book in the confident tones suitable to a manuscript-in-hand, a manuscript called "The Devil and Cotton Mather":

"This study in sadism is one of the most remarkable psychological portraits in the whole field of biography. Miss Porter's chief concern is with the prolonged emotional debauch that was Cotton Mather's hidden life, expressing itself outwardly in the cruelty, superstition, and intolerance which made the old divine famous as a savage witch-burner of colonial history. . . . As a narrative of religious ecstasy and righteousness, the bigotry and superstition of the Salem witchcraft mania, as a psychological study of a morbidly diabolical figure, and as a portrait in a conscience that found cruelty a means to self-approbation, this biography of Cotton Mather challenges the imagination, and provokes the thoughtful mind to speculate a little longer on the mystery of human nature."

Liveright gave Miss Porter an advance of $300 to complete her research, and she agreed to deliver the manuscript in time for fall publication. A second advance of $300 followed the next year. In June, 1929, KAP wrote from Bermuda asking for an additional $250, explaining that she had had to read more than 400 books for the project, but that its completion had been delayed by her need to write other things in order to support herself. She promised two

184

chapters every week until the book was finished and Liveright, reminding her that the book had now been listed three times in his catalogues, sent the money. A few instalments reached him. Then KAP wrote to ask that Liveright stop announcing the book. Well, he responded, in a tone that now sounds poignant, was it possible that he might be able to see the book by the fall of 1930? No other parts of the book arrived; instead, in 1930, she published, with Harcourt, Brace, *Flowering Judas* which brought her first fame—crowned nine years later with *Pale Horse, Pale Rider*.

In 1931 Robert McAlmon reported, in *Being Genuises Together*, that Katherine Anne Porter was secluded in Paris writing a biography of Cotton Mather.

So I went to call on the 85-year-old writer at her apartment on the 15th floor of a building in College Park, Maryland, to ask her about her progress in the book on Cotton Mather because I had heard she was working on it once again. Approaching her 86th birthday, she is somewhat frailer than her customarily frail self, a tiny, beautifully groomed, sharp, and humorous woman, at times disarmingly (and perhaps not quite honestly) self-deprecating: "My stories are real. The people were there. I'm just a reporter." At other times she is, justifiably, proud of her reputation: "*I'm* not going to write my autobiography. Every book I pick up these days has something about me in it, right or wrong. So I don't have to bother."

She wears the heavy lenses that follow a double cataract operation, her nightgown is covered with an elegant blue voile negligée; she explains that she has been resting and writing. Her voice is high and soft, she takes short quick breaths, and talks well and volubly: "I'm a great talker, probably too much. Once I get my teeth in your ear, you're done for." She seems to ramble, but she always remembers her starting point and returns to it gracefully.

How did she come to get interested in Mather? KAP remembers a picture in her sister's textbook of a Puritan wearing a wig, and her sister saying of it: "That man caused witches to be burned." From this developed her lifelong interest in both Mather and witchcraft (although now, she tells me, she believes that no witches were burned, only Negroes). She had realized, too, that 1928 would mark the 200th anniversary of Mather's death and thought that no important work had yet been written about him. As it happened, Ralph P. and

Louise Boas published a biography in 1928 (reprinted in 1964), and
Robert Middlekauff and J. P. Wood wrote another in 1971. Unmen-
tioned by KAP was Barrett Wendell's fine work on Cotton Mather
(1891).

Was she still at work on him? No. Four sections of the projected
book were published in *Accent, Hound and Horn,* and *Partisan
Review,* from 1934 to 1942. But she is not immediately concerned
with finishing it and will not work on it again "until it can all be
finished at once." Eleven chapters, or about half, are done. "Everything else is in order, but it's not *written* yet," she says. She recalls
Liveright's advance with some scorn: "Five hundred dollars for all
that work and all that reading and research. And I had to do other
writing to support myself." (It wasn't until 1962, with *Ship of Fools,*
that she earned really substantial income from her writing.)

The published portions of her work on Mather are auspicious.
Accent (spring and summer, 1942) carries two accounts of the early
life of Mather, beautifully written, and without the usual infelicities of
scholarly style. She writes as a novelist dealing carefully but imag-
inatively with the history of a life. The sections are called, somewhat
formidably. "Affectations of Praehiminicies," and the tone for the
book is set when she speaks of Mather's "unwearying pursuit of a
single idea . . . the single aspiration of Cotton Mather to identify
publicly and unmistakably his personal interests and ambitions with
the will of God."

But now she is occupied with another, entirely different book, this
one also a history ("I don't think I will write any more fiction"), but of
the Sacco-Vanzetti case. She is well into it, she says, promised it to
her publisher (now the Atlantic Monthly Press) on December 1, but
recently extended that date to early February.

Why Sacco and Vanzetti? KAP reminisces about her interest in the
case during the years she lived in Mexico, about her contributions to
the cause, "if only 25 cents now and then." In 1927 she went to
Boston for the final appeals and hearings, picketed the governor's
office, was arrested briefly once, maybe twice. But never, she hastens
to add, was she held in jail overnight. She remembers the few hours
she spent in a cell as terrible. No books or papers, no cigarettes, and
no light were permitted. "But I always got out in time for dinner."
She was assigned to a committee of the Defense group which

transcribed the letters of Sacco and Vanzetti on the typewriter, and these both affected and inspired her to her present work. And she talks of the night they all waited in the street watching for the flicker of light that would signal the execution. She regards the case as another, terrible example of American witchhunt.

After this book, she is planning to write another history, of a medieval murder case. "I won't tell you any more about it, because someone else might take the idea." There are other plans, other ideas, and not all her traveling is done. For her birthday celebration on May 15 she will go to Brownwood, Texas, where she was born, the "black dirt" country of her youth. She has been invited by the president of Howard Payne College, in Brownwood, to celebrate among familiar surroundings; promises she will be taken to revisit all the places she remembers so well. As she talks she lingers lovingly on details of her mother, her father's life, her family, which she traces back to its settlement in Wales in 1648.

Meanwhile she lives comfortably in two apartments, the wall between them broken down. The recent death of her friend and agent, Cyrilly Abels, has saddened her, and during the interview she holds in her lap a picture of Cyrilly and her husband Jerome.

Preparing to leave, I could not resist asking her why she had decided to settle in College Park. Her response was a long recounting of her odyssey through the years, from one house to another in Mexico, the U.S., and Paris, most of them increasingly unsatisfactory because people could too easily "get to me" and so disrupt the writing life to which her primary allegiance has always gone.

In 1966, living in Spring Valley, she was given an honorary degree by the University of Maryland. At the time she was ill, so a procession of students, faculty, and administration came to her house, in full academic regalia, to bestow the degree. She was impressed with the mannerliness and grace of the whole affair, began to think of Maryland as "my university." "I couldn't have a better one," she says proudly, and then adds: "I never set foot in a university until the day I went to teach in one." She remembers her convent education with much pleasure, claiming her family thought it quite good for her. "And so it was," she says.

But why College Park?

"Oh yes, well." She was tired of wandering and impressed by Dr.

Wilson H. Elkins and his university (Elkins was also, she discovered, a small-town boy from Texas). So she took a townhouse near the university, gave that up because of a serious fall on the stairs, and came to her present place in the same complex of buildings. Grateful to the university and its president, she offered them a considerable portion of her private library if they would house it. They did, in a fine room furnished with her furniture and lined with glass cases holding much of her working library and many editions the rare book people have bought to add to her volumes. Pictures of her family and friends line the walls: over the fireplace is a large oil painting of KAP which she wanted hung there.

Her conversation often turns to the subject of her serious illnesses and her close brushes with death (at least three times), experiences which convince her of a kind of immortality. After these it is not difficult for her to conceive of the real thing. But, she says, "Life is running away from me—at an unusual speed." In the next breath, she returns to her literary plans, her deadlines (which her life has been spent *not* meeting because her concept of art is that it cannot be timed in any way), and the projects still to be worked on.

"The past is past—and I'm glad of it," she says. And then, as I leave, "one-half my work is still undone." Seeing that small, indominable figure standing at the door, her head held in the same erect, jaunty, graceful way it is in her youthful pictures, it seems that she will be here to do it all. Even the Cotton Mather biography.

A Fine Day of Homage to Porter

Joan Givner/1976

From *The Dallas Morning News*, 23 May 1976. Reprinted by permission of *The Dallas Morning News*.

Years ago, Katherine Anne Porter countered Thomas Wolfe's dictum that you can't go home again with the firm reply: "Nonsense, it's the only place you can go." She proved her statement this month by returning to celebrate her 86th birthday in Brownwood, Texas, where she was born.

The occasion, really a birthday party, was organized by Howard Payne University, which awarded her an honorary degree and arranged the Katherine Anne Porter Symposium, an event not to be confused with the usual academic conference where intellectual heavyweights meet to spar and compete. This is not to say that there was any lack of vigorous intellectual activity during the two days of papers, but that there was so much more.

There was Brownwood itself, a little gemstone of a country town and never lovelier than at this time of year. The fields were full of wild flowers. The mourning doves were brooding in the live oaks in the green and growing spring landscape which Miss Porter has celebrated so often in her writing.

Delegates to the conference came from distant parts of the United States and Canada. Many were from Texas, and their special gift to the out-of-state visitors was the reading of Porter's stories in her native speech. A pleasant young woman from Baylor University evoked perfectly the character of Miranda, Porter's fictional representative. Another Baylor professor with a fine ear for regional speech and a talent for speaking it read an unforgettable paper on the regional imagery in "Noon Wine."

Then there was the hospitable welcome of the Howard Payne faculty. Surely no conference was ever arranged with such good will and such a sure sense of what was fitting to the occasion. These amiable people entertained, chauffeured and patiently explained everything from chiggers to bluebonnets. At no point was adherence to a prearranged schedule allowed to interfere with the wishes of the delegates or the honored guest. Informality, good humor and adaptability were the order of the day, and larger institutions with experienced conveners might well envy the success of this group.

But, of course, hosts and delegates were united by their admiration and affection for Katherine Anne Porter and it was her presence which made the conference so special. She attended the Howard Payne University graduation, accepted her own honorary degree and delighted students by, on her own initiative, handing out the diplomas. For students, faculty and visitors alike, the highlight of the two days was her presence and her speech at the Symposium banquet.

She began by saying that her speech was not only unprepared and unrehearsed, but also she didn't even know what she was going to say before she said it. The remark was deceptive. She once said that she came from a long line of story-tellers whose stories had shape and meaning. To hear her speak is to understand this fact, for it is clear that, if she does not plan speeches, she creates them spontaneously with such skill that they naturally assume a shape.

With the same artistry used in creating her short stories and holding taut the thread of her themes, she wove together two incidents. They were inspired by the Mexican wedding gown, bought for $16 years before, which she had not planned to wear, but had decided at the last minute would be appropriate to her birthday party. She noted that we all create an ambience, an atmosphere around us and the dress had done this for her. Accordingly, she recalled a traveling exhibition of Mexican Art which she helped organize in the '20s, but which had been apparently lost and she had wept for its loss.

Many years later she had, quite unexpectedly, found it again in Paris, with all the beautiful objects still intact. She told the story merrily in the laughing, gay voice once described as that of "someone coquetting with an old beau." But she ended on a somber note, declaring anew her conviction that "nothing is ever lost." She spoke her faith firmly and simply, an unbelievably fragile figure with white hair and robed entirely in white.

Someone remarked (not unkindly) that the white dress resembled a Christening gown. The observation was perceptive, for the interming of birth, marriage, and death was the theme of her day's activities and her speech no less than it is of her fiction.

Her other story was of her visit earlier in the day to the country cemetery in which her mother had been buried at this same spring time, so many years ago. The visit was a repetition of an earlier pilgrimage to the grave which she had made midway in her own mortal life. That was in 1936 when she came to the cemetery, wrote a poem there and buried it in her mother's grave. At the end of her speech she read the poem, "Anniversary in a Country Cemetery."

There was a feeling as she read that something had come full circle for Katherine Anne Porter on this day. A pattern had been completed, all loose ends gathered and tucked in, and nothing lost. Finally, a large birthday cake was brought in, presents given and Happy Birthday sung. Unlike her character, Granny Weatherall, she did not blow out her candles and they burned steadily.

To all those who had gathered in Brownwood, this was a day of homage to a small gallant Texan, whose only wish is that she be "read and remembered." They left dedicated to the carrying out of that wish.

Index

A

Abels, Cyrilly, 155, 187
Accent, 186
Aeschylus, 20
Agee, James, 31
American Caravan, 9
Anderson, Sherwood, 119
Aristotle, 93
Atl, Dr. (Gerardo Murillo), 127
Atlantic Monthly, 30, 64, 74
Atlantic Monthly Press, 117, 118
Augustine of Hippo, Saint: The Confessions
  of Saint Augustine, 99, 164
Austen, Jane, 80
Austin, Texas, 35, 99

B

Baldwin, James, 65
Bankhead, Tallulah, 39
Barnes, Djuna, 151
Barry, Jeanne du, 166
Basel, Switzerland, 11–12, 37, 66, 115, 118
Baton Rouge, Louisiana, 14, 15, 153
Baylor University, 189
Beach, Sylvia, 150, 169
Beauvoir, Simone de: The Second Sex, 76
Bedford, Sybil, 153
Berlin, Germany, 66, 166–67, 178, 179
Bermuda, 37, 184
Best-Maugard, Adolfo, 121, 122, 125, 126
Bible, 53
Bishop, John Peale, 31, 58, 119
Boas, Ralph P., and Louise: Cotton Mather:
  Keeper of the Puritan Conscience, 185–86
Boni & Liveright, 184
Book-of-the-Month Club, 117
Boone, Daniel, 76, 81, 142
Boone, Jonathan, 76, 81, 160
Boston, Massachusetts, 178, 186–87
Brace, Donald, 114, 118

Brant, Sebastian: Narrenshiff, 66, 118
Bremerhaven, Germany, 40, 66, 97, 115,
  129
Brontë, Emily: Wuthering Heights, 80, 89,
  106, 181–82
Brown v. Board of Education, 39
Brownwood, Texas, 158, 187, 189, 191
Buda, Texas, 35
Burroughs, William, 134; Naked Lunch, 112
Bushman, Francis X., 83

C

Cable, George Washington, 57
Caldwell, Erskine, 42, 46–47, 48
California, 126. See also Hollywood,
  California
Calvin, John, 59, 60
Cape Ann, Massachusetts, 117, 130
Capote, Truman, 147
Carillo, Felipe, 131, 148
Carroll, Lewis: Alice in Wonderland, 182
Case, Anna, 74
Cator, Libby, 156
Century, 30, 108, 141
Chaucer, Geoffrey, 106, 176, 181
Chicago, Illinois, 10, 83, 139, 143, 165
Churchill, John Spencer, 135
Cicero, Marcus Tullius, 153
Civil War, 48, 56, 57, 58, 59
Clark, Eleanor, 180
Clarke, Kenneth, 182
Clemons, Walter, 49, 68, 133; The Poison
  Tree, 133
Cliburn, Van, 35
Cocteau, Jean, 146
College of Notre Dame, 173
College Park, Maryland, 142, 153, 159, 162,
  167, 170, 176, 177, 185, 187–88
Connecticut, 68, 95
Connolly, Cyril, 153
Conrad, Joseph, 62

Cooke, Alistair, 182
Copard, A. E.: "A Field of Mustard," 146
Corpus Christi, Texas, 3
Coucy, Chatelain de, 138
Covarrubias, Miguel, 10, 124–25, 126
Cowley, Peggy Baird, 148
Crane, Hart, 131–32, 148, 165
Crowinshield, Frank, 124
Crume, Paul, 15, 168
Cuba, 66, 149

D

Dallas, Texas, 16, 160
Dallas News, 168
Dante, 80, 106, 181
Denver, Colorado, 10, 16, 84, 139, 143, 160, 165
DeVoto, Bernard, 44–45
Dialogos, 120
Díaz, Porfirio, 113, 121
Dickens, Charles, 80, 106
Doherty, Mary, 90, 123
Doré, Gustave, 80
Dos Passos, John, 47, 48
Doylestown, Pennsylvania, 15, 37, 75, 95, 115, 128
du Maurier, Daphne, 100

E

Eckman, William, 35
Eisenstein, Sergei: *Thunder Over Mexico,* 11
Elchner, Sister Maura, 173, 174–75
Eliot, George, 94
Eliot, T. S., 62, 65, 104, 141, 147, 151–52; *The Cocktail Party,* 151
Elkins, Dr. Wilson H., 187–88
Ellison, Ralph, 65
Enciso, Jorge, 122, 125
Erasmus, Desiderius, 66
Erskine, Albert, Jr., 140, 153, 165
Esquire, 177
Essanay Film Company, 10, 83

F

Faulkner, William, 42, 47, 50, 51, 52, 57, 168; *Sanctuary,* 174; *The Sound and the Fury,* 50
Feeley, Sister Kathleen, 173, 174, 176
Fitzgerald, F. Scott, 63, 87, 132, 141; *The Great Gatsby,* 63; *Tender Is the Night,* 63, 87

Fleming, Ian, 112
Ford, Ford Madox, 132, 149, 171
Ford, Julie, 149
Forster, E. M.: *A Passage to India,* 89
Fort Worth, Texas, 6, 165
Fort Worth Critic, 165
Freud, Sigmund, 24–25, 94
Friedan, Betty, 156; *The Feminine Mystique,* 156
Fulbright exchange program, 182

G

Gamio, Manuel, 122, 125
Garrett, George, 49, 68, 133
Genet, Jean, 166
Geneva, Switzerland, 118
Georgetown, Washington, D.C., 69, 71, 74, 78, 156
Germany, 37. *See also* Berlin, Germany; Bremerhaven, Germany
Glasgow, Ellen, 42
Goebbels, Joseph, 165, 167
Goering, Hermann, 165, 167, 179
Goldman, Emma, 167
Gordon, Caroline, 42, 43–49, 53, 54, 56, 59, 66, 67, 97, 115, 119, 133; *None Shall Look Back,* 133
Goyen, William, 34, 68
Grentzer, Rose Marie, 138, 156
Guerrero, Xavier, 126

H

Harcourt, Brace, and Company, 117, 185
Hardwick, Elizabeth, 147
Hardy, Thomas, 80, 104, 170
Harrison, Barbara, 137, 138
Harrison Press, 137
Harte, Bret, 100
Hawkes, John, 134; *The Lime Twig,* 112
Hegel, Georg, 54
Heine, Heinrich, 54
Hemingway, Ernest, 62–63, 95, 114, 121, 141, 147, 150–51, 168, 169; "Big Two-Hearted River," 63; *The Old Man and the Sea,* 73
Hemingway, Mary, 151
Hitler, Adolf, 67, 165, 166–67, 178
Holloway, Gay Porter (sister), 82, 159
Hollywood, California, 3, 73, 165
Homer, 80, 106, 181
Hound and Horn, 129, 186
Howard Payne College, 187, 189–90

Howells, William Dean, 117
Hughes, Richard: *A High Wind in Jamaica*, 89
Humphrey, William, 49, 133; *Home From the Hill*, 33–34, 50; *The Ordways*, 133

I

Indian Creek, Texas, 33, 35, 74, 99, 142, 158, 164
Institute of Contemporary Arts, 28
International Festival of the Arts, Paris, France, 126–27
Ireland, 73, 75

J

James, Henry, 33, 63, 73, 80, 104, 106, 170; "The Beast in the Jungle," 62; *The Turn of the Screw*, 17–27
Joan of Arc, Saint, 146, 181
Johnson, Rhea, 156–57
Johnson, Samuel, 90, 107, 176
Jones, John Paul, 81
Jones, Madison, 42, 43, 45–46, 50–52, 55, 57, 58, 59
Jong, Erica, 181
Joyce, James, 62, 104, 169; *Dubliners*, 30, 62; *Ulysses*, 62

K

Keats, John, 150
Kirstein, Lincoln, 129
Klein, Herbert, 166
Koontz, John Henry, 110, 160
Kyle, Texas, 33, 35, 37, 99, 164

L

Lafayette, Marquis de, 81
Lardner, Ring, 168
Lawrence, Seymour, 117, 147–48, 155
Lee, Gypsy Rose, 111
Library of Congress, 28, 138, 156
Little, Brown & Company, 117
Liveright, Horace, 184, 186
Long, Huey, 67
Lopez, Hank, 120
Louisiana, 70, 72, 74, 82, 83, 115, 139. *See also* Baton Rouge, Louisiana; New Orleans, Louisiana

Lowell, Robert, 119, 147
Lozano, Manuel Rodríguez, 125

M

McAlmon, Robert: *Being Geniuses Together*, 185
McCarthy, Joseph, 67
McCarthy, Mary, 55, 63, 93; *Memoirs of a Catholic Childhood*, 63
Mademoiselle, 31
Mailer, Norman, 112, 134
Mansfield, Katherine, 30
Marot, Clement, 138
Mather, Cotton, 185–86. *See also* Katherine Anne Porter: works: *The Devil and Cotton Mather*
Matisse, Henri, 103
Maxwell, William, 183
Mérida, Carlos, 124
Mexico, 10, 37, 40, 63, 66, 67–68, 70, 78, 85–86, 87, 101, 107, 113–14, 120, 121–28, 131, 141, 147, 148, 165, 167, 175–76, 178, 186, 187; Obregón revolution, 86, 121–24, 148, 163. *See also* Mexico City, Mexico; Vera Cruz, Mexico
Mexico City, Mexico, 12–13, 120, 122
Michaels, Sidney: *Dylan*, 152–53
Middlekauff, Robert: *The Mathers: Three Generations of Puritan Intellectuals*, 186
Miller, Henry, 102, 134; *Tropic of Cancer*, 102
Mitchell, Margaret: *Gone with the Wind*, 100
Modotti, Tina, 127
Molière, 101
Moore, Marianne, 105, 151, 152
Montaigne, Michel de, 80, 107
Montgomery County, Pennsylvania, 81
Morley, Thomas: "Now is the Month of Maying," 156
Moses, Grandma, 44
Moss, Howard, 168
Mussolini, Benito, 66, 67

N

Nacho, Tatâ, 121
Nation, 178
National Institute of Arts and Letters, 74
New Orleans, Louisiana, 15, 75, 83, 99, 115, 128, 153, 160, 175
New Republic, 178
New York City, 9, 63, 86, 107–08, 114, 121,

124–25, 132, 134, 139, 140, 141, 146, 147, 165, 167
New York Review of Books, 147
New York Times, 56
New Yorker, 168, 183

O

Obregón, Alvaro, 148
O'Connor, Flannery, 42, 44, 45, 46, 48–49, 50, 52, 53, 54–55, 57, 58, 133; "Some Thoughts on the Grotesque in Southern Fiction," 52
O'Connor, Frank, 183

P

Paris, France, 37, 73, 78, 114, 121, 132, 137, 138, 148, 150–51, 153, 185, 187
Parker, Dorothy: "Big Blonde," 168
Partisan Review, 186
Percy, Walker, 57
Petrarch, 91
Picasso, Pablo, 103
Playboy, 158
Pollock, Jackson, 104, 166
Porter, Colonel Andrew, 81
Porter, Catherine Anne (grandmother), 10, 35, 38, 80, 81, 99, 100, 106, 143, 159, 160, 163, 166, 181
Porter, Gene Stratton, 13
Porter, Harrison Boone (father), 37, 61, 83, 109, 113, 122, 159, 160, 164, 187
Porter, Horace, 81
Porter, Katherine Anne, awards, fellowships, and honorary degrees, 8, 12, 40, 66, 76, 148, 153, 162, 163, 165, 174–78, 187, 189, 190; biography, 32, 33, 37–38, 70, 81–84, 99, 164, 185; and book reviewing, 15, 33, 136, 165; clothing of, 135, 154, 161; on Communism, 12, 28–29, 47, 114, 147–48, 167; and cooking and food, 12, 135–36; and death, 162–63, 164, 171, 172, 175, 188; education of, 9–10, 33, 70, 74, 99–101, 105, 106, 142, 159, 165, 175, 187; and family and family history, 9–10, 15–16, 37, 45, 79, 80, 81, 99–100, 108–09, 120, 142, 160, 164, 187; on fascism, 40; and ghostwriting, 11, 15, 165; and illness, 3, 6–7, 10, 16, 84, 85, 163, 165, 170–71, 188; and journalism, 10, 16, 83, 84, 136, 143–44, 160, 165; on language, 93–94, 102–03, 134, 177–78,

180–81, 182; on the "lost generation," 87, 104, 120–21; and marriage, 10, 108–09, 110, 137, 139, 145, 160, 163, 165, 179; and Mexican art, 125–27, 148, 165, 190; on minorities, 40, 167; and moon shot, 158, 160–61; and movies, 10, 83, 130–31, 139, 143–44, 165; and politics, 11, 12, 122, 147, 177–78; on pornography, 102; and readings and lectures, 28, 29, 32, 33, 34–35, 73, 100, 106, 115, 136, 142, 163, 165, 174, 179, 182; on sex, 109–10, 181; and short story anthology, 145; and singing career, 83–84; and the South, 45, 82–83; as stylist, 8–9, 14–15, 92–93; on symbolism, 54, 55–56, 64–65, 93; and teaching, 3–5, 10, 32, 100, 111, 115, 165, 179; and television, 182; on the United States, 39–40, 127–28; Werra, S.S.: voyage on, 40, 66, 71, 75, 96–97, 115, 129, 148, 165; on being a woman, 77, 94–95, 178; on women's liberation, 155–56, 160, 181; on writing, 11, 13, 30–32, 33, 34, 35, 36–37, 41, 46, 62, 70–71, 79, 84–85, 86–94, 95, 97–98, 101, 105, 106, 107, 114, 118–19, 120, 133–34, 136, 137, 154, 161, 174, 181, 183; work process, 8, 9, 11, 15, 43, 44, 63, 64, 72, 88, 90–91, 95–96, 129–30, 142, 179–80; on the young, 101–02; works: "Affectation of Praehiminicies," 186; "After a Long Journey," 66–67; "Anniversary in a Country Cemetery," 191; "A Christmas Story," 140; The Collected Essays and Occasional Writings of Katherine Anne Porter, 137, 145, 155; The Collected Stories of Katherine Anne Porter, 140; "The Cracked Looking Glass," 114; The Days Before, 29, 74, 137, 179; The Devil and Cotton Mather, 12, 14, 160–61, 171–72, 177, 184–86, 188; "The Fig Tree," 183; "Flowering Judas," 62, 64, 89–90, 91, 93, 95, 114, 122–24, 129, 175, 180, 185; Flowering Judas, 8, 62, 64, 66, 74, 97, 136, 141, 148, 162, 165, 167; "The Grave," 65; "Hacienda," 11; Hacienda, 134; "He," 178; "The Hermit of Halifax Cave" (juvenilia), 9, 63, 105, 142–43; "Holiday," 47, 53, 63–64, 76, 96; "The Jilting of Granny Weatherall," 180–81, 191; Katherine Anne Porter's French Song Book, 137, 138, 140, 156; "The Leaning Tower," 168, 179; The Leaning Tower and Other Stories, 74, 114, 162, 165, 167–68; "A Little Incident in the Rue de l'Odéon," 169; "Magic," 114; Many Redeemers:

"Legend and Memory" (published as "The Old Order" stories), 10; "María Concepción," 11, 30, 64, 92, 107, 108, 123, 141–42; *The Never-Ending Wrong*, 186–87; "No Safe Harbor." *See Ship of Fools*; "Noon Wine," 12, 15, 34, 35–38, 43, 64, 67, 72, 74, 75, 89, 95, 115, 128, 133, 140, 168, 175, 188; "Noon Wine: The Sources," 35, 36; "Old Mortality," 15, 34, 43, 67, 72, 75, 95, 113, 115, 128, 140; *Outline of Mexican Popular Arts and Crafts*, 125, 148; "Pale Horse, Pale Rider," 15, 16, 67, 72, 75, 85, 115, 128, 139–40, 160, 165, 170, 175; *Pale Horse, Pale Rider*, 9, 72, 74, 75, 114, 162, 165, 167–68, 179, 185; "Portrait: Old South," 168; "Rope," 9, 44, 64; *Ship of Fools* (novel), 40–41, 61, 62, 65–66, 67–68, 69, 71–73, 75–76, 95, 96, 97–98, 99, 109, 111, 112–13, 114, 115–17, 120, 128–30, 135, 140, 142, 145, 148–49, 153, 154, 158, 160, 162, 163, 165, 166, 175, 179, 186; *Ship of Fools* (movie), 130, 173–74; "Theft," 64; "The Wooden Umbrella," 169; work in progress, 14, 63, 73, 172, 187
Porter, Mary Alice (mother), 159, 160, 164, 187, 191
Porter, Paul (brother), 159
Porter, William Sydney (O. Henry), 9, 76, 80–81, 100, 142, 160
Pound, Ezra, 62, 147
Powers, J. F., 76, 133; *Morte d'Urban*, 133
Pressly, Eugene, 12, 43, 110, 118, 149–50, 153, 165
Prettyman, E. Barrett, 155
Pritchett, V. S., 153

R

Ransom, John Crowe, 105
Reed, John, 167
Rivera, Diego, 10, 114, 127
Rocky Mountain News, 10, 16, 139, 165
Rome, Italy, 73, 173–74
Ronsard, Pierre de, 80
Rosenfeld, Paul, 123
Ross, Harold, 183
Roth, Philip: "The Conversion of the Jews," 76, 146
Rovelstad, Howard, 155
Rubin, Louis D., 43–60
Ruffin, Edmund, 48
Russell, Bertrand, 182

S

Sacco, Nicola, 147, 178, 186–87
Salinger, J. D., 65
San Antonio, Texas, 99, 113, 121, 158–59, 161, 163
Saroyan, William, 63
Sartre, Jean-Paul, 76
Sennett, Mack, 138, 143
Sergeev-Tzensky, S.: "Living Water," 145–46
Sévigné, Madame Marie de, 109
Shakespeare, William, 20, 32, 106, 177, 181; *Othello*, 27; sonnets, 79–80, 91
Sibon, Marcelle, 127
Sill, George, 141–42
Siqueiros, David, 127
Sitwell, Edith, 146–47
Smith, William J., 156
Smollett, Tobias, 80
Southern Review, 140
Southern fiction, 42–60
Southwest Review, 15, 30, 168
Spain, 37, 121, 179
Spivacke, Harold, 138, 156
Spring Valley, Virginia, 135, 187
Stein, Gertrude, 104, 107, 169; *Four Saints in Three Acts*, 103–04
Sterne, Laurence, 63, 91; *Tristram Shandy*, 92
Stevens, Wallace, 105
Stevenson, Robert Louis, 34, 106–07
Story, 12
Stromberg, Hunt, 10
Stuart, Jesse, 32
Styron, William, 51–52, 87–88; *Lie Down in Darkness*, 50–51; *Set This House on Fire*, 87
Sutherland, Donald, 169
Swanson, Gloria, 10
Switzerland, 37. *See also* Basel, Switzerland; Geneva, Switzerland

T

Talmadge, Herman, 45
Tate, Allen, 17–27, 31–32, 36, 58, 66, 105, 119, 147, 152, 180, 181, 182
Taylor, Peter, 49–50, 132–33, 168; "Bad Time," 49; *Miss Leonora When Last Seen*, 133
Teresa of Avila, Saint, 84
Texas, 33, 34, 83, 113, 121, 139, 142. *See also* Austin, Texas; Brownwood, Texas; Buda, Texas; Corpus Christi, Texas; Dallas,

Texas; Fort Worth, Texas; Indian Creek, Texas; Kyle, Texas; San Antonio, Texas
Thackeray, William, 80, 106
Thomas, Dylan, 152–53
Thomas Aquinas, Saint, 99, 164
Thompson, Virgil, 103–04; *Four Saints in Three Acts*, 103–04
Time, 117
Times Literary Supplement (London), 58
Turgenev, Ivan, 80
Turnbull, Roberto, 126, 131
Twain, Mark, 117

U

University of Maryland, 135, 138, 154, 155, 157, 161, 187–88
University of Michigan, 150
University of Texas, Austin, 34–35, 68
University of Virginia, 116–17, 168
University of Wichita, 61–62

V

Van Doren, Carl, 15, 107, 108, 111, 141
Van Doren, Mark, 17–27, 111, 182
Vanity Fair, 124
Vanzetti, Bartolomeo, 147, 178, 186–87
Vera Cruz, Mexico, 40, 66, 71, 96, 115, 129, 148
Villa, Francisco (Pancho), 167
Virginia, 81, 120
Voltaire, 164; *Complete Works of Voltaire*, 61; *Philosophical Dictionary*, 80

W

Warren, Robert Penn, 36n, 62, 105, 147, 180, 183; *Night Riders*, 14
Washington, George, 81
Washington and Lee University, 117
Weinstein, Jerome, 155, 157, 187
Welty, Eudora, 47, 52, 62, 63, 132, 133, 147; *A Curtain of Green*, 133; *The Golden Apples*, 133; *The Ponder Heart*, 133; *The Wide Net*, 133
Wendell, Barrett: *Cotton Mather: The Puritan Priest*, 186
Wescott, Glenway, 133, 136, 137, 138, 147, 171; *The Pilgrim Hawk*, 133
Wesleyan College, 42, 60
Wheeler, Monroe, 137, 138
White, Katharine Angell, 183
Wilson, Edmund, 58, 94, 148, 153–54
Windsor, Duke and Duchess of, 151
Wolfe, Thomas, 42, 52, 189
Wood, James Playsted: *The Admirable Cotton Mather*, 186
Woodlawn Sanatorium, Dallas, Texas, 3–5, 84
Woolf, Virginia: *To the Lighthouse*, 89
Wright, Richard, 65

Y

Yaddo artists' colony, 75, 76, 147
Yeats, William Butler, 95, 104, 170

Z

Zapata, Emiliano, 167, 178